A Century of Education

Education is a 'country's biggest business' and the most important shared experience of those who live in it.

A Century of Education provides an accessible, authoritative and fascinating overview of the role and nature of education in the twentieth century. Eminent historian of education Professor Richard Aldrich has assembled a team of contributors, all noted experts in their respective fields, to review the successes and failures of education in the last century and to look forward to the next.

A succinct overview of twentieth-century social, economic, political and intellectual developments in the first chapter is followed by ten topics: primary, secondary, further, and higher education, together with central and local government, teachers, pupils and students, special educational needs, curriculum, and qualifications and assessment. Each chapter has four sections: a review of the educational situation in 2000; a similar assessment in 1900; changes and continuities throughout the century; and a conclusion reviewing the lessons for today and tomorrow.

A Century of Education is a work of information, interpretation and reference, which demonstrates the strengths and weaknesses of education during the twentieth century and identifies educational priorities for the twenty-first. For anyone interested in what has become the most important issue of our time, this unique book is destined to become a classic text.

Richard Aldrich is Professor of History of Education and Head of the History and Philosophy Group at the Institute of Education, University of London.

A Century of Education

Edited by Richard Aldrich

London and New York

First published 2002
by RoutledgeFalmer
2 Park Square, Milton Park, Abingdon, Oxon, OX14 4RN

Simultaneously published in the USA and Canada
by RoutledgeFalmer
270 Madison Ave, New York NY 10016

RoutledgeFalmer is an imprint of the Taylor & Francis Group

Transferred to Digital Printing 2005

Typeset in Sabon by Taylor & Francis Books Ltd

British Library Cataloguing in Publication Data
A catalogue record for this book is available from the British
Library

Library of Congress Cataloging in Publication Data
A catalogue record for this book has been requested

ISBN 0–415–24322–X (hbk)
ISBN 0–415–24323–8 (pbk)

Contents

Contributors

Richard Aldrich is Professor of Education and Head of the History and Philosophy Group at the Institute of Education, University of London. He is a former President of the International Standing Conference for the History of Education and of the UK History of Education Society.

Bill Bailey is Senior Academic in the School of Post-Compulsory Education at the University of Greenwich. He has published articles and chapters on the history and recent development of vocational and further education in England.

Ian Copeland is Senior Lecturer in the School of Education at the University of Reading. His research and publications focus upon the development of policy and provision for pupils experiencing difficulties in the state education system.

Peter Cunningham is Reader in the History of Education at Homerton College, Cambridge. His research interests include the primary curriculum and the status and training of primary teachers in the twentieth century.

Philip Gardner is Senior Lecturer in the School of Education at the University of Cambridge and a Fellow of St Edmund's College. He is co-director with Peter Cunningham of an ESRC-funded enquiry into the impact of wartime evacuation upon teacher attitudes and practice.

Peter Gordon is Emeritus Professor of Education at the Institute of Education, University of London. He has written widely on the history of education, with particular reference to curriculum, as well as on aspects of educational policy.

Roy Lowe is Professor of Education at the University of Wales, Swansea and President of the UK History of Education Society. He has written extensively on aspects of the history of education in Britain and the USA.

Gary McCulloch is Professor of Education at the University of Sheffield and editor of the journal, *History of Education*. His numerous publications include three volumes on grammar, secondary technical and secondary modern schools in the twentieth century.

Paul Sharp is Senior Lecturer and Chair of the School of Education at the University of Leeds. He has directed a number of funded research projects and published widely on the development of the English school system, higher education and the 16–19 curriculum.

Ruth Watts is Reader in the History of Education at the University of Birmingham. Her recent publications include *Gender, Power and the Unitarians in England 1760–1860* (1998) and articles on gender and imperialism and on the cultural history of women and science.

Alison Wolf is Professor of Education at the Institute of Education, University of London and Executive Director of its International Centre for Research on Assessment. She is an Executive Editor of *Assessment in Education* and has written widely on assessment issues and qualifications and the labour market.

Acknowledgements

Philip Taylor commissioned this book; Anna Clarkson and her colleagues at RoutledgeFalmer have guided its progress and seen it into print. The ten contributors have responded generously to my editorial requests. Averil Aldrich and Judy Morrison have provided valuable assistance in the preparation of the final manuscript. I am most grateful to them all.

Richard Aldrich
Institute of Education
University of London
July 2001

Abbreviations

A	Advanced level
ACHMI	Audit Commission and Her Majesty's Inspectorate
AS	Advanced supplementary level
AT	Attainment target
AUT	Association of University Teachers
BEC	Business Education Council
BERA	British Educational Research Association
BoE	Board of Education
BTEC	Business and Technician Education Council
CAC	Central Advisory Council
CAT	college of advanced technology
CGLI	City and Guilds of London Institute
CNAA	Council for National Academic Awards
CRE	Commission for Racial Equality
CSE	Certificate of Secondary Education
CSG	Curriculum Study Group
CSIE	Centre for Studies in Inclusive Education
CTC	city technology college
CVCP	Committee of Vice-Chancellors and Principals
DCDEC	Departmental Committee on Defective and Epileptic Children
DES	Department of Education and Science
DfE	Department for Education
DfEE	Department for Education and Employment
DSA	Department of Science and Art
EOC	Equal Opportunities Commission
ERA	Education Reform Act
ESN	educationally subnormal
ESRC	Economic and Social Research Council
FE	further education
FEDA	Further Education Development Agency
FEFC	Further Education Funding Council

GB	Great Britain
GCE	General Certificate of Education
GCSE	General Certificate of Secondary Education
GDP	gross domestic product
GIST	Girls into Science and Technology
GM	grant maintained
GNVQ	General National Vocational Qualification
GPDST	Girls' Public Day School Trust
HEFCE	Higher Education Funding Council for England
HMI	Her/His Majesty's Inspectorate
HMSO	Her/His Majesty's Stationery Office
ILEA	Inner London Education Authority
IQ	intelligence quotient
ISCHE	International Standing Conference for the History of Education
IT	information technology
ITB	Industrial Training Board
JMB	Joint Matriculation Board
KS	Key Stage
LCC	London County Council
LEA	Local Education Authority
LEC	Local Enterprise Council
LMS	local management of schools
LSB	London School Board
LSC	Learning and Skills Council
MoE	Ministry of Education
MP	Member of Parliament
MSC	Manpower Services Commission
NCC	National Curriculum Council
NCTA	National Council for Technological Awards
NCVQ	National Council for Vocational Qualifications
NFER	National Foundation for Educational Research
NSPCC	National Society for the Prevention of Cruelty to Children
NSSU	National Special Schools Union
NUT	National Union of Teachers
NVQ	National Vocational Qualification
O	Ordinary level
OECD	Organization for Economic Co-operation and Development
Ofsted	Office for Standards in Education
ORACLE	Observational, Research and Classroom Learning Evaluation
PGCE	Post-Graduate Certificate in Education
QAA	Quality Assurance Agency

QCA	Qualifications and Curriculum Authority
RAE	Research Assessment Exercise
RCBDD	Royal Commission on the Blind, the Deaf and Dumb, etc.
RCEEA	Royal Commission on the Elementary Education Acts
RSA	Royal Society of Arts
SAT	standard assessment task
SCAA	School Curriculum and Assessment Authority
SEAC	School Examinations and Assessment Council
SEN	special educational needs
SMS	secondary modern school
SSEC	Secondary School Examinations Council
STS	secondary technical school
TEC	Technician Education Council
TEC	Training and Enterprise Council
TES	*Times Educational Supplement*
TGAT	Task Group on Assessment and Testing
TOPS	Training Opportunities Scheme
TSA	Training Services Agency
TSO	The Stationery Office
TUC	Trades Union Congress
TV	television
TVEI	Technical and Vocational Education Initiative
UFC	Universities Funding Council
UGC	University Grants Committee
UK	United Kingdom
USA	United States of America
USSR	Union of Soviet Socialist Republics
VET	vocational education and training
WRNAFE	Work-Related Non-Advanced Further Education
YOP	Youth Opportunities Programme
YTS	Youth Training Scheme

Key events in education in the twentieth century

1900   *Board of Education* established; Consultative Committee to advise Board on matters referred to it.

1901   *Cockerton Judgment*: restricted school board expenditure to elementary education.

1902   *Balfour Education Act*: creation of Local Education Authorities following abolition of school boards; voluntary (Church) schools given rate aid.

1903   *Robert Morant* appointed first Permanent Secretary at the Board of Education.

1904   *Report of Interdepartmental Committee on Physical Deterioration*: drew attention to the health and well being of school children.

1904   *Elementary Code*: encouraged a more enlightened approach to the curriculum.

1904   *Secondary School Regulations*: prescribed a subject-based curriculum.

1905   *Handbook of Suggestions*: replaced central control of the curriculum.

1907   *Free Place Regulations*: allowed free places for up to 25 per cent of secondary school population.

1907   *School Medical Service* established by Board of Education.

1911   *Report of Consultative Committee on Examinations in Secondary Schools*: recommended system of public examinations at 16.

1914   *Elementary Education (Defective and Epileptic Children) Act*.

1915   *Department of Scientific and Industrial Research* established to sponsor research in universities.

1917   *Secondary School Examinations Council* established to administer School Certificate examinations.

1918   *Fisher Education Act*: school-leaving age raised to 14; part-time schooling from 14 years of age; 50 per cent of approved LEA expenditure to be met by government.

1919   *University Grants Committee* established.

1919   *Burnham Committee*: established national pay scales for elementary teachers.

1919   *Report of Committee on Adult Education (Smith)*: recommended establishment of university extra-mural departments.

1921   *Report of Committee on National Expenditure (Geddes)*: led to a reduction of £6.5 million in the education estimates of 1922.

1922   *Secondary Education for All* published.

1922   *British Broadcasting Company* established.

1923   *Report of Consultative Committee on Differentiation of the Curriculum for Boys and Girls in Secondary Schools*: pointed out ways in which girls were disadvantaged by the existing curriculum.

1926   *Report of Consultative Committee on the Education of the Adolescent (Hadow)*: recommended the separation of primary and secondary education at the age of 11 and the establishment of 'modern' as well as grammar secondary schools.

1929   *Report of Joint Departmental Committee on Mental Deficiency (Wood)*.

1931   *Report of Consultative Committee on the Primary School (Hadow)*: curriculum was to be thought of in terms of activity rather than facts to be acquired.

1931   *Report of Committee on National Expenditure* (May): led to further cuts in educational expenditure including a ten per cent reduction in teachers' salaries.

1933   *Report of Consultative Committee on Infant and Nursery Schools (Hadow)*: recommended separate infant schools and national provision of nursery school education.

1936   *Education Act*: school-leaving age to be raised to 15 in September 1939, but postponed by outbreak of war.

1938   *Report of Consultative Committee on Grammar and Technical High Schools (Spens)*: recommended a tripartite system of education according to ability; rejection of multilateral solution; endorsement of junior technical schools.

1943   *White Paper on Educational Reconstruction* published.

1943   *Report of Secondary School Examinations Council on Curriculum and Examinations in Secondary Schools (Norwood)*: supported a tripartite division of secondary education into grammar, technical and modern schools.

1944   *Butler Education Act*: created a Ministry of Education with central advisory councils for England and Wales; ended feepaying in maintained schools; public education to be organized in successive stages – primary, secondary and further; compulsory schooling to be raised eventually to 16; county colleges to be established to continue education for school-leavers to the age of 18.

1944   *Report of Committee on Public Schools and the General Education System (Fleming)*: examined possible links between public schools and the state system.

1944   *Report of Committee to consider the Supply, Recruitment and Training of Teachers and Youth Leaders (McNair)*: recommended raising teachers' status and three years' training.

1945   *Report of Special Committee on Higher Technological Education (Percy)*: recommended upgrading of selected technical colleges to colleges of advanced technology.

1945   *Handicapped Pupils and School Health Regulations*: led to a rapid expansion of special schools.

1946   *Report of Barlow Committee on Scientific Manpower*: ten-year programme to double the number of scientists at the universities.

1947   *School-leaving age* raised to 15.

1948   *Cambridge University* admitted women to degrees.

1951   *General Certificate of Education* at Ordinary and Advanced Levels introduced.

1955   *National Council for Technological Awards* established.

1956   *White Paper on Technical Education*: creation of colleges of advanced technology; regional colleges to cater for day release students.

1958   *Local Government Act*: replaced specific central grant for education with a general grant for all local services.

1959   *Report of Central Advisory Council. 15 to 18 (Crowther)*: proposed a 20-year programme to ensure that by 1980 half of all pupils continued in full-time education until 18.

1960   *Report of Departmental Committee on the Youth Service in England and Wales (Albermarle)*: recommended expansion of work in Youth Service.

1960   *Report of Committee on Secondary School Examinations (Beloe)*: recommended Certificate of Secondary Education.

1961   *Commonwealth Immigration Act.*

1962   *Curriculum Study Group* established within the Ministry of Education.

1963   *Report of Central Advisory Council. Half our Future (Newsom)*: considered the education of children of average ability between 13 and 16.

1963   *Report of Committee on Higher Education (Robbins)*: recommended expansion of higher education by the creation of new universities; colleges of advanced technology to be designated as universities.

1964   *Department of Education and Science* replaced the Ministry of Education.

1964   *Schools Council for Curriculum and Examinations* established.

1964   *Council for National Academic Awards* established.

1965   *Race Relations Act*: creation of Race Relations Board.

1965   *Circular 10/65*: LEAs required to propose schemes for comprehensive reorganization on lines laid down by the DES.

1966   *White Paper on Polytechnics and other Colleges*: led to designation of 30 polytechnics.

1967   *Report of the Central Advisory Council. Children and their Primary Schools (Plowden)*: recommended expansion of nursery schooling; introduction of concept of educational priority areas; transfer to secondary schools at 12 plus; importance of the relationship between school and home.

1968   *First Report of Public Schools Commission (Newsom)* on boarding education.

1969   *First Black Paper* published.

1969   *Open University* received its charter.

1969   *Report of Committee on Technician Courses and Examinations (Haslegrave)*: recommended establishment of Technician Education Council and Business Education Council.

1970   *Second Report of Public Schools Commission (Donnison)* on direct grant grammar schools.

1970   *Commission for Racial Equality* established.

1970   *Circular 10/70* replaced *Circular 10/65*: LEAs to decide the future organization of secondary education in their areas.

1972   *School-leaving age* raised to 16.

1972   *Report of Committee of Enquiry into Teacher Education and Training (James)*: recommended reorganization of teacher training into three cycles.

1972   *White Paper on A Framework for Expansion*: colleges of education to cease to be monotechnic institutions.

1973   *Manpower Services Commission* established with responsibilities for training and employment.

1975   *Sex Discrimination Act*: Equal Opportunities Commission set up.

1975   *Direct Grant List* for secondary schools ended.

1976   *Education Act*: to compel reluctant LEAs to introduce comprehensive education.

1976   *Commission for Racial Equality* established with powers of investigation and enforcement of laws against racial discrimination.

1976   *James Callaghan's speech* at Ruskin College, Oxford, inaugurated the education debate.

1976   *William Tyndale* controversy and the *Auld Report*.

1977   *Taylor Report* recommended a governing body for each school.

1978   *Special Educational Needs. Report of Committee of Enquiry into Education of Handicapped Children and Young People (Warnock)*: introduced the concept of special educational needs.

1979   *Education Act*: Conservative government repealed 1976 Act on comprehensive schools.

1980   *Education Act*: introduced assisted places at independent schools.

1980   *A Framework for the School Curriculum* issued by the DES.

1981   *Education Act*: special educational needs, identification and provision.

1981   *West Indian Children in Our Schools. Interim Report of the Committee of Inquiry into the Education of Children from Ethnic Minority Groups (Rampton).*

1983   *White Paper on Teaching Quality* published.

1983   *Technical and Vocational Education Initiative*: introduced specialized technical and vocational education for the 14–18 age range.

1983   *Youth Training Scheme* replaced Youth Opportunities Programme and provided a year's foundation training for unoccupied 16- or 17-year-old school leavers.

1984   *Secondary Examinations Council and School Curriculum Development Committee* replaced Schools Council.

1984   *Education (Grants and Awards) Act*: enabled the Secretary of State to support specific educational initiatives with grants.

1985   *Education for All. Report of the Committee of Inquiry into the Education of Children from Ethnic Minority Groups (Swann).*

1986   *General Certificate of Secondary Education* replaced GCE O and CSE examinations.

1986   *Education (No 2) Act*: dealt with composition and powers of governing bodies, freedom of speech, sex education.

1986   *National Council for Vocational Qualifications* established.

1987   *Teachers Pay and Conditions Act*: marked the ending of the Burnham Committee and the designation of 1,265 minimum hours per year for teachers.

1988   *Education Reform Act*: national curriculum and national testing; open enrolment; opting out; local management of schools; abolition of ILEA; abolition of university teachers' tenure; independence of polytechnics and colleges.

1988   *National Curriculum Council and School Examinations and Assessment Council* replaced School Curriculum Development Committee and Secondary Examinations Council.

1989   *Universities Funding Council* replaced University Grants Committee.

1991   *Training and Enterprise Councils* established.

1992   *Further and Higher Education Act*: further education and sixth-form colleges removed from LEA control; polytechnics granted full university status.

1992   *White Paper on Choice and Diversity* published.

1992   *General National Vocational Qualifications* introduced.

1993   *School Curriculum and Assessment Authority* replaced National Curriculum Council and School Examinations and Assessment Council.

1993   *Office for Standards in Education* established.

1994   *Teacher Training Agency* established.

1994   *Code of Practice on the Identification and Assessment of Pupils with Special Educational Needs* issued.

1995   *Department for Education and Employment* established.

1997   *National Literacy Strategy* introduced for primary schools.

1997   *Qualifications and Curriculum Authority* formed by merger of National Council for Vocational Qualifications and School Curriculum and Assessment Authority.

1998   *Quality Assurance Agency* established for higher education.

1999   *Green Paper on Teachers: Meeting the Challenge of Change* published.

1999   *Institute for Learning and Teaching* established for teachers in higher education.

2000   *Learning and Skills Act*: established learning and skills councils to plan and finance all post 16 education and training outside the universities.

2000   *Review of the National Curriculum in England*: citizenship and personal, social and health education to be added to the National Curriculum.

2000   *General Teaching Council* established.

Introduction

Richard Aldrich

Purpose and plan

The purpose of this book is to provide an account and interpretation of education in England during the twentieth century.[1] This is a large undertaking, for one hundred years of educational history are not easily contained within a single volume. Nevertheless the ten topics considered here – primary, secondary, further and higher education, together with central and local government, teachers, pupils and students, special educational needs, curriculum, qualifications and assessment – provide a substantial coverage of the formal dimensions of the subject. They encompass both major educational themes and categories that might have been identified at any point in the century, and other topics and terminology that may be seen as reflecting current issues. This combination is the stuff of history. Many of the questions we ask of the past are a reflection of contemporary concerns.

History may be defined as a record of human and other events with particular reference to the dimension of time: past, present and future. Historical study has two main purposes. The first is to furnish an account of past events. The second is to provide an interpretation of those events and by so doing to locate ourselves, both as individuals and as members of society, within historical time. Such location is particularly appropriate in the early years of a new century and a new millennium.

There are books by single authors and there are edited collections. *A Century of Education* has been planned to combine the best of both worlds. It is one entity in terms of overall subject matter and design, and draws upon a methodology employed by the editor in previous works;[2] nevertheless, each of its ten chapters is written by an expert in that particular field. A single format is employed for the overall structure of chapters, but within that format each contributor has been free to provide evidence and interpretation in a style most appropriate to her or his analysis of the particular theme. Each chapter begins with a brief review of the situation in the year 2000, followed by a similar appraisal of that at the beginning of the twentieth century. The central section encompasses the years between. The overall theme for this section is that of changes and continuities. Within this theme contributors have adopted different forms of organization and interpretation. This is demonstrated by the varying emphases placed upon such elements as chronology, primary sources, frameworks of explanation and methodology. Indeed, this book may be seen as a reflection of the current state of part of the historiography of history of education in England. It also provides some insights into the way in which the discipline's several elements and field of study are construed and constructed within personal, departmental and institutional contexts.

In his chapter on primary education Peter Cunningham draws upon a range of archaeological, pictorial, technological and other evidence in charting the rise of the primary school. This chapter and that on teachers by Philip Gardner both demonstrate the rich store of evidence collected by these Cambridge-based scholars for recent research projects and publications.[3] Gary McCulloch's contribution provides an important synthesis of research undertaken for three volumes on different types of secondary school,[4] and may be seen as an extension of the work of one of his illustrious predecessors at the University of Sheffield, John Roach.[5]

The chapter on further education by Bill Bailey of the University of Greenwich reflects his wide experience of this field, as befits a former editor of the journal, *The Vocational Aspect of Education*. Similarly, Roy Lowe of the University of Wales, Swansea who writes on higher education is a former editor of *History of Education* and has recently edited a substantial four-volume collection of major themes in this field.[6] Paul Sharp's chapter on central and local government draws not only upon his own previous work,[7] but also upon the substantial corpus of research and publications in educational administration that has proceeded from scholars at the University of Leeds.[8]

Pupils and students, the recipients and consumers of education, have too often been hidden from history. Their centrality for history of education in an age which is more concerned with the outcomes of education than its inputs, and which places learning above teaching, however, cannot be in doubt. In her chapter on this topic Ruth Watts of the University of Birmingham examines the dimensions of gender, ethnicity and social class. In so doing she draws on traditions which have often emphasized the failures, rather than the achievements, of education in England in the twentieth century.[9] This theme is continued and finds a more specific focus in the next contribution. Ian Copeland of the University of Reading draws upon his substantial record of research and publication in the history of special educational needs to examine issues of learning difficulty.[10] In the penultimate contribution Peter Gordon, former head of the Curriculum and History and Humanities departments of the Institute of Education,

University of London, reviews the curriculum history of the twentieth century.[11] Finally Alison Wolf of the Institute's Mathematical Sciences group and director of its International Centre for Research on Assessment, brings comparative and historical perspectives to bear on issues of qualifications and assessment.

Contexts, changes and continuities

As indicated above, the theme of educational changes and continuities lies at the heart of each chapter of this book. It also provides an organizing principle for the drawing of conclusions. Education, however, does not take place in a vacuum. It reflects, and at times challenges, the social, economic, political and intellectual contexts of its age. The purpose of this second section is to identify some of the key twentieth-century changes and continuities in those contexts within which education must be located.

Viewed from a comparative perspective the continuities may appear substantial. The United Kingdom is still a monarchy with a national anthem entitled 'God save the Queen'. Its parliament still includes an unelected second chamber – the House of Lords. The Church of England remains an established church with the monarch at its head. Foreign observers still remark on the hierarchical nature of English society and of many of its institutions, including those of education – most notably the public schools and the ancient universities of Oxford and Cambridge.

Yet in spite of such continuities the twentieth century was also an era of substantial changes. The nature and extent of such changes may be gauged by our reactions to the England of 1900 – which now appears as imperialist, racist, aristocratic and patriarchal, and fundamentally divided along lines of gender and social class.[12] Notwithstanding the levelling effects of the Liberal government of Asquith and the First World War, even in 1922 the richest five per cent of the population would still own more than 80 per cent of the nation's wealth.[13] In contrast, researchers such as Charles Booth and Seebohm Rowntree showed that at the turn of the century large sections of the population, some 30 per cent in London, were mired in deep poverty. Many men and women eked out lives of unrelieved drudgery. For the 94 per cent of men and 35 per cent of women who were in paid employment, hours were long and holidays a rarity. Three-quarters of the workforce were engaged in some type of manual tasks.[14]

On 1 January 1901 a leading article in *The Times* considered prospects for the century ahead. Despite the initial reverses of the Boer War,[15] the tone was supremely confident.

> We enter upon the new century with a heritage of achievement and of glory, older, more continuous, and not less splendid, than that of any other nation in the world. Our national character, as the ordeal of the

past year has abundantly shown, has lost nothing of its virility and doggedness when put to the proof of war.

Our Constitution has developed from a personal Monarchy limited by the power of an hereditary aristocracy into a democratic system of the most liberal kind, knit together by a THRONE to which all of the self-governing communities of the Empire are profoundly attached.

This transition has been effected without any of those violent breaks with the past which in less happy lands than ours have robbed the victories of freedom of the blessings and advantages they naturally produce.

The system that now prevails in England and her colonies, broad-based upon the people's will, possesses a strength, stability and flexi-bility of which no other can boast. With such an instrument of government, with our vast accumulations of wealth, widely diffused among the community, and, above all, with a people prosperous, contented, manly, intelligent and self-reliant, we may look forward with good hope to the storms and conflicts that may await us.[16]

Although, even in January 1901, that vision of a triumphant, unparal-leled nation, prosperous, contented and democratic, at the centre of the largest empire the world had ever seen, was not universally shared, few could have predicted the magnitude of the conflicts and changes that were to lie ahead. The long Victorian summer was followed by a brief Edwardian autumn but the nation's strength and confidence would be sapped by two world wars, the loss of empire and relative economic decline. In 1900 the United Kingdom was the most prosperous country in the world, with the highest gross domestic product (GDP) per capita. During the twentieth century GDP increased some fourfold,[17] but there was a substantial decline in relative terms. Indeed, by 1975 the British economy was in poor shape and GDP per head had fallen to fifteenth among the countries of the Organization for Economic Co-operation and Development (OECD).[18]

In the first decade of the twentieth century new perspectives on the nature and extent of British democracy were provided by the Labour movement and the campaign for female suffrage. During the First World War the much-vaunted qualities of virility and doggedness of British troops were frequently brought to nothing by the sheer incompetence of their officers – 'lions led by donkeys', indeed. After the War there were few 'homes fit for heroes', and it soon became clear that Germany could not be 'made to pay'. The 1920s and 1930s saw economic upheaval and unem-ployment of an unprecedented kind. The rise of Fascist dictatorships in Europe produced a rapid deterioration in international relations, and by 1939 the nation was at war once more.

Unlike 1914 there was little exultation. Following the retreat from

Dunkirk and the fall of France, avoidance of defeat, rather than victory, seemed the most that could be achieved. No longer could it be maintained that this was the greatest nation on earth in economic terms, but a sense of moral superiority still led many to trust in God and the empire to see Britain through. Thus in October 1940, at the height of the Blitz, Sir Cuthbert Headlam confided in his diary.

> We are a strange race which, if God did not love, must inevitably go under. We come through our troubles not because we deserve to do so, but because God likes us I suppose because we do possess qualities of courage and endurance when we are up against it, and possess the qualities, too, which makes the world a better place – a sense of justice and fair play, a willingness to see the other fellow's point of view, and a horror of cruelty and unfairness between man and man. I believe, that in their heart of hearts even these dictators realize that the British Empire is a real necessity in the world which they cannot replace.[19]

It was widely presumed that Winston Churchill, whose bulldog image and spirit had brought the nation through a period of 'blood, toil, tears and sweat' in which she experienced 'her finest hour', would lead the Conservative Party to victory in the general election of July 1945. Churchill's status as an architect of victory and his determination not to preside over the break-up of the British Empire, however, had little appeal for a nation determined on radical economic and social change. The Labour government of Clement Attlee granted independence to India in 1947 and to Burma in the following year. Key sections of production and distribution were brought under state control by a vigorous programme of nationalization – which included coal mines, gas and electricity, civil aviation, railways and road transport, and the Bank of England. The Welfare State, which promised an end to poverty and want, was epitomized by the National Health Service, introduced in 1948.

Conservative governments were in power for 13 years from 1951 but the 1960s, the so-called 'Swinging Sixties', brought substantial social change. Student protest and satirical television exemplified by the programme, *That was the week that was*, led to widespread bewilderment, not least among members of the Establishment. Censorship was challenged,[20] and issues such as abortion, the contraceptive pill, divorce and homosexuality brought to the fore. New icons, the Beatles and the Rolling Stones, Mary Quant and Twiggy, gave the country an unaccustomed leadership in popular music and fashion. From 1964 a Labour government was led by Harold Wilson, whose emphasis upon science and technology and apparent ease with modern communications presented a sharp contrast to the two previous Conservative Prime Ministers, Harold Macmillan, 'the last Edwardian', and his successor, Sir Alec Douglas-Home.[21] By 1979, however, devaluation, inflation, shoddy goods, minimal economic growth and poor industrial relations culminating in the 'winter of discontent', indicated that the country had reached a new low. As Correlli Barnett concluded of the post-war years:

> The dreams of 1945 would fade one by one – the imperial and Commonwealth role, the world power role, British industrial genius, and, at last, New Jerusalem itself, a dream turned to a dank reality of a segregated, subliterate, unskilled, unhealthy and institutionalised proletariat hanging on the nipple of state maternalism.[22]

Radical change now proceeded from the political right and many of the reforms of the previous 35 years were reversed. Public utilities were privatized and the powers of local councils, trade unions, and some professions severely reduced. Relative economic decline was halted; consumer wealth and purchasing power increased. The collapse of communist and socialist regimes in central and eastern Europe seemed further to endorse the triumph of capitalism. This shift in the national economic and social agenda was so successful that Conservative governments under Margaret Thatcher and John Major won four successive electoral victories. The 'New Labour' Party led by Tony Blair, victorious in 1997 and 2001, reshaped its policies in a Conservative mould.

Thus in spite of the survival of such institutions as the monarchy and the state church, by the year 2000 England was very different from what it had been a century before. Few now believed that the English were God's chosen race, indeed fewer than ten per cent of people regularly attended any Christian church, while the words of the National Anthem seemed increasingly archaic in a more inclusive age. Imperial grandeur had been replaced by continuing concerns about globalization, closer integration into the European community and devolution of powers and diversification of cultures within the United Kingdom itself. Aristocratic power had much diminished, symbolized by the metamorphosis of some of the great estates into theme parks. Patriarchal and racial attitudes were challenged and the rights of women and of members of ethnic minorities safeguarded by legislation.

Nevertheless, in spite of overall relative economic decline and of regional pockets of poverty, in the year 2000 the people of England were more prosperous than ever before. Wealth was more broadly shared. Car ownership, overseas holidays, travel by plane, which for the first half of the century were luxuries available only to a small minority, were now commonplace. The communications revolution of the twentieth century, moreover, embraced not only new means of transport but also developments such as radio, cinema, television, video, computers and the Internet which had considerable implications for education.

This section has provided the briefest of surveys of twentieth-century social, economic, political and intellectual changes and continuities for the purpose of providing some contexts. In the ten succeeding chapters this mixture of changes and continuities is examined in depth with specific reference to a century of education.

Notes

1 England, which has by far the largest population of the four countries which currently constitute the United Kingdom, is the focus of this book. Nevertheless, the distinctive educational values, systems and histories of Scotland, Wales and Northern Ireland do not entirely preclude the use in places of the term, British.

2 See, for example, R. Aldrich, *Education for the Nation*, London, Cassell, 1996 and R. Aldrich, D. Crook and D. Watson, *Education and Employment: the DfEE and its Place in History*, London, Institute of Education, 2000.

3 See, for example, P. Gardner and P. Cunningham, 'Oral history and teachers' professional practice: a wartime turning point?', *Cambridge Journal of Education*, 1997, vol. 27, no. 3, pp. 331–42.

4 G. McCulloch, *Philosophers and Kings: Education for Leadership in Modern England*, Cambridge, Cambridge University Press, 1991; *The Secondary Technical School: A Usable Past?*, London, Falmer, 1989; *Failing the Ordinary Child? The Theory and Practice of Working Class Secondary Education*, Buckingham, Open University Press, 1998.

5 J. Roach, *A History of Secondary Education in England, 1800–1870*, London, Longman, 1986; *Secondary Education in England 1870–1902: Public Activity and Private Enterprise*, London, Routledge, 1991.

6 R. Lowe (ed.) *History of Education: Major Themes*, London, Routledge, 2000.

7 See, for example, P.H.J.H. Gosden and P. Sharp, *The Development of an Education Service: the West Riding, 1889–1974*, Oxford, Martin Robertson, 1978; P. Sharp and J. Dunford, *The Education System in England and Wales*, London, Longman, 1990.

8 Home of the *Journal of Educational Administration and History*, edited for many years by Peter Gosden and W.B. Stephens.

9 See, for example, the several writings of England's most notable historian of education, Brian Simon, and the publications of the University of Birmingham-based Centre for Contemporary Cultural Studies, including *Unpopular Education: Schooling and Social Democracy in England since 1944*, London, Hutchinson, 1981. The chapter by Roy Lowe, himself for many years a member of staff at the University of Birmingham, also demonstrates connections with these traditions.

10 See, for example, I. Copeland, *The Making of the Backward Pupil in Education in England, 1870–1914*, London, Woburn Press, 1999.

11 See R. Aldrich (ed.) *In History and in Education: Essays Presented to Peter Gordon*, London, Woburn Press, 1996, for a review of his work.

12 See D. Cannadine, *Ornamentalism: How the British Saw Their Empire*, London, Allen Lane, 2001 for a recent discussion of the relationship between empire and social class.

13 A.H. Halsey with J. Webb (eds) *Twentieth-Century British Social Trends*, London, Macmillan, 2000, p. 7. In 1994 the share of the richest five per cent was 25 per cent.

14 Ibid. These figures are for 1911. By the end of the century manual workers had declined to a third.
15 1899–1902.
16 *The Times*, 1 January 1901.
17 Halsey with Webb, op. cit., p. 6.
18 *The Times*, 27 January 1997. Although in 2000 the UK still had the world's fourth largest economy.
19 S. Ball (ed.) *Parliament and Politics in the Age of Churchill and Attlee: the Headlam Diaries, 1935–1951*, Cambridge, Cambridge University Press, 1999, p. 225. Headlam, who had served on the General Staff in the First World War, was a Conservative MP and junior minister on various occasions between 1924 and 1951.
20 In 1960 Penguin Books was successfully defended by Michael Rubinstein, when prosecuted for obscenity for publishing an unexpurgated text of D.H. Lawrence's novel, *Lady Chatterley's Lover*.
21 Labour was in power 1964–70 and 1974–9, The intervening Conservative government of Edward Heath was brought down by the oil crisis, three-day week and miners' strike.
22 C. Barnett, *The Audit of War*, London, Macmillan, 1986, p. 304.

Chapter 1

Primary education

Peter Cunningham

The situation in 2000

In the year 2000 the work of British primary schools is highly visible and politically contested. Whether visibility derives from their contentiousness or vice-versa, and how the relationship between these two features has changed over the course of a century, poses an interesting question for historians of education. Primary teachers currently suffer an uneasy relationship with the State and complain that their work and their schools have become a political football. Compulsory education of children between the ages of five and 11 is managed and conducted within a statutory curriculum framework, but pedagogical style varies from teacher to teacher and from school to school, reflecting the individuality of the teachers and the ethos of individual schools. A new departure in the closing years of the century was the launch of 'national strategies' for literacy and numeracy which sought to impose some uniformity on teaching method, as the introduction of a national curriculum ten years earlier had done on the content of what primary school children learned. The account below will follow two themes in primary education: curriculum discourse between State and teachers, and increasing visibility of the primary school which brought that discourse into the public arena.

There are competing claims in the description and explanation of changing practice in primary schools. New Labour's Green Paper in the spring of 2001 claimed achievement of a 'transformation' in primary education over their term of office from 1997 to 2000, illustrated by a rise from 65 to 75 per cent in the proportion of children gaining level 4 in English at Key Stage (KS) 2 and a similar achievement in maths from 59 to 72 per cent. Important as these indicators may be to short-term policy the measures reflect a narrow definition of primary education, and their significance as measures of change is open to question. So, too, are the explanations offered for this achievement:

> The wholehearted commitment of governors, teachers and non-teaching staff across the country has been the key to the success so far

in raising standards of English and mathematics. Every day, in all 18,000 primary schools, they are using their professionalism to take forward the national strategies and integrate them with the wider curriculum. All the evidence shows that primary heads and teachers are now enthusiastically committed to the teaching methods they have learnt from the national strategies.[1]

From this account it would appear that professional culture took a sudden turn, fired by enthusiasm for government strategies which at last solved the problem of how to teach. Historians may reserve their judgement on this narrative of 'transformation', but the claim is of interest as evidence of a presumed need to restore public confidence in primary schools through political propaganda, a confidence which political propaganda had in previous years been bent on undermining.

Study of the professional press might produce a contrasting view, one of low morale, of teacher disaffection and a failure to recruit new staff, given the bureaucratic direction of their work over the past decades.[2] Pressures arising from increased visibility and accountability of primary teachers at the turn of the century are illustrated by the case of Marjorie Evans, a primary headteacher accused of physical and mental abuse towards children, whose case was publicly pursued through conviction by magistrates, reprieve on appeal, lengthy investigation by the Local Education Authority (LEA) and by a tribunal of school governors before eventual acquittal.[3] This visibility and accountability affects children's experience of primary education too, currently through increasingly intensive and continuous testing and reporting, and through the ranking of their schools in league tables. League tables are based on the results of standard assessment tasks (SATs) which echo the scholarship and eleven-plus examinations of previous eras. The scholarship exam in the first half of the century affected relatively few, the eleven-plus later constituted a single terminal assessment point for all, but now assessment impinges throughout primary school from baseline assessment on entry through KS1 and KS2 SATs, with intermediate forms of assessment increasingly applied.

Within the primary age range children may be taught in separate infant and junior schools, in first and middle schools or in all-through primaries; the schools may be secular or denominational. They may be large institutions with hundreds of pupils, more typically found in urban areas, or small schools with rolls of less than a hundred serving rural populations. The national curriculum structure is overlaid upon this institutional variety, in three Key Stages. A Foundation Stage caters for children from the age of three (some primary schools have nursery classes or other pre-school provision closely attached) until the end of the first year of compulsory schooling, when they have reached the age of five. Over the age of five, children move on from 'Reception' classes to follow Key Stage One for two years, and then proceed to Key Stage Two for a further four years.

Applying the parameters of primary education in 2000 determines a concentration on the age range 5 to 11. The century dawned, however, with schools defined less by age range than by social class, and elementary schools began the century with the heritage of providing a working-class education within a compulsory state system (although its success had also attracted many of the middle classes too). The compulsory age of schooling in 1900 was 5 to 13, although 'babies' had been admitted from the age of three. Official recognition, in the 1926 Hadow Report, of 'adolescence', a construct emerging from physiological, psychological and sociological study of growth, begins to rationalize a break in schooling at 11. 'Babies' had meanwhile been excluded from elementary schools but nursery provision, sometimes closely associated with the schools, was an increasing focus for attention. In the Hadow Reports of 1931 and 1933,[4] the nursery/infant and junior phases within primary education were increasingly sharply distinguished, and in many areas separate schools provided for each phase. The 1944 Education Act, in establishing secondary education for all, put the official seal on universal primary education almost by default, and by that time a quite distinctive 'culture' of primary education had emerged, informed by developmental psychology. A later attempt during the 1960s to extend this culture up the age range led some local authorities to provide 'middle schools' (for ages 8 or 9 to 13 or 14) reinforced in some instances by practical considerations of providing new school buildings for an expanding cohort of children and for comprehensive secondary provision. The corollary of the middle school was the 'first school' which embraced the infant and 'lower junior' age ranges.

Whatever changes have taken place over time in primary education, any attempt at explanation has to extend beyond government policy. Working our way back across the century by revisiting classrooms past, the evidence speaks as much of cultural and technological transformations as of policy change. Comparing the classroom of 2000 with that of 1975 a proliferation of information technology might appear the most striking feature. Over the past 25 years the microcomputer has become central to learning activity in the primary school. Desktop computers, laptops and palmtops as part of the classroom furniture, sometimes a separate computer suite, and children regularly engaged on the Internet, are an increasingly common sight. Teachers have become managers not only of children but also of complex technical resources. A quarter of a century earlier, however, a succession of visual and technological aids, most notably video, had already made a significant difference to the style of interaction between teachers and pupils and the nature of children's learning. In 1950, classes were perhaps 50 per cent larger than they are now with groups of some 40 to 50 as the norm, and partly as a consequence of these ratios relationships between children and teachers were more formal. A variety of teaching resources, books and equipment facilitated more flexibility in teaching styles and a modicum, at least, of independent learning. Children were beginning to move a little more freely and with less regimentation about the classroom and the school. Retreating to the classroom of 1900 the numbers of children per teacher would be far greater again, with classes up to twice the size they are now, and teaching styles consequently much more rigid and regimented in the main. Relationships between teacher and pupils were reflected in, but also determined by, the design and use of space, desks fixed in long rows facing the front. A striking contrast, too, would lie in the children's appearance, their general state of physical health, nourishment and clothing. Such perceptions forcibly remind us that understanding historical change in primary education requires far wider considerations than teaching style and performance indicators.

Change over time has to be explored, therefore, in a variety of dimensions, such as government policy nationally and locally, the structures of primary schooling which result, the physical environment of primary school buildings and classrooms, the prescribed curriculum and the teacher's role, curriculum in practice and the lived experience of teachers and children. These dimensions intersect and interact, and the priorities adopted in examining them will determine the sources on which we draw.

Curriculum history has a long pedigree going back to Birchenough and Bramwell but has more recently shifted its focus from the prescribed to the enacted curriculum.[5] Oral history has offered a route to uncovering the pupil's voice,[6] and that of the teacher.[7] Depaepe and others have preferred to use the teachers' press as a source for classroom history, arguing that professional journals facilitate Geertz's 'thick description': 'They enable us to look behind the scenes at classroom practice and to gauge the strategy, ulterior motives, reservations and hidden meanings behind pedagogical and didactic practice'.[8] Professional journals cover practical matters as well as pedagogical and general social issues, documenting for historians the links between the two. Another way into the history of classroom activity has been more archaeological, drawing on pictorial evidence and on artefacts.[9] This approach has amongst other merits that of focusing attention on technology, otherwise surprisingly taken-for-granted.[10] The technology of primary curriculum and pedagogy through magic lanterns, slide projectors, radio, cine-projectors, television and computers has had untold impact on the classroom as a space and on teaching and learning. Latterly National Curriculum record keeping brought filing cabinets into the primary classroom, the literacy and numeracy strategies boosted 'big books', whiteboards and overhead projectors. The teachers' press is rich with historical sources in the form of manufacturers' and retailers' advertisements and in critical discussion.

The situation in 1900

'Primary' schools were so designated in revolutionary France and recognized by Webster's *Dictionary* in 1828, but the legislation that introduced universal schooling in England and Wales established 'elementary' as the preferred label. Public elementary schools retained this statutory designation until 1944, and the label remained in popular use. Meanwhile the term primary was increasingly adopted in professional discourse from the later nineteenth century onwards and gained official sanction in the Board of Education's Consultative Committee reports (the Hadow reports) of 1926 and 1931.[11]

A growing body of published writings on elementary education in the years around 1900 provides ample documentation for the aims and intended methods of teaching. Our understanding of these elementary schools at the turn of the nineteenth century is also helped by an abundance of visual evidence, as many buildings remain from the School Board period[12] and furniture and artefacts survive in schoolroom museums up and down the country. Above all they coincide with an era when photography became an important ritual and medium of communication so that school and class photographs abound in local archives. Visual images of unsmiling children in crowded and cramped classrooms offer clues to the experience of primary education at the time. Apparatus such as Froebel's 'Gifts' laid out for use, children's work displayed, for example rows of identical line drawings, and on the walls framed pictures of monarchs or Christian images offer detailed evidence for curriculum. As rich and as treacherous as any written document, however, school photographs offer multiple readings.[13]

Elementary schools of circa 1900 live on, too, in the published memoirs of those who taught or learned in them. F.H. Spencer recalled his early years as a teacher in the 1890s, much of it with the upper standards of teenagers but also in the middle of the school:

> This meant arithmetic and English (grammar, composition, reading, dictation, spelling – all still regarded as separate subjects), geography and history, drill (still the only form of physical education, though it developed into barrack-yard physical jerks of a long-discarded type), science, with experiments which by no means always succeeded, and drawing (done in my later years at this school with coloured chalks on sheets of brown paper), Scripture, singing (though I never really attained the facility with the tonic sol-fa, accomplishment of most of my colleagues) – everything, in fact. It was gruelling work in the middle school, with fifty to sixty boys of all ranges of ability ... and the clever boys were kept droning through work they had already mastered.[14]

Spencer also dwelt on the plentiful corporate punishment, caning and 'not too vicious but sometimes quite hearty ear-boxing', though he argued that to infer from this that elementary teachers were brutal or cruel would be quite wrong.[15]

Changes and continuities

Against this background described by Spencer, the Board of Education issued a new set of Regulations for Elementary Schools in 1904. The Regulations conveyed both liberal and instrumental aims. The purpose of the Public Elementary School was to 'form and strengthen the character and to develop the intelligence' of children, to assist both girls and boys, 'according to their different needs, to fit themselves, practically and intellectually, for the work of life'. In that task the school should aim to enlist the interest and co-operation of the parents and the home to help children 'not merely to reach their full development as individuals, but also to become upright and useful members of the community'. Such breadth and coherence represented a considerable departure from the mechanical and increasingly complex curriculum previously laid down to facilitate 'payment by results'. But even more constructive was the enhancement of these broad aims by a handbook of *Suggestions for the Consideration of Teachers and others concerned in the work of Public Elementary Schools*, published the following year. The *Suggestions* have frequently been cited as a landmark both in the official acknowledgment of a more child-centred approach to elementary education and in the State's recognition of a more independent role for the elementary teacher:

> The teacher must know the children and must sympathize with them, for it is of the essence of teaching that the mind of the teachers should touch the mind of the pupil ... and though the teachers can influence only a short period of the lives of the scholars, yet it is the period when human nature is most plastic, when good influence is most fruitful.[16]

One professional response was a welcome from the journal *School World*, 'the book is a fine piece of work and it runs on a high level ... it is a new and a brave thing to say what is said in these suggestions to the primary teachers of England'.[17] It was agreed that primary schooling was predominantly about the training of character, and that children should progress through it according to their own state of readiness. But this general welcome was not without reservation, and the criticisms made tell us something about the primary school as seen from the inside by teachers. *School World* argued that public opinion was only just awakening to the State's responsibility for the physical welfare of the young, and the key to the teacher's work, it argued, was knowledge of the child's body. Physical education, so well catered for in the independent schools to which politicians sent their own sons, was still woefully neglected in public elementary schools. *School World* also noted absence of consideration for the teacher's status, for conditions of work such as over-filled classes, as a result of which primary teaching remained 'an unpopular and comparatively empty profession ... On this subject, surely the most important of all connected with primary education, the *Suggestions* are silent.'[18]

Birchenough looked back on this first decade of the twentieth century as one of 'great and fruitful activity' in which the focus turned to education for alert and disciplined intelligence, for qualities of imagination and sympathy, for robust character which were the foundation of good citizenship.[19] Not only Deweyan but also Pestalozzian and Herbartian principles of relevance, concreteness and interest informed a more integrated and child-centred curriculum, with investigative methods in elementary science, a nature study movement and handicraft with a new purpose.[20] The sense of a new discourse about the role of primary education was reinforced by Liberal reforms of 1906 and 1907 introducing school meals and a school medical service which made the elementary schools on a national scale much more than simply educational institutions, as vehicles for improving the nation's health and nutrition.

In 1927 a revised *Handbook of Suggestions* was published by the Board of Education, reflecting what Birchenough celebrated as 'the growth of an altogether higher professional standard' than that which had pertained 20 years previously.[21] It marked a significant advance of thinking about the curriculum in its more liberal view of history and science, and in the aesthetic and practical side of schoolwork, in drawing, music and handicraft. Closely allied to these curricular emphases was a concern for the quality of the school environment, identifiably influenced by the Duchess of Atholl, Parliamentary Secretary to the Board of Education.[22] New technology worked alongside new attitudes in creating more visual interest within the classroom. A good deal of space was given in the teachers' press to the 'Schoolroom Beautiful'.[23] Increasing availability and improving quality of pictorial reproduction encouraged more visual stimulus in the classroom. In January 1927, Evans Brothers, publishers of *Teachers World*, began publication of the impressive *Pictorial Education* which offered large-scale and high-quality photographs for the classroom wall, and later that year the Board of Education produced a report on the use of pictures in schools.[24] Technological progress may thus be seen impinging on primary classrooms alongside pedagogical theory in contributing to motivation and gaining the children's interest. The new *Handbook of Suggestions* of 1927 was greeted in the professional journals as a 'sane and liberal statement' of work that could be done and was already being done 'by the best and most experienced teachers', and the professional autonomy it implied was welcomed. It was a 'challenge to independent thought', underlining the sense of excitement about innovation and was considered more accessible in its style. There was no apparent irony intended when a commentator in *Teachers' World* asked 'Are we old-fashioned in our methods? If we are, it is the beginning of the end. In this progressive world it is perilous to be out of date.'[25]

For the public at large in the 1920s schools became more visible through local open days and education weeks. The combined effect of a statutory requirement to consult with their citizens on planning educational provision, and of municipal pride, spurred some LEAs to publicize their schools. In 1922 West Ham planned a 'civic educational festival', 'a special week in which a striking and cheerful display should be given of the hugely interesting and varied educational work of all kinds now going on in the borough'.[26] Many teachers gave freely of their own time in planning and realizing these events. Young children themselves were also becoming more 'visible', their emotional and intellectual growth understood and expressed as an object of scientific investigation through both Freudian psychoanalytic perspectives and Piagetian developmental psychology. A leading exponent of these trends in British primary education was Susan Isaacs, whose books were widely read and much reprinted and who also exerted an influence through official channels.[27]

In 1937 the need for a substantially revised edition of the *Suggestions* after only a decade was seen as evidence by one contemporary of the speed and degree of change in educational discourse.[28] The stress was on 'education rather than instruction, the study of the child more than the subject-matter'. Particular attention was paid to the adoption by junior schools of the good practice that was seen to have characterized the education of infants, and full account was taken of the new visual aids, school broadcasts and the use of books. 'The richness of school life at its best stands revealed', reflecting the 'idealism and devotion' which Birchenough considered now informed the work of elementary education.[29]

Evidence from professional journals suggests that by 1937 new approaches to education were far more established and accepted, though not without controversy. The *Handbook of Suggestions* was enthusiastically welcomed by *The Schoolmaster and Woman Teacher's Chronicle* (hereafter, for brevity, *The Schoolmaster*) for being more than purely statements of ideals but 'unavoidable responses to changed conditions', 'reasonable and practical' as well as 'liberal and noble'.[30] The President of the Board of Education offered his own personal commendation of the new *Handbook*, focusing on three themes: a shift of emphasis from the subject to the child, a transformation of the teacher's function from training to superintending growth and development, and a good environment to foster mental and physical growth.[31] The *Journal of Education* greeted the new *Handbook* as 'very much suggestions rather than instructions', but noted, too, 'a tendency in some quarters to regard the book as a sort of pedagogic Bible', and expressed reservations about its sometimes 'unduly rosy view' and 'somewhat complacent exposition'.[32]

The *Schoolmaster* aligned itself with progressivism generally, and indeed 'progressivism' was seen to embody the cause of general educational advance.[33] A sense of irrevocable change was as strong as that of impending world conflict in much of the professional journalism. In April 1937 a presidential address to the National Union of Teachers (NUT) described the way in which during the last 25 years extended freedom in schools and educational advancement had gone hand-in-hand with increased knowledge and growing control of natural forces,[34] and F.H. Spencer, Chief Inspector of Education for the London County Council (LCC) was reported as observing of progress since 1902, that 'children today are more alert, more resourceful, more original, more civilized and vastly happier'.[35] This phenomenon was seen as a product of economic and cultural change of which the new education had not only been a beneficiary but in which it had also played its part. Euphoria about new methods, however, was tempered by recognition of material obstacles, including excessive class sizes and inadequate or inferior resources.[36] Inadequate facilities constituted a major obstacle to improvement; for example there were still 999 schools on the official Board of Education 'black list' of schools with defective premises, which received continuing publicity.[37] There were also cynical voices, as in a letter from a teacher questioning the extent of practical classroom teaching experience of the authors of the *Handbook of Suggestions*,[38] and an exchange of correspondence in the pages of *The Schoolmaster* about 'stunts' and 'fads'.[39] A front-page article appeared in the same journal under the banner headline: 'FACTS ARE THE MAIN THING: A Good Word for the Old Way of Teaching'.[40] Sir Percy Jackson, retiring Chairman of the West Riding Education Committee, recognized teaching as a profession wielding great power,[41] while Oliver Stanley, President of the Board of Education, stressed the need for education in a democracy and claimed that the schools were 'steadily winning a hold on the esteem and affection of the people'.[42] In *The Schoolmaster's* judgment the new *Handbook of Suggestions* published in April 1937 revealed not just liberal idealism, but a strategic response to developing international tension by asserting the teachers' role in the maintenance not only of a fit and healthy population but also the spirit of freedom in contrast with authoritarian states.[43] From another political angle, the Trades Union Congress (TUC) publication *Education and Democracy* argued that the main purpose of modern education was to extend liberty and that this purpose must inform both teaching method and curriculum.

For the public at large in the 1930s schools became more visible through publications such as the National Union of Teachers', *The Schools at Work*.[44] This folio volume contained 52 pages of sepia photographs to:

> represent very fairly the purpose which actuates the schools and the methods which that purpose employs. Not the least striking feature of this work is the marked contrast revealed in the conditions in the schools fifty years ago as compared with those of today.[45]

One double-page spread showed the varied activities of an infant school day, including learning out of doors, learning through play and a percussion band. In representations of juniors the 'three Rs' were more prominent but there was also much art and craft, some of it in specialist accommodation, though predominantly with children sitting in rows. There was an emphasis in pictures and text alike on child-centredness, on the teachers' professionalism and on a sense of national pride, schooling and the freedom of teachers as 'a most characteristic episode in our island story'.[46] A less complacent image of the schools for public consumption was provided by one of a critical series of social documentary films sponsored by the gas industry in the later 1930s. Basil Wright's *Children at School* (1937) was a moving critique of the poor physical condition of many of the nation's elementary schools.[47] The outbreak of war brought schools to the public attention in a new way as they were evacuated from the big cities: images of orderly groups of children in their teachers' care.[48]

For the 1950s and 1960s the most accessible evidence of change in primary education survives today in the visual form of school buildings. After the war, immediate priority was given to accommodating new secondary schools, and protests were heard, as before, about the scandalous neglect of the primary school building stock. But new primary school buildings which did slowly appear still speak eloquently through their architectural forms of changing relationships between teachers and children, and of a changing curriculum. In counties such as Hertfordshire which pioneered advances, the schools from this period, even after half a century of use, continue to provide an inspiring and generous environment of light and space, though by modern standards costly to heat and to maintain.[49] Classrooms became more flexible, allowing for group work and specialized activities such as creative work, scientific investigation and library research, whilst circulation spaces such as the traditional corridor were adapted to become part of the learning environment. Educational texts and teachers' journals of the time, more generously illustrated than before, offer photographic evidence of children engaged informally on a variety of activities within a more integrated curriculum. Historians need to question the representativeness of their sources, remembering that the most photogenic environments were the most photographed, whilst hundreds of thousands of children continued to labour in traditional class-rooms under more formal pedagogies aimed primarily at achievement in the selection process of the eleven-plus examination. Nevertheless, these visual images of progressivism embody a discourse which generated new expectations of primary education.

The pre-war *Handbook of Suggestions* was not supplanted until the end of the decade. This new handbook acknowledged the educational phase in its simpler title: *Primary Education*. Progressive practices were still contested and the new handbook was indicative of a good deal of compromise between conflicting views on primary practice, but it certainly gave some official endorsement to the activity methods that had been emerging in the new primary schools.[50] *Teachers World* viewed the new guidance as a 'milestone', one which marked primary education as having 'come into its own – a stage of education with a life and philosophy of its own'.[51] However, there is evidence of a live debate in the professional press between 'traditional' and 'progressive' teaching methods and doubts were raised for example about the variety of practice.

> We usually pride ourselves, and boast to the rest of the world, about the freedom that we enjoy to do pretty much as we like in our teaching. [but] ... One of the snags is that many teachers don't know quite why they adopt certain styles or methods. They may have done them when they were young; or they may have adopted them from some head, or writer, or lecturer, who may or may not have had sound educational reasons for his system; or they may have just blundered into them.[52]

The broader cultural context of primary education at this time was an increasing affluence and a rising standard of living. Technology now available to enliven the educational experience of primary children was enticingly promoted in the pages of the professional press. Full-page advertisements of Junior Nature Study films from the Rank G.B. Film Library promised to arouse in children an interest in the natural world around them, using time-lapse photography to record seasonal changes in flora and fauna and microphotography to render minute structures in more easily perceptible scale. Balsa wood for junior crafts, historical and scientific models enabled 'a valuable introduction to the scope and limitations of natural wood, and to three-dimensional thinking', 'practice in measuring, hand and eye training, and the development of manual skill' as well as offering 'the emotional stimulus of achievement'. Advertisements for art materials, plasticine, pottery equipment and stage lighting held up the model of a rich and creative curriculum, even to those readers whose own practice in school may have been more limited. Publishers of children's books and schoolbooks, increasingly illustrated and attractively printed, were entering a boom period. Series of information books by publishers such as Ladybird and A. & C. Black were well advertised, and at the beginning of the new school year *The Schoolmaster* reported the Children's Book Show organized by the Juvenile Group of the Publishers' Association at the National Book League.[53]

Lavishly reported by the teachers' journals was a National Education Exhibition organized by the NUT at Olympia, echoing flamboyant consumer exhibitions such as Ideal Homes and the Motor Show. This exhibition created a public stage for the developing primary curriculum, offering teachers and the general public alike an impressive view of the range of activities, of new teaching methods and of the technologies employed in them.[54] *Teachers World*, with its marked tendency of pique towards the NUT, was somewhat carping at the allegedly limited coverage of primary education in the exhibition.[55]

By 1963 primary education had received a sufficiently high profile for the Minister of Education to accede at last to pressure for a major enquiry and he gave a new remit to the Central Advisory Council for Education, chaired for this purpose by Bridget Plowden. Following more than three years of investigation and discussion this massive review was published under the significant title of *Children and their Primary Schools*, offering a survey which began with the child, its physical and intellectual development, family and neighbourhood before covering the organization of school and the curriculum. Plowden generated a high level of publicity and visibility for primary education. The Report itself celebrated the ever more visible and visual primary classroom, through photography in black and white and in colour.[56] Its long enquiry coincided with the introduction of a second public service TV channel and with colour television, and significant use of this medium was made to raise the public profile of primary education. A film on primary education, *I Want To Go To School – Children at Work and Play*, was produced by the NUT and was given three separate screenings on TV in 1960.[57] Growing public interest stemmed in part from increasing concerns and arguments over eleven-plus selection, especially as governments began to respond to these concerns by promoting comprehensive secondary schools.

Raising the visibility of primary education was soon to backfire, however, in the media coverage received by the troubled William Tyndale School in the mid-1970s. The youth revolt of the 1960s, culminating in campus unrest in the year after the Plowden Report, invited critics to propose a quite spurious connection between the two. Educational institutions at all levels, new universities, the new comprehensives and now the primary schools proved a hunting ground for journalists seeking out the roots of this cultural turmoil and television proved a dramatic medium for investigative documentary. At William Tyndale School, a somewhat anarchic regime, and consequent parental disquiet and tension between school governors and the local education authority, generated a number of televisual events in the form of protests, demonstrations and strikes. A protracted enquiry conducted by Robin Auld QC for the Inner London Education Authority (ILEA) kept the events in the media spotlight for much of 1976 and provided a pretext rather than a reason for the Prime Minister's unusual intervention in educational matters. James Callaghan made his portentous Ruskin speech in October of that year.

A second kind of visibility, not unconnected with the first, was produced by a growing trend of empirical research. Primary education as a topic for social scientific research was well established by Blyth's sociological study in 1963. One criticism directed at the Plowden Report had been its insufficient and partial research of classroom practice, and pedagogical debates emerging from Plowden revealed a dearth of knowledge about how primary teachers taught. Researchers in university departments of education began to make good this dearth through observation of primary classrooms, and the publication in 1976 of findings by Neville Bennett of Lancaster University, and later by the ORACLE research team at Leicester University, served to fuel as well as to inform public debate.[58] This growth of university-based research was also associated with post-graduate and in-service training as the academic qualifications for primary teaching, its expectations and occupational status, were raised.

Government, too, was prompted to conduct its own investigations, exemplified in a survey conducted by Her Majesty's Inspectors (HMI), *Primary Education in England*, 1978.[59] Secretary of State Shirley Williams hailed the survey as an up-to-date and objective professional assessment, made through traditional inspection and statistical techniques.[60] Welcoming its publication in 1978 a leader in *The Times* observed that the problems of primary education had been much discussed on the basis of anecdotal impressions, political prejudice and decontextualized statistics, to which HMI now brought a more candid, sober and experienced view. The resulting picture was less bleak than often portrayed where good working relationships between teachers and children were accompanied by attention to literacy and numeracy, resulting in gradually rising standards of reading between 1955 and 1976. This was in contrast to the view of stagnation in reading that had aroused concern when identified by an earlier report of 1972 by the National Foundation for Educational Research (NFER). Her Majesty's Inspectors supported the view that basic skills were more successfully learned when embedded in a broader curriculum of high quality, and to this end they set a higher priority on more specialist teaching than on reducing class sizes. Moreover teachers were identified as underestimating the abilities of and failing to extend the most able children, especially those from immigrant or deprived backgrounds.[61] In fact it was the latter point that made the front-page headline for *The Times*: 'Clever pupils' potential unfulfilled', and on the inside pages 'Primary schools have low standards in most subjects apart from basic skills'. The response of the NUT was to hope that evidence of the high priority given to the three Rs would end the sniping that schools had had to endure.[62] The *Times Educational Supplement (TES)* identified a sharp contrast between the tone of the *Primary Survey* and that of the Department of Education and Science (DES) 'Yellow Book' that had provided the briefing for Prime Minister Callaghan's Ruskin speech two years before. The earlier document (echoing Black Paper themes) had spoken of 'uncritical application of informal methods', a 'lack of discipline' and a failure to achieve satisfactory results in formal subjects, especially maths. By contrast the HMI survey found 75 per cent of teachers were 'mainly didactic' in their teaching, and only 20 per cent of classes observed employed a satisfactory combination of methods, implying a far less widespread application of informal methods than had been assumed. The 20 per cent of teachers who were 'mainly exploratory' in their teaching style, however, were apparently less successful in the reading and maths scores achieved.[63]

In 1986 the House of Commons Education, Science and Art Committee addressed the state of primary education, after an enquiry lasting three years and including visits to 51 schools. The title of its report, *Achievement in Primary Schools*,[64] was significantly nuanced by contrast with that of Plowden, the emphasis having now moved from 'children' to 'achievement'. The committee also distanced itself historically from Plowden by contrasting the economic and political context 20 years on: economic recession, job anxiety, rising public expectation, retrenchment in public expenditure and a general questioning of authority.[65] Plowden's philosophy, it claimed, had reflected a prevailing spirit of the time, an optimism about the ability of society to secure general social improvement and about the prospect of technology delivering an ever-increasing standard of living. But increasing competition in world markets, a debate on standards and a demand for accountability had changed the climate. Moreover indices of economic disadvantage and social breakdown had increased with unemployment rising more than fourfold (from three-quarters of a million in 1971 to three and a quarter million in 1986) and divorce figures almost doubling (from 80,000 in 1971 to 158,000 in 1984). National Society for the Prevention of Cruelty to Children (NSPCC) figures for rates of child abuse were beginning to rise sharply in the 1980s.[66] The committee re-emphasized the substantial and crucial importance of primary education in forming a foundation for future attitudes and achievement, and stressed the complexity and skill required of nursery and primary teachers against a continued undervaluing of this phase both in status and resources. The changing historical context was underlined by Willam van Straubenzee, the committee's chairman, as he launched the report: 'The importance of the subject is such that the nation will have to face up to it. What was seen as adequate in previous generations would not be adequate today.'[67]

The *TES* expressed its view that politicians and public alike were being told to 'put up or shut up' on primary education, that the only way to raise standards would be to spend more money. Primary schools needed more teachers (one per class was insufficient), primary teachers needed to be paid on a par with their secondary colleagues, and schools had to be better resourced. In its opinion the committee had provided 'a useful handbook on the state of primary education and a resounding call for the nation to take its primary children and teachers more seriously'.[68] *The Teacher* saw the report as a pat on the back: 'MPs like what they see in primaries' offering 'support for NUT policies'. A special conference of the Union, 'A Firm Foundation: the nation's primary schools', was convened and addressed by Secretary of State, Kenneth Baker, arguing that primary education, too often overlooked, was now at the top of his agenda. Baker's address as reported in *The Times* sounded less congratulatory in tone, however, with a warning against complacency as he repeated earlier HMI concerns about weak curriculum planning, lack of depth in science and failure to stretch the most able.[69] Teachers attending the conference demanded more staff, time and money to do the job, but also voiced resentment at the idea that they needed telling how to do it.[70]

There were, however, mixed messages in public discourse on primary education. At the annual conference of the British Association for the Advancement of Science support for an exploratory curriculum came from an unexpected quarter. Graham Anthony, industrial director of the Engineering Council, supported topic work, pupil-centred projects, open-ended learning and across-the-curriculum approaches, claiming 'This is what engineering is about – pulling together ideas from different parts of the curriculum ... then putting them together to get an answer.' Thus primary teachers were effectively 'meeting the challenge of science and technology to safeguard Britain's industrial and commercial future'.[71]

Against the background of concerns expressed in 1978 about the 'whole curriculum' and in 1986 about 'standards of achievement', the inauguration of a national curriculum in 1988 appears with hindsight as an almost inevitable development, though powerful voices had continued to hold such an idea as anathema. A dramatic and fundamental feature of the National Curriculum which emerged was its construction of young children's learning in terms of 'core subjects' defined as English, mathematics and science, distinct from humanities, creative arts and physical education which were somewhat ambiguously designated 'foundation subjects' but clearly regarded as of less importance. However, a visible and visual impact on the primary classroom resulted from the energetic response of educational publishers for whom the National Curriculum had laid a golden egg. All sorts of attractive new teaching materials and teaching aids, colourful posters and books epitomized by the innovative publications of Dorling Kindersley, adorned classroom walls and bookshelves with the noticeable result, fully intended by the government, that classrooms became more uniform across the country. Teachers busy with bureaucratic tasks had proportionately less time for displays of children's work, on which great emphasis had been placed in previous decades, and published materials were more frequently substituted for children's work in maintaining the principle that the classroom should be an attractive and educative space.

Accountability meant a new kind of visibility for primary education, the hostile gaze of a new inspection regime ushered in by the Office for Standards in Education (Ofsted) in 1993 and public exposure for primary schools through the publication of league tables. Government also continued to pressurize primary teachers and undermine their professional credibility in the 1990s through the promotion of tabloid rhetorics such as 'Back to basics' and the proposal of a 'Mums' army' for the staffing of infant classes with unqualified helpers. More instrumental was the development of 'national strategies' for literacy and numeracy, hatched under the Conservative governments of the mid-1990s, but implemented with the fairly seamless transition of policy on primary education under New Labour from 1997. These strategies shifted the balance of authority even further from the teacher to the State, in that not only curriculum but pedagogy, too, was now being dictated. The strategies included tight prescription of how they were to be taught. Although this further erosion of professional autonomy was initially repugnant, teachers were won over as the teaching plans and materials were reasonably well designed. Under pressure of frequent inspection it would clearly be safer to follow prescribed methods, and the ease of planning reduced some of the bureaucratic burden that had built up with assessment, recording and reporting.[72]

Conclusion

Over the course of the century primary education became distinctive and highly visible. More than with secondary schools, parents enjoy greater access to the institution and a closer relationship with the class teacher. The sense of partnership between school and home in rearing and educating younger children, echoing the advocacy of home–school co-operation from as early as the 1905 *Suggestions*, has become almost a cultural norm and runs much deeper than a mere government policy. A perception of the early years of child development as critical to later 'success' has shifted the policy spotlight increasingly to primary schools. The immediate future may bring even more focus on pre-school provision, in which the primary schools have a significant, though far from exclusive, stake. Early years education is identified as a critical investment for the

future by families and by the nation. The impact of technology on information and learning will continue to modify pedagogy, and the appearance
of primary classrooms will continue to change, reflecting this. Technology
is one aspect of cultural change that alters the appearance of primary
education in parallel with other social institutions. Other social and
cultural changes in the state of health, standard of living and family structure have had a significant impact on primary schools over the twentieth
century and will continue to do so in the twenty-first. Earlier maturity and
an increasing sophistication of 11-year-olds, as well as the ever more
complex world of knowledge, is making demands on primary teachers in
the upper age range, and the traditional and distinctive primary model of
the generalist class teacher is likely to disintegrate under these demands.

It is less clear how the tension between professional autonomy and state
determination of curriculum and teaching methods will be resolved.
Measurement of outcomes and hence pervasive testing and inspection
appears to have become an inevitable consequence of accountability, to
which no end is in sight. Yet teacher supply has faltered as bureaucratic
mechanisms of accountability have tended to stifle the altruism and
creativity that attracted recruits to primary teaching.[73] Younger children
present more of an attraction to many potential teachers, so that the
teacher shortages are less acute in primary than in secondary, but current
pupil–teacher ratios, so much greater in maintained than in independent
primary schools, may hinder recruitment as much as they may be seen to
hamper school effectiveness. The twenty-first-century primary school
already sees more ancillary workers, such as teaching assistants, and the
organizational tyranny of discrete class units is beginning to dissolve.

Undoubtedly the perceived national importance of primary education
and conflicts between teacher professionalism and state control of
curriculum and pedagogy will ensure a continuing high level of visibility
for primary education.

Key reading

Successive editions of the *Handbooks of Suggestions* up to the 1959
edition cited in this chapter, and subsequently guidance published by the
Schools Council, HMI, the National Curriculum Council (NCC), School
Curriculum and Assessment Authority (SCAA) and the Qualifications and
Curriculum Authority (QCA), offer insights into official aspirations for
primary curriculum and teaching method. Books of guidance for primary
teachers written by educationists and teacher trainers may be grounded
more in principle than policy, though they also represent ideals rather than
contemporary practice: J. Welton, *Principles and Methods of Teaching*,
London, W.B. Clive, 1906 with new editions in 1912 and 1924; M. Sturt
and E. Oakden, *Matter and Method in Education*, London, Kegan Paul,

Trench, Trubner, 1928, 2nd edn, 1931; M.V. Daniel, *Activity in the Primary School*, Oxford, Blackwell, 1947; L. Marsh, *Alongside the Child in the Primary School*, London, A. & C. Black, 1970; A. Pollard, *Reflective Teaching in the Primary School*, London, Cassell, 3rd edn, 1997. Teachers' journals provide a rich source of insights into the primary class-room from the teacher's point of view, especially *Teachers World* (from 1913 to 1976), *Junior Education* (1976–) and *Child Education* (1924–), *The Schoolmaster* (journal of the NUT which became *The Teacher* from 1962), and for the second half of the century the *Times Educational Supplement* becomes increasingly attentive to primary education, especially from the Plowden period onwards.

Commentaries by educationists early in the twentieth century and, as the century progressed, increasing volumes of research by university-based educationists provide important documentary sources for practice: F.H. Hayward, *The Primary Curriculum*, London, Ralph Holland, 1909; W.K. Richmond, *Purpose in the Junior School*, London, Alvin Redman, 1949; W.A.L. Blyth, *English Primary Education: a sociological description*, London, Routledge and Kegan Paul, 1965; M. Galton, B. Simon and P. Croll, *Inside the Primary Classroom*, London, Routledge and Kegan Paul, 1980; P. Mortimore and others, *School Matters: the junior years*, Wells, Open Books, 1988. Official reports and surveys by HMI supplement these sources.

Biographical and autobiographical sources for children and teachers give a more intimate view of individual experiences of primary education: V. Bell, *The Dodo*, London, Faber and Faber, 1950; G. Holmes, *The Idiot Teacher*; London, Faber and Faber, 1952. Ethnographic studies later amplify this type of account, for example, M. Armstrong, *Closely Observed Children: the diary of a primary classroom*, Richmond, Writers and Readers, 1980. Film and video sources may be found increasingly for the later decades of the century, and a readily available oral source lies in the memories of teachers and children.

Early historical accounts include: T. Raymont, *History of the Education of Young Children*, London, Longmans, 1937; C. Birchenough, *History of Elementary Education in England and Wales*, London, University Tutorial Press, 3rd edn, 1938. The pursuit of a more child-centred approach to the curriculum has been examined by R.J.W. Selleck, *Primary Education and the Progressives 1914–1939*, London, Routledge and Kegan Paul, 1972 and by P. Cunningham, *Curriculum Change in the Primary School since 1945*, London, Falmer, 1988. R. Lowe (ed.) *The Changing Primary School*, London, Falmer, 1987 offers historical analysis of various aspects such as school governance, relationships with parents and primary school architecture covering from 1945, while N. Thomas, *Primary Education from Plowden to the 1990s*, London, Falmer, 1990 deals more exclusively with policy and curriculum. C. Richards and P. Taylor (eds) *How Shall We*

School Our Children? Primary education and its future, London, Falmer, 1998 considers providers, participants and procedures, and R. Alexander, *Culture and Pedagogy: International Comparisons in Primary Education*, Oxford, Blackwell, 2000 analyses British primary education, within its recent historical and cultural context, in a comparative perspective.

Notes

1 Department for Education and Employment, *Schools: Building on Success*, London, February 2001, p. 28.
2 For example, an account of a disillusioned teacher of infants: H. Wilce, 'I Quit', *Times Educational Supplement*, 9 March 2001.
3 *Times Educational Supplement*, 23 March 2001.
4 Board of Education, *Report of the Consultative Committee on the Primary School*, London, HMSO, 1931; Board of Education, *Report of the Consultative Committee on Infant and Nursery Schools*, London, HMSO, 1933.
5 C. Birchenough, *History of Elementary Education in England and Wales*, London, University Tutorial Press, 3rd edn, 1938; R.D. Bramwell, *Elementary School Work 1900–1925*, Durham, University of Durham Institute of Education, 1961; I. Goodson and S. Ball (eds) *Defining the Curriculum: Histories and Ethnographies*, London, Falmer, 1984.
6 S. Humphries, *Hooligans or Rebels?*, Oxford, Blackwell, 1981; for more recent periods, children's perceptions have been researched and recorded: A. Pollard, D. Thiessen and A. Filer (eds) *Children and their Curriculum: the Perspectives of Primary and Elementary School Children*, London, Falmer, 1997.
7 P. Cunningham and P. Gardner, *Elementary School Teachers 1918–1939: Text and Testimony*, London, Woburn Press, (forthcoming 2002); P. Cunningham, *Being a Primary Teacher in the Twentieth Century*, CREPE Occasional Papers no. 13, Warwick, Centre for Research in Elementary and Primary Education, University of Warwick, 2000.
8 M. Depaepe *et al. Order in Progress: Everyday Education Practice in Primary Schools – Belgium, 1880–1970*, Leuven, Leuven University Press, 2000, p. 40.
9 I. Grosvenor, M. Lawn and K. Rousmaniere, *Silences and Images: The Social History of the Classroom*, New York, Peter Lang, 1999.
10 Lowndes's classic study, however, offered useful detail on aspects of classroom technology: G.A.N. Lowndes, *The Silent Social Revolution*, Oxford, Oxford University Press, 2nd edn, 1969, p. 134.
11 Matthew Arnold (1861) and T. Huxley (1877) cited in *Oxford English Dictionary*; F.H. Hayward (ed.) *The Primary Curriculum*, London, Ralph Holland, 1909.
12 M. Seaborne, *Primary School Design*, London, Routledge and Kegan Paul, 1971; M. Seaborne and R. Lowe, *The English School: Its Architecture and Organisation*, vol. 2, 1870–1970, London, Routledge and Kegan Paul, 1977.
13 I. Grosvenor, 'On visualising past classrooms', in Grosvenor, Lawn and Rousmaniere, op. cit.; M. Banks, 'Visual anthropology: image, object and interpretation', and B. Winton, ' "The camera never lies": the partiality of photographic evidence', in J. Prosser (ed.) *Image-Based Research: A Sourcebook for Qualitative Researchers*, London, Falmer, 1998.
14 F.H. Spencer, *An Inspector's Testament*, London, English Universities Press, 1938, p. 192.

15 Ibid., pp. 192–3.
16 Board of Education, *Handbook of Suggestions for the Consideration of Teachers and Others Concerned in the Work of Public Elementary Schools*, [Cd. 2638] London, HMSO, 1905, pp. 14–15.
17 *School World*, October 1905, pp. 371–3.
18 *School World*, October 1905, p. 371.
19 Birchenough, op. cit., p. 177.
20 Birchenough, op. cit., p. 448.
21 Birchenough, op. cit., p. 449.
22 A graduate of the Royal College of Music and one of the earliest women MPs: R. Betts, 'Parliamentary women: women Ministers of Education, 1924–1974', in J. Goodman and S. Harrop (eds) *Women, Educational Policy-Making and Administration in England*, London, Routledge, 2000, pp. 175–80.
23 Antecedents for this concern might be found in the work of Harriet Finlay-Johnson, but in *Teachers World* at this time the exponent was headmaster Samuel Clegg (father of Alec Clegg, later Director of Education for the West Riding and active in promoting a more aesthetically pleasing environment in schools): *Teachers World*, 2 September 1927, Special Supplement; see also *Journal of Education*, April 1927, p. 239, and October 1927, p. 726.
24 *Journal of Education*, February 1927, p. 142; *Teachers World*, 4 January 1928, title page.
25 *Teachers World*, 22 June 1927; 1 July 1927 p. 734.
26 West Ham LEA, 'Forward West Ham: An Educational Handbook for Parents and Citizens, and Programme of the West Ham Education Week, June, 1922, London, 1922, pp. 30–1; *Teachers World*, 28 September 1927, p. 1290; 5 October 1927, p. 6.
27 S. Isaacs, *Intellectual Growth in Young Children*, London, Routledge and Kegan Paul, 1930; S. Isaacs, *Social Development in Young Children: A Study of Beginnings*, London, Routledge and Kegan Paul, 1933; Board of Education, op. cit., 1931; Board of Education, op. cit., 1933.
28 Birchenough, op. cit., p. 450.
29 Ibid.
30 *The Schoolmaster and Woman Teacher's Chronicle*, 15 April 1937, title page, p. 758.
31 *The Schoolmaster*, 22 April 1937, p. 782.
32 *Journal of Education*, June 1937, p. 383.
33 *The Schoolmaster*, 20 May 1937, p. 966.
34 *The Schoolmaster*, 2 April 1937, p. 611.
35 *Journal of Education*, July 1937 p. 465.
36 *The Schoolmaster*, 2 April 1937, p. 632, 6 May 1937, p. 913.
37 *The Schoolmaster*, 29 July 1937, p. 171.
38 *The Schoolmaster*, 6 May 1937, p. 913.
39 *The Schoolmaster*, 4 February 1937, p. 232, 4 March 1937, p. 448.
40 *The Schoolmaster*, 12 August 1937. A critical review by Robert Lynd, essayist and social commentator, of Stephen Potter's celebrated book, *The Muse in Chains*.
41 *The Schoolmaster*, 14 January 1937, p. 47.
42 *The Schoolmaster*, 21 January 1937, p. 94.
43 *The Schoolmaster*, 15 April 1937, title page and p. 758.
44 NUT, *The Schools at Work, being a pictorial survey of national education in England and Wales*, London, Evans Brothers Ltd, n.d. [1931].
45 Ibid., p. 5.

46 Ibid., p. 7.
47 P. Cunningham, 'Moving images: propaganda film and British education, 1940–45', *Paedagogica Historica*, 2000, vol. 36, no. 1, pp. 389–406.
48 Ibid.; P. Cunningham and P. Gardner, '"Saving the nation's children": teachers, wartime evacuation in England and Wales and the construction of national identity', *History of Education*, 1999, vol. 28, no. 3, pp. 327–37.
49 S. Maclure, *Educational Development and School Building: Aspects of Public Policy 1945–1973*, Harlow, Longman, 1984; M. Seaborne, 'The post war revolution in primary school design', in R. Lowe (ed.) *The Changing Primary School*, London, Falmer, 1987; P. Cunningham, 'Open plan schooling: last stand of the progressives?', in Lowe, ibid.; A. Saint, *Towards a Social Architecture: the role of school-building in post-war England*, London, Yale University Press, 1987.
50 C. Richards, 'Yet another "crisis" in primary education?', *British Journal of Educational Studies*, 2001, vol. 49, no. 1, pp. 4–25.
51 *Teachers World* (Primary Edition), 27 November 1959, p. 1.
52 *Teachers World* (Primary Edition), 13 May 1959, p. 1.
53 *The Schoolmaster*, 9 October 1959.
54 *The Schoolmaster*, May and June 1959, passim.
55 *Teachers World* (Primary Edition), 5 June 1959, p. 1.
56 R. Aldrich, 'The Plowden Report, 1967: a visual study in primary school location, space and learning', unpublished conference paper, ISCHE XX, Kortrijk, Belgium, 1998.
57 P. Cunningham, *Curriculum Change in the Primary School since 1945: Dissemination of the Progressive Ideal*, London, Falmer, 1988, p. 173.
58 W.A.L. Blyth, *English Primary Education: a sociological description*, London, Routledge and Kegan Paul, 1965; P. Ashton and others, *The Aims of Primary Education: A Study of Teachers' Opinions* (Final report from the Schools Council Aims of Primary Education Project 1969–72 based at the University of Birmingham School of Education), London, Macmillan, 1975. The Observational, Research and Classroom Learning Evaluation (ORACLE) project reported in 1980.
59 Department of Education and Science, *Primary Education in England: A Survey by HM Inspectors of Schools*, London, HMSO, 1978 (included juniors but not infants).
60 *The Teacher*, 29 September 1978, p. 1.
61 *The Times*, 27 September 1978.
62 Ibid.
63 *Times Educational Supplement*, 29 September 1978. *The Teacher* noted that the survey of more than 500 schools had taken place between 1975 and Easter 1977, beginning before the launch of the 'Great Debate' in November 1976: *The Teacher*, 22 September 1978, p. 11.
64 House of Commons Education, Science and Art Committee, *Achievement in Primary Schools*, HC 1985–86, 40–1.
65 Ibid., para. 1.7.
66 Ibid., paras 3.3, 3.4, 3.5, 3.25.
67 *The Teacher*, 29 September 1986, p. 1.
68 *Times Educational Supplement*, 26 September 1986.
69 *The Times*, 2 October 1986.
70 *The Teacher*, 6 October 1986, p. 1.
71 *The Teacher*, 8 September 1986, p. 6. The British Association was a high-profile forum in which public debate on the curriculum could surface, as in

1937 when H.G. Wells sparked a furore with radical ideas for modernization of the elementary school curriculum. *The Schoolmaster*, 9 September 1937, p. 362; *Journal of Education*, October 1937, pp. 675–82.

72 A further mechanism in this modification of the teachers' pedagogical role and autonomy was the preparation by the Qualifications and Curriculum Authority of curriculum guidance for 'foundation subjects'; model schemes of work were published to support teachers from 1998 as curriculum requirements for foundation subjects were temporarily suspended to facilitate a concentration on 'the basics'. Once again, teachers understandably seized on the convenience of these materials which were quite well designed, but were also seen as 'authoritative'.

73 P. Cunningham, *Being a Primary Teacher in the Twentieth Century*, CREPE Occasional Papers no. 13, Warwick, Centre for Research in Elementary and Primary Education, University of Warwick, 2000.

Chapter 2

Secondary education

Gary McCulloch

The situation in 2000

At the end of the twentieth century, secondary education was compulsory for all children between 11 and 16 years of age, with more than half of the age group staying on to the age of 18. It sought to cater for all abilities and aptitudes, while enforcing a national curriculum and an examination system that ensured a comparable educational programme in every school in the country. Yet it was widely perceived as being in a state of crisis. A frequent criticism has been that it is socially divided, between the large majority of secondary schools funded by taxation but free at the point of delivery, and the seven per cent of secondary schools that are independent of the State and supported by parental fees.[1]

The commentators Adonis and Pollard have recently complained that, more than any other in the western world, the school system in England is based on a division between state and private (so-called 'public') schools, with prestige and resources going mainly to the latter rather than to the former. The Conservative politician, George Walden, described this division as a 'Berlin Wall', the basis for a 'two-nation education system'.[2] Nick Davies, a journalist with the newspaper, *The Guardian*, also emphasized the differences between state and private schools in a series of trenchant articles on 'Schools in crisis'. Divided by a strip of land in Brighton, on the south coast, at the private school Roedean almost every pupil secured at least five top grades in GCSE examinations taken at the age of 16, while only ten per cent of pupils attending Stanley Deason secondary school could achieve the same marks.[3] The two private King Edward VI schools in Birmingham charged annual fees of £4,900 and boasted a new design centre, new language and computer laboratories, a covered swimming pool, and a teacher–pupil ratio of 1:12. By contrast, the state school, Bordesley Green, also in Birmingham, had 'lots of concrete, windows and draughts', received funding of £2,232 per pupil, and had a teacher–pupil ratio of 1:16.[4] The leading independent school, Eton College, a boys' boarding school for 13 to 18-year-olds, charged annual fees of over

£12,000 in 1995; when London state school pupils spent a week there, newspapers celebrated a meeting of the 'Bash Street Kids' and 'Lord Snooty and his pals'.[5]

Within the state sector, too, there are many social differences, especially between schools located in affluent suburbs and those in the inner cities. Cases of spectacularly failing schools in the poorer areas of the country have become commonplace. Ridings School in Halifax, West Yorkshire, was forced to close temporarily in 1996 because of assaults by pupils on teachers. According to a report in *The Independent*, 16-year-old pupils took a whole French lesson to draw a table and write 'la table' under it, a religious studies lesson consisted of drawing a church, and up to three-quarters of the pupils were absent in some lessons. Yet, at the same time, 'It was also a school of stark contrasts. An orderly class was taught well next door to a classroom in which chaos reigned.'[6] Hackney Downs School in London was another example of seemingly intractable problems which in this case led to the permanent closure of the school.[7]

Other schools were not in the headlines but suffered from chronic difficulties with outdated and inadequate facilities, an issue that the new Labour government was struggling to address as the century reached its end.[8] Social differences and inequalities were readily apparent between different secondary schools within the same city, a phenomenon assiduously followed by many parents who sought to exercise a preference over the best school for their children. Equally, it remained true that schools in similar areas with comparable intakes of pupils could perform very differently in terms of examination results, while in many cases schools could demonstrate year on year improvements in the performance of their pupils that defied the nature of the environment in which they worked.[9] Although its many critics could describe secondary education as 'a system in which too many children are condemned to a life of failure', plagued by poor standards and inadequate facilities,[10] there were still significant successes to be found.[11] Nonetheless, after a century of development, secondary education continued to be fiercely contested over fundamental issues relating to its purposes, character, and role.

The situation in 1900

To what extent can we find the origins of these controversies in the character of secondary education as it was first established? In 1900, the modern system of state secondary education in England was in its most crucial stage of development. It is most instructive to recall the nature of the issues being addressed, and how they were resolved, at this pivotal moment. The decisions taken at this time asserted a key role for state involvement as distinct from a dependence on local and voluntary provision, for an organized system of central and local administration as opposed to a confusing range of agencies, and for clear lines of demarcation between secondary education and elementary and technical provision rather than an overlap between them.

Although the term 'secondary education' was current throughout the nineteenth century, imported originally from France,[12] only in the final decade was there a successful attempt both to define and organize it in a systematic way. In the mid-1890s, it was the subject of a Royal Commission led by James Bryce which was invited to consider 'what are the best methods of establishing a well-organised system of Secondary Education in England, taking into account existing deficiencies'.[13] The Bryce Report, published in 1895, noted that the ground of secondary education was 'already almost all covered with buildings so substantial that the loss to be incurred in clearing it for the erection of a new and symmetrical pile cannot be contemplated'. At the same time, it acknowledged, 'these existing buildings are so ill-arranged, so ill-connected, and therefore so inconvenient, that some scheme of reconstruction seems unavoidable'.[14] The task facing the Commission was in its own view 'nothing less than to complete the educational system of England, now confessedly defective in that part which lies between the elementary schools on the one hand and the Universities on the other, and to frame an organisation which shall be at once firm and flexible'.[15] It developed for this purpose a broad and inclusive definition of secondary education, seeking to embrace technical instruction within it. According to the Bryce Report, secondary education:

> teaches the boy [sic] so to apply the principles he is learning, and so to learn the principles by applying them, or so to use the instruments he is being made to know, as to perform or produce something, interpret a literature or a science, make a picture or a book, practise a plastic or a manual art, convince a jury or persuade a senate, translate or annotate an author, dye wool, weave cloth, design or construct a machine, navigate a ship, or command an army.[16]

Ultimately, therefore, secondary education might be described as 'education conducted in view of the special life that has to be lived with the express purpose of forming a person fit to live it'.[17] It remained to be seen how best to provide for such an ideal.

Among the existing 'buildings' identified by the Bryce Report were the socially elite 'public schools' such as Eton, Harrow, Rugby and Winchester, independent, fee-paying and mainly boarding schools at the height of their power and prestige in the late Victorian era. There were also a large number of local endowed, proprietary and private schools, highly varied in standards and fee levels. Some of the school boards responsible for elementary education had also developed 'higher grade' elementary schools which in many cases were offering an alternative form of secondary education for the urban artisan and lower middle class. Several agencies were involved in funding, inspecting and providing examinations for these different kinds of schools. The Bryce Report recommended that a central authority should be created that would be responsible for the whole of secondary education, 'not in order to control, but rather to supervise the Secondary Education of the country, not to override or supersede local action, but to endeavour to bring about among the various agencies which provide that education a harmony and co-operation which are now wanting'.[18] Local authorities would be established that would be responsible to this central authority. Moreover, three grades of secondary schools would be defined, within which the so-called higher grade elementary schools would be accepted as secondary schools of the third grade.

The political negotiations that ensued to bring about a comprehensive system of state secondary education brought some of Bryce's proposals to fruition, but abandoned others. The Board of Education created in 1900 provided a central authority. The local education authorities (LEAs) introduced under the Education Act of 1902, supplanting the school boards, were to be responsible for secondary schools in their own area. However, the higher grade school experiment was stopped in its tracks, and secondary education under the auspices of the State was soon redefined as principally academic in character. As Reeder has argued, overall, 'bureaucratic and legislative intervention in the period 1897–1904 entailed the development of an educational system which differentiated between the higher elementary (including the technical) sector and the secondary sector, not only in terms of administrative control, but in the type of curricula offered and in pupil intakes and occupational outcomes'. Secondary education remained confined to a small elite, accessible through the payment of fees or through competitive scholarships from the elementary schools.[19]

The prefatory memorandum to the Regulations for Secondary Schools issued in 1904 clarified the nature and purposes of secondary education under the new regime. It defined 'secondary schools' as including 'any Day or Boarding School which offers to each of its scholars, up to and beyond the age of 16, a general education, physical, mental and moral, given through a complete graded course of instruction of wider scope and more advanced degree than that in Elementary Schools'.[20] Instruction in such schools would be general in nature, with specialization in any given area permitted only after general education had been completed to an advanced stage. The course of instruction also needed to be complete in giving a full treatment to different areas up to the age of 16. A minimum number of hours each week was also specified for English subjects (English language and literature, geography and history), languages (ancient or modern), mathematics and science.

The beginning of the twentieth century, therefore, marked the establishment of the modern era of secondary education in England. It was fiercely contested between a number of rival agencies and interests. In retrospect, too, the outcomes of these reforms have often been held responsible for the subsequent problems that the system was to encounter. Simon, in particular, characterized the 1902 Act as a wrong turning that effectively reinforced the social divisions between elementary and secondary education.[21] Vlaeminke has complained of the 'lost opportunity' represented by the abolition of the higher grade schools.[22] Certainly, the system as it was introduced did entrench social differences, even if it also held out at least some opportunity for social advancement. It now remains to explore how the lofty ideals of Bryce and the rigid certainties of the 1904 Secondary School Regulations were eventually to degenerate into the seemingly intractable problems of secondary education at the end of the twentieth century.

Changes and continuities

Over the twentieth century as a whole, several features were dominant in secondary education in England. The most obvious trend was one of growth, in pupil numbers, schools, and length of schooling. Underlying this trend were a number of tensions, social as well as educational in nature, that had been evident at the beginning of the century and that persisted despite a rapidly changing social context and many determined attempts to reform the system. The academic tradition remained dominant, and was buttressed by an infrastructure of assessment and examinations that became if anything stronger over the course of the century. There was a major tension between educating the social and academic elite and catering for the remainder of the age group which constituted the majority. At the same time, the independent or 'public' schools survived and even prospered as a separate system. These persistent tensions in turn encouraged a continuing debate over the nature of secondary education that was never fully resolved.

In examining these features as they developed in more detail, it is convenient to divide the century into three key phases of development in secondary education. The first runs from the Education Act of 1902, which established a system of state secondary education, to the Education Act of 1944, which introduced free secondary education for all pupils from 11 to 15 years of age. The second is from 1944 until 1965, a period during which an initial experiment with a so-called 'tripartite system' of different types of secondary schools eventually gave way to a model of a single type of school designed for all abilities and aptitudes, the comprehensive school. Lastly, the period from 1965 until 2000 witnessed the establishment of a system of comprehensive schools, but also increasing dissatisfaction that led to a range of new initiatives that were intended to improve opportunities for different groups of pupils.

1902–1944

The new model of grant-aided secondary education was soon consolidated in the decade that followed the Education Act of 1902 and the Regulations of 1904. The number of pupils at secondary schools began to grow, especially under the Liberal government after 1906. Under a major free place scheme introduced in 1907, up to one-quarter of the pupil intake was to be reserved for elementary school pupils who passed a qualifying examination. By 1911, over 82,000 former elementary school pupils were at secondary school, comprising about 60 per cent of the total intake, and about one-third of these received free secondary education.[23] Yet strong doubts remained over the opportunities offered to the mass of the population to progress to secondary schools. At the time of the outbreak of the First World War in 1914, of every 1,000 pupils of 10 to 11 years of age attending elementary schools, only 56 went on to a secondary education, a situation that has led the historian, Brian Simon, to conclude that the odds against such children receiving a free secondary education still stood at 40 to 1.[24]

There were many, indeed, who were willing to contend that educational opportunities for working-class children had actually declined in the first decade of the twentieth century. In 1907, for example, one Rochdale teacher, J.H. Brittain, inquired: 'Is it as easy now, as ten or twelve years ago, for the child of the self-sacrificing worker to obtain education higher than elementary in our large towns?' Brittain had himself taught in a higher grade school in the 1890s, which had prepared boys to go on directly to universities in some cases. Now, he complained, 'Rightly or wrongly I feel that under the administration of the Board during the past ten years the working man has been "jockeyed" out of facilities which the splendid enterprise of the great school boards gained for him.'[25]

Public and political interest in educational reform increased during the First World War, culminating in the Education Act of 1918, but economic and industrial problems in the early 1920s led to a period of retrenchment in education. In this context, the Labour Party, emerging as the main opposition party to the Conservatives, and seeking to offer a radical alternative, argued in favour of extending secondary education to all children. The key expression of this policy was a report entitled *Secondary Education For All*, produced by the influential historian R.H. Tawney. This work declared that secondary education should be regarded as the right of all, 'secondary education being the education of the adolescent and primary education being education preparatory thereto'.[26] The division of education into elementary and secondary was, it insisted, 'educationally unsound and socially obnoxious'.[27] On the other hand, it acknowledged that there should be more than one type of secondary school, and that 'local initiative and experiment' should be encouraged. Thus, it continued,

> There is no probability that what suits Lancashire or the West Riding will appeal equally to London or Gloucestershire or Cornwall, and if education is to be an inspiration, not a machine, it must reflect the varying social traditions, and moral atmosphere, and economic conditions of different localities. And within the secondary system of each there must be more than one type of school.[28]

This approach suggested that secondary education should be defined not in terms of a particular kind of curriculum or ethos, still less as an expression of social distinctions, but simply in relation to the age range of pupils.

This reappraisal of the nature and meaning of secondary education was continued in 1926 through the publication of a report by the Consultative Committee of the Board of Education (the Hadow Report) under the title *The Education of the Adolescent*. This accepted that secondary education was being interpreted in an unduly narrow way. It proposed instead that the term 'elementary' should be abolished in favour of the word 'primary', and that the name secondary should be given to 'the period of education which follows upon it'.[29] The schools that currently were described as secondary schools would be called by the name of grammar schools, while other, newer forms of secondary school would be called modern schools. Thus, it concluded, 'On such a scheme there will be two main kinds of education – primary and secondary; and the latter of these two kinds will fall into two main groups – that of the grammar school type, and that of the type of the modern school.'[30] It conceded that such a change would involve a fundamental shift in attitudes: 'We admit that we are here walking on difficult ground, and that there are fires burning beneath the thin crust on which we tread.'[31] Nevertheless, it was clear as to the practical outcome of what it was proposing:

> It is that between the age of eleven and (if possible) that of fifteen, all of the children of the country who do not go forward to 'secondary education' in the present and narrow sense of the word, should go forward none the less to what is, in our view, a form of secondary education, in the truer and broader sense of the word, and after spending the first years of their school life in a primary school should spend the last three or four in a well-equipped and well-staffed modern school (or senior department), under the stimulus of practical work and realistic studies, and yet, at the same time, in the free and broad air of a general and humane education, which, if it remembers

handwork, does not forget music, and, if it cherishes natural science, fosters also linguistic and literary studies.[32]

On this view, secondary education would be defined simply in terms of the education of a particular age range, but there would be different types of secondary education catering for different kinds of needs.

Others expressed alarm at the possible implications of such a development. One such was Dr Cyril Norwood, who had been one of the leading headmasters of the new type of secondary school after the Education Act of 1902. As headmaster of Bristol Grammar School between 1906 and 1916, he had transformed the fortunes of the school before going on to be headmaster at two leading public schools in succession, Marlborough College and Harrow School. In the 1920s, he was also chairman of the Secondary School Examinations Council, which reported to the Board on examination matters. He noted that the number of pupils in grant-aided secondary schools had already grown from under 100,000 in 1904–5 to almost 400,000 in 1925. If there were further expansion, and pressure to alter the curriculum of such schools, the 'great work of establishing a sound tradition of Secondary education that has been accomplished in the last twenty five years' would be seriously undermined.[33] This signalled a determination to preserve the character of the existing form of secondary education for those pupils who were able to benefit from it. In turn, it raised difficult questions as to how to differentiate between pupils who were fitted for different forms of secondary education, and whether these would be accorded parity of esteem. Such were the 'fires burning beneath the thin crust on which we tread', of which the Hadow Report had been acutely aware but which it failed to assuage.

During the 1930s, there was little further reform in secondary education, partly due to economic problems and partly because of the conservative nature of both the National Government and the Board of Education in this period. Nevertheless, the debate that had begun about the character of secondary education did not subside, but instead became a key area of contention. Sir Michael Sadler, one of the main architects of the new secondary education of the earlier part of the century, observed 'an upthrust of new strata of the community into the plane of secondary education', but predicted a growing tension between 'the furtherance of the common interest and the fostering of an elite'.[34] The Board of Education's Consultative Committee made another attempt to resolve this tension through a further major report on secondary education (the Spens Report), published in 1938. This proposed that there should be not only the two forms of secondary school, grammar and modern, that the Hadow Report had recommended, but that 'technical high schools' should also be regarded as providing secondary education. Moreover, it added, the inequalities and differences that existed between the older and newer forms of secondary schools should be addressed so that 'parity of status' could be achieved between them. It argued that 'The barriers between different types of secondary school which we seek to remove are the legacies of an age which had a different educational and social outlook from our own.'[35] This meant that the conditions under which the schools operated should be equalized, and also that a new Secondary Code should be introduced to include modern schools as well as grammar and technical high schools: 'The meaning of the word "secondary", which has no statutory definition, would, thus, be extended to include in official regulations part of what falls at present under the statutory definition of "public elementary school", as well as various forms of "higher education".'[36] However, there was already a great deal of scepticism, including within the Board of Education itself, as to whether such 'parity' would be convincing, and the Spens Report was being quietly shelved even before the onset of the Second World War created a temporary diversion from plans for reform.[37]

By 1941, the war itself had stimulated a widespread interest in reforming ideas for a post-war society. In these new circumstances, secondary education became central to agitation for a wholesale reconstruction of the educational system. As early as September 1940, Tawney could perceive what he saw as 'new and fruitful possibilities' that might lead to the creation of 'a universal system of secondary education, embracing schools varying in educational type and methods, but equal in quality'.[38] This was indeed a key tenet of the White Paper, *Educational Reconstruction*, which was eventually produced in July 1943. According to this White Paper, the education system would be recast to provide for successive stages of primary, secondary, and further education. After the age of 11, 'secondary education, of diversified types but on equal standing, will be provided for all children', and in secondary schools 'the standard of accommodation and amenities will be steadily raised to the level of the best examples'.[39] It went on to propose that children of 11 should be classified for different types of schools not through the results of a 'competitive test', but based on their school records supplemented by intelligence tests and parental wishes. It was clear, indeed, that the interests of the child were paramount: 'The keynote of the new system will be that the child is the centre of education and that, so far as is humanly possible, all children should receive the type of education for which they are best adapted.'[40] The White Paper also argued that the 'academic training' characterized by the existing secondary schools would be unsuitable for the majority of pupils.[41]

The implications of the new scheme that were implicit in the White Paper were spelled out in graphic detail in another report published the following month. This was a Board of Education report on the curriculum and examinations of secondary schools, produced by a committee under the chairmanship of (now Sir) Cyril Norwood. The latter took the opportunity to expand on his ideals of secondary education which he had been developing over the previous 40 years. Part I, Chapter I of the report, 'The nature of secondary education', provides a classic statement of the aims of secondary education in general and the range of types within it. According to the Norwood Report it was the business of secondary education 'first, to provide opportunity for a special cast of mind to manifest itself, if not already manifested in the primary stage, and, secondly, to develop special interests and aptitudes to the full by means of a curriculum and a life best calculated to this end'.[42] In order to cater for such special interests and aptitudes, it identified three 'rough groupings'. First, there were pupils who were interested in 'learning for its own sake', who were best suited to the academic curriculum of the grammar schools. Second, there were those whose interests and abilities lay in 'applied science or applied art', and these should be catered for in the technical schools. Last, many pupils, who dealt 'more easily with concrete things than with ideas', would be especially well suited for the modern schools.[43] Overall, it concluded, 'under such a reorganisation all children would have the opportunity of the education best suited to them; for variety of type and alternative courses within the type are essential to any satisfactory system of secondary education'. The three types of school, moreover, would be accorded 'parity of conditions', but would need to win 'parity of esteem' themselves. Pupils would thus be given 'equivalence of opportunity', that is, 'the opportunity to receive the education for which each pupil is best suited for such time and to such a point as is fully profitable to him'.[44] It was under these strictures that 'secondary education for all' was at last to be achieved, or so it seemed.

Meanwhile the independent schools had survived virtually unscathed from the debate over secondary education. They had been undermined by broader social and cultural changes which brought into question the ideals of education for leadership that had given the elite public schools such authority.[45] Many had also suffered as a result of financial problems. In the reforming euphoria of the Second World War, many critics insisted that the public schools should be abolished entirely, or at least be brought within the state system of education.[46] By the end of the war, nevertheless, they remained a separate system, comprising an alternative form of provision based on parental fees that was attractive to many because of its established social prestige. The Education Act of 1944 made no attempt to intervene in the independent schools. For those pupils in the statutory system, however, secondary education, defined as 'full-time education suitable to the requirements of senior pupils', would be provided free to all, with schools in every area

> sufficient in number, character, and equipment to afford for all pupils opportunities for education offering such variety of instruction and

training as may be desirable in view of their different ages, abilities, and aptitudes, and of the different periods for which they may be expected to remain at school, including practical instruction and training appropriate to their respective needs.[47]

No mention was made of different kinds of schools, nor yet of parity of esteem, but the issues that went unremarked in the legislation were to be fundamental problems in an era of secondary education for all.

1944–1965

For at least a decade after the 1944 Education Act, a determined attempt was made to develop a 'tripartite' system of secondary education based on three different types of schools, grammar, technical and modern. The Ministry of Education, which had succeeded the Board under the legislation of 1944, was anxious to promote this demarcation as far as possible in the different local areas, while the LEAs varied widely in their attitudes. Both the Labour governments under Clement Attlee, 1945–51, and Winston Churchill's Conservative government that followed, strongly endorsed this general policy. They preferred to maintain this approach rather than an alternative that was increasingly mooted during this time, of developing multilateral or comprehensive schools designed for all abilities and aptitudes. Nevertheless, by the 1950s it was becoming widely apparent that the tripartite system, insofar as it existed at all, was not a success, and a new debate ensued to find a fresh way forward. This dilemma was resolved, temporarily at least, when the new Labour government elected on a narrow majority in 1964 decided to encourage all LEAs to reorganize their secondary schools into a system of comprehensive education.

The New Secondary Education, a pamphlet issued by the Ministry in 1947 and probably the most significant policy statement in this area in the late 1940s and 1950s, had no reservations as to the future development of secondary education. It expressed full confidence that 'The new conception of secondary education will make a revolutionary change in education in England and Wales.'[48] For the first time, it declared, 'genuine secondary education' would now be provided for all children over 11, as 'the right of all, and no longer the privilege of a few'.[49] Nevertheless, doubts were quick to emerge, even within the Ministry itself. The chief inspector for secondary schools, R.H. Charles, noted privately as early as September 1945 that there was already 'undoubtedly a widespread view that the division in the Norwood Report of children into three categories is really theoretical and artificial, and that if it is pressed and translated into bricks, mortar and regulations, it will have anything but a happy social effect'.[50] Such anxiety was also vividly reflected in *School and Life*, the first report to be produced by the new Central Advisory Council for Education, which had succeeded the former Consultative Committee.[51]

The grammar schools themselves were acutely aware of imminent challenge to their position. In 1946, the Incorporated Association of Head Masters took it upon itself to warn publicly of a 'threat to the grammar schools', claiming that a confusion between the ideas of uniformity and equality was endangering the achievements and the prospects of such schools.[52] Eric James, High Master of Manchester Grammar School, attempted in this uncertain context to defend and redefine the ideals of the grammar schools. He praised the achievement of the Education Act of 1902 in making possible a new form of equality of opportunity in which an able minority from all social backgrounds was able to gain access to an advanced form of education, thus producing a social and political elite based neither on birth nor on wealth, but on ability or 'merit'.[53] It was this view that was satirized to devastating effect in the later 1950s in Michael Young's work, *The Rise of the Meritocracy*.[54] According to Harry Rée, the Headmaster of Watford Grammar School, only an 'act of blindness' could undermine the grammar schools 'in view of the essential contribution they are prepared to make to the development of education and society in the years ahead'.[55] Nevertheless, the position of the grammar schools was soon to become rapidly more insecure.

The Ministry did not issue detailed instructions to show how different schools should be provided for different 'types' of pupil, but it did specify that grammar and technical provision together should constitute about 20 to 25 per cent of the age range. In practice, provision for secondary technical schools (STSs) was much less than had been anticipated. By 1955, only 4.4 per cent of the total number of pupils in maintained and assisted secondary schools attended an STS. At the local level, while 76 of the 83 county borough LEAs kept at least one school described as secondary technical, the distribution of these schools was highly irregular in county areas.[56] At the end of the decade more than 40 per cent of LEAs did not provide any secondary technical education at all.[57] The STSs that did exist also varied greatly in character, from those that continued to recruit pupils at 13 as the former junior technical schools had done in the inter-war period, to those that imitated the grammar schools and developed an increasingly academic approach. Many lacked suitable accommodation and resources, which encouraged parental suspicions that they were not at all equal to the grammar schools. In 1959 the Crowther Report, *15 to 18*, argued strongly that the STSs could play a vital part in the development of what it called an 'Alternative Road', distinct from and complementary to 'the academic tradition which inspires and is embodied in our grammar schools and universities'.[58] Nevertheless, by this stage it was already too late to change attitudes towards the STSs as separate schools.

The failure of the STSs meant that what had been intended to develop as a tripartite system was instead effectively a bipartite system of grammar and modern schools in many local areas. The secondary modern schools (SMSs), moreover, also did not attract the broad support that had been hoped. SMSs were intended to provide for the needs of about three-quarters of secondary school pupils up to the minimum leaving age, which was raised in 1947 from 14 to 15. They were to be non-selective in their admission of pupils. It was also expected that they would remain free from the constraints of examinations so that their curriculum could develop in a distinctive manner to cater for the particular needs of their pupils. In the early 1960s, there were nearly 4,000 SMSs in England and Wales, with over 1.5 million pupils who had not been selected at the age of 11 either for a grammar school or for a technical school. Underlying the apparently successful establishment of the SMSs, nonetheless, was a range of persistent difficulties. Many of the schools that were based in inner city areas proved to be ' "secondary" only in name', the 'depository of the unsuccessful – the rag bag into which children who have not made the grade are put'.[59] Schools in areas such as Merseyside, it was suggested, 'do not and cannot yet provide a true secondary education within the full meaning of that term', and were separated from the grammar schools by a 'gaping and almost unbridgeable chasm'.[60] On the other hand, some SMSs based in the more affluent suburbs began to imitate some of the traditions of the grammar schools and introduced examinations.[61]

The palpable differences between the kinds of provision offered by the grammar schools on the one hand and the modern schools on the other placed increasing pressure on the prime instrument of selection, the eleven-plus examination. Sir David Eccles as minister of education acknowledged privately in 1955 that 'The most political problem in education is the 11+ examination and the Socialist proposal to abolish it by rolling up all secondary schools into comprehensive schools.'[62] At the same time, the recurrent debate over the meaning of secondary education surfaced once again, this time in acknowledgement of the fact that the aspirations behind 'secondary education for all' remained unfulfilled. In response to this latter issue, the Newsom Report on children with average and below average ability, published in 1963, proposed that 'an education that makes sense' for such pupils would be practical, realistic and vocational in character, with clear limits placed on what would be expected of them. This outlook implied a distinctive curriculum for the non-academic majority of the age group whatever the kind of school that was provided for them.[63]

Such were the issues surrounding secondary education when the Labour Party was returned to office in 1964. The new government soon seized the opportunity to promote a national policy of comprehensive education, as the Conservatives had long feared. However, it did so by means of a circular, 10/65, encouraging LEAs to reorganize on a comprehensive basis, rather than through legislation that would require them to do so.[64] The government's policy had already been approved by the House of Commons in January 1965 in the following terms:

> That this House, conscious of the need to raise educational standards at all levels, and regretting that the realisation of this objective is impeded by the separation of children into different types of secondary schools, notes with approval the efforts of local authorities to reorganise secondary education on comprehensive lines which will preserve all that is valuable in grammar school education for those children who now receive it and make it available to more children; recognises that the method and timing of such reorganisation should vary to meet local needs; and believes that the time is now ripe for a declaration of national policy.[65]

This approach was viewed as decidedly timid and a missed opportunity by critics of academic selection who wished to see a fully comprehensive system,[66] but reflected awareness of continuing strong parental support for the established grammar schools in many parts of the country. Meanwhile the public schools remained inviolate, the focus of a further ineffective inquiry in the 1960s,[67] but continuing to provide an exclusive education for a social elite, and acting as a beacon for parents who were discontented with the character of state secondary education.

1965–2000

The period from 1965 until the end of the century witnessed the establishment of the comprehensive school as the main form of provision of secondary education in England and Wales. It was also a period during which criticisms of secondary education persisted and indeed grew, and new approaches were developed that served to undermine the comprehensives themselves. Despite the reforms that had taken place and the further expansion that occurred over this time, the debates over the nature and purposes of secondary education had clearly not been resolved.[68]

By the end of the 1960s, comprehensive reorganization was well under way, with over 1,300 comprehensive schools already in existence including nearly one-third of secondary school age pupils, and many more being planned for the future. Although the Conservative Party was returned to office in 1970, and immediately reversed Circular 10/65 with the issue of its own Circular 10/70, the process as a whole could not be reversed. Many grammar schools were 'saved' from closure or merging into comprehensives, either by moving to a different local area with another LEA, or through the use of powers under section 13 of the 1944 Education Act to challenge LEA proposals to reorganize particular schools. Nevertheless, within 30 years of the publication of Circular 10/65, over 90 per cent of pupils of secondary school age were being educated in comprehensive schools.[69]

Underlying this major development, there remained many difficult issues that were not fully addressed. One major point of contention was the fact that there were still clear differences between secondary schools, whether in terms of academic achievement or in relation to their social intake of pupils. The Labour minister of education, Michael Stewart, insisted in the 1960s that in a comprehensive system 'no child will be put in a position of being sent to a school which is accepted from the start as not possessing as good facilities as some other schools for advanced academic education'.[70] However, many LEAs and officials at the new Department of Education and Science (DES) were well aware that as comprehensive schools would recruit pupils principally on a neighbourhood basis, they would tend to be different in 'middle-class areas' from those in 'poor, socially under-privileged areas'.[71] Commonwealth immigration in large urban centres in the 1960s heightened differences between secondary schools in terms of both class and ethnicity. In schools that were reorganized from being SMSs to become comprehensives, the underlying continuities were often readily apparent. Especially in districts where grammar schools were retained, such comprehensive schools were often simply the old SMSs in a new guise. The nature of the comprehensive school depended at least partly on whether it was a former grammar school or a former SMS, whether it was in an LEA with a largely manual or non-manual population, and whether it offered sixth-form courses.[72]

Continuity from earlier tripartite patterns of provision was especially striking in relation to curriculum and assessment. The comprehensive schools inherited General Certificate of Education (GCE) Ordinary (O) and Advanced (A) level examinations for the academically able, and Certificate of Secondary Education (CSE) examinations for the less able. These separate examinations served different courses that echoed the former grammar/secondary modern divide. As Goodson has observed:

> As in the tripartite system, so in the comprehensive system, academic subjects for able pupils are accorded the highest status and resources. The triple alliance between academic subjects, academic examinations and able pupils ensures that comprehensive schools provide similar patterns of success and failure to previous school systems.[73]

The ultimate effect, explored in the early 1980s in Ball's study of a co-educational comprehensive school, *Beachside Comprehensive*, was a resilient pattern of low achievement on the part of working-class pupils. Ball also found that streaming of classes on the basis of academic ability exacerbated differences in educational opportunity.[74]

These continuing problems, present from the early years of the spread of comprehensives, worsened during the 1970s in the context of economic and industrial conflict. Comprehensive education was increasingly held responsible on the one hand for allegedly declining academic standards, and on the other for not producing the skilled modern workforce that was needed for the 'world of work'. Such anxiety was expressed in forceful terms by the then Labour Prime Minister, James Callaghan, in a key speech at Ruskin College, Oxford, in October 1976.[75] This intervention led to a self-styled 'Great Debate' on education that again revealed a deep-seated uncertainty about the nature and purposes of secondary education. For example, in November 1978 the Chairman of the Schools Council for the Curriculum and Examinations, John Tomlinson, pointed out that the 'political promise of Secondary Education for All', far from being achieved in 1944, remained an 'unsolved conundrum'. Secondary education, he continued, was no longer given 'solely for the brainy by the brainy', as it had been 40 years before. Another approach was therefore required, according to Tomlinson, to educate all up to the age of 16, which had become the school-leaving age in 1972–3. This should involve more 'real experience', and a celebration of making as well as of thinking.[76]

The Conservative government that came to power under Margaret Thatcher in 1979 pursued these issues with renewed vigour and determination. The Technical and Vocational Education Initiative (TVEI), launched originally as a pilot scheme from 1983, was an attempt to promote diversity in the curriculum for 14 to 18-year-olds within the secondary schools that might be especially suited to the non-academic majority of pupils. However, the initiative attracted strong criticism from educational groups on the basis that it would encourage greater divisions in the comprehensive schools.[77] As the TVEI became established in the schools, these initial anxieties began to subside until a fresh initiative sought to create a new class of secondary schools, city technology colleges (CTCs). The CTCs, announced by Kenneth Baker as Secretary of State for Education in 1986, would be new secondary schools that were outside the influence of LEAs, designed specifically to offer a 'new choice of school' with a strong technological element in the curriculum.[78] The impact of the CTCs proved to be transitory and limited, especially because of difficulties of funding and the logistics of founding a new type of secondary school. More important was the overall thrust of government policy that they came to symbolize, away from a single model of secondary school and towards a greater emphasis on 'choice' and 'competition' between a diverse range of schools. This trend continued under the general provisions of the Education Reform Act of 1988, also introduced by Baker. It was celebrated in the White Paper, *Choice and Diversity*, published soon after the Conservatives' fourth successive general election victory in 1992, which envisaged the spread of grant-maintained schools, self-governing but funded directly by a central agency.[79]

The final years of the Conservative government in the mid-1990s, there-fore, were marked by a deepening and bitter debate about the record of the comprehensive schools and whether they should be maintained, improved, or abandoned. On the one hand, many critics argued that the comprehensive schools had failed to achieve results. David Blunkett, then the shadow spokesperson on education and employment for the opposi-tion Labour Party, argued in a lecture to the Social Market Foundation in February 1996 that comprehensive schools had failed successive genera-tions of pupils over the previous 30 years and needed to change. According to Blunkett, indeed, 'In spite of more than fifty years of universal state secondary education and thirty years of comprehensive education, the pattern of excellence at the top and chronic under-performance at the bottom persists.'[80] On the other hand, there were many who defended the record of the comprehensive schools and sought to maintain their role.[81]

These debates reached a form of culmination with the general election of 1997. John Major as Prime Minister went into the general election campaign with an emphasis on the merits of choice and diversity that was stronger than ever. He espoused the return of grammar schools as centres of academic excellence, a notion that was symbolized in a desire that he expressed for a 'grammar school in every town'. By contrast, the Labour Party leader, Tony Blair, condemned the idea because it would mean a return to the system of the eleven-plus examination and the two-tier system of grammar schools and secondary modern schools. He was anxious to 'refine and redefine' the comprehensive schools, but rejected the idea of reviving the secondary moderns.[82] During the election campaign, the Conservative Party became embroiled in controversy over proposals to introduce a programme costing £360 million that would allow up to 720 secondary schools to select pupils by aptitude or academic ability.[83] It continued to advocate the development of new grammar schools, and this again served to direct attention towards the spectre of the SMSs. Thus the final general election of the twentieth century, which the Labour Party eventually won by an unprecedented margin, replayed in a rather surreal fashion the debates over secondary education that had been fought out to no clear conclusion over the past 50 or even 100 years.

Conclusion

During the twentieth century, secondary education was transformed from an elite form of educational provision, remote from the experience of the majority of the population, to become compulsory and universal, a familiar and important part of all families and lives. For many, it repre-sented the final stage of schooling, while for an increasing number it formed an intermediate phase between primary and tertiary education. Throughout the century it was an object of attention in its own right, often the focus of contending forces among educators, policy makers and the public at large. Despite its successful establishment, indeed, it appeared to become increasingly controversial, to the extent that by the end of the century there were many who regarded it as ultimately a failed, or at least a deeply flawed project. The reasons for these discontents lay both in the elite origins of secondary education and in its relationship with the wider society as the century wore on.

Hence, over the twentieth century as a whole, the fires consumed the thin crust on which the Hadow Report of 1926 had trodden. At the end of the century, Bryce's vision of secondary education as 'education conducted in view of the special life that has to be lived with the express purpose of forming a person fit to live it' remained as elusive as it had been a century before. The ideal of 'secondary education for all', which appeared to have been achieved in 1944, had also failed to be fully realized.

And yet all passion was not spent as the recurrent debate over secondary education continued into the twenty-first century. In 2001, the Labour government, contemptuous of what its official spokesman described as the 'bog-standard comprehensive', but at the same time 'building on success', launched a fresh initiative to provide more specialist schools, church schools, city academies and schools sponsored by business, faith or voluntary groups alongside foundation, community, grammar and secondary modern schools. The Green Paper, *Building on Success*, published in February 2001, looked forward to a 'post-comprehensive' era in which every secondary school would develop a distinctive ethos and tailor teaching to the needs of individual pupils.[84] The experience of the past 100 years had served to render the earlier ideals of secondary education virtually unrecognizable in their outcome, and did not appear to bequeath a clear path forward to the future, but evidently it had not dimmed the zeal of reformers. It must be hoped that in the twenty-first century, ways will be found to complete the tasks that in the twentieth century were left undone.

Key reading

Brian Simon's four-volume work, *Studies in the History of Education*, is especially strong on the history of secondary education, and the second, third and fourth volumes are all useful on twentieth-century developments up to 1990. John Roach's two-volume study of secondary education in the nineteenth century is important for earlier developments: *A History of Secondary Education in England, 1800–1870*, London, Longman, 1986 and *Secondary Education in England, 1870–1902*, London, Routledge, 1991. A three-volume work on the tripartite dimensions of secondary education in the twentieth century by Gary McCulloch explores public and grammar schools and ideals of 'leadership': *Philosophers and Kings:*

Education for Leadership in Modern England, Cambridge, Cambridge University Press, 1991; the development and failure of the secondary technical schools: *The Secondary Technical School: A Usable Past?*, London, Falmer, 1989; and the history of working-class secondary education, in particular the secondary modern schools: *Failing the Ordinary Child? The Theory and Practice of Working-Class Secondary Education*, Buckingham, Open University Press, 1998. Classic work on secondary education in the twentieth century includes Harry Judge, *A Generation of Schooling*, Oxford, Oxford University Press, 1984; A.M. Kazamias, *Politics, Society and Secondary Education in England*, Philadelphia, University of Pennsylvania Press, 1966; Olive Banks, *Parity and Prestige in English Secondary Education*, London, Routledge and Kegan Paul, 1955; and Harold Dent, *Secondary Education For All*, London, Routledge and Kegan Paul, 1949. To these general accounts may be added Reese Edwards's study of the secondary technical schools: *The Secondary Technical School*, London, University of London Press, 1960; William Taylor on secondary modern schools: *The Secondary Modern School*, London, Faber and Faber, 1963; Frances Stevens on grammar schools: *The Living Tradition*, London, Hutchinson, 1960; and E.C. Mack on public schools: *Public Schools and British Opinion since 1860*, New York, Columbia University Press, 1941. The extensive literature on the development of comprehensive schools since the 1960s includes Stephen Ball's ethnographic study: *Beachside Comprehensive*, Cambridge, Cambridge University Press, 1981; Alan Kerckhoff *et al.*, *Going Comprehensive in England and Wales*, London, Woburn Press, 1996; Caroline Benn and Clyde Chitty, *Thirty Years On*, London, Penguin, 1997; and Richard Pring and Geoffrey Walford (eds) *Affirming the Comprehensive Ideal*, London, Falmer, 1997.

Notes

I am grateful to the Leverhulme Trust for its support for the research projects, 'The life and educational career of Sir Cyril Norwood' (F118AU) and 'Education and the working class' (F118AB), on which this chapter is partly based.

1 For other general surveys of secondary education in this period, see for example, R. Lowe, 'New perspectives on the evolution of secondary school education in the UK', in B. Moon, S. Brown and M. Ben-Peretz (eds) *Routledge International Companion to Education*, London, Routledge, 2000, pp. 642–52; B. Simon, *Education and the Social Order, 1940–1990*, London, Lawrence and Wishart, 1991; H. Judge, *A Generation of Schooling: English Secondary Schools since 1944*, Oxford, Oxford University Press, 1984; A. Kazamias, *Politics, Society and Secondary Education in England*, Philadelphia, University of Pennsylvania Press, 1966; O. Banks, *Parity and Prestige in English Secondary Education: A Study in Educational Sociology*, London, Routledge and Kegan Paul, 1955; and H. Dent, *Secondary Education For All: Origins and Development in England*, London, Routledge and Kegan Paul, 1949.

2   A. Adonis and S. Pollard, *A Class Act: The Myth Of Britain's Classless Society*, London, Penguin, 1998, chapter 2; G. Walden, 'The school wall won't fall down', *The Independent*, 31 July 1995; see also G. Walden, *We Should Know Better: Solving The Education Crisis*, London, Fourth Estate, 1995.

3   N. Davies, 'Education – the great divide', *The Guardian*, 6 March 2000.

4   A. Adonis and M. Bright, 'So you thought all schools were equal', *The Observer*, 1 February 1998.

5   'Brains, beaks and tailcoats', *The Independent*, 5 September 1995.

6   J. Judd, 'School that was a lesson in failure', *The Independent*, 7 November 1996.

7   See, for example, Maureen O'Connor, Elizabeth Hales, Jeffrey Davies and Sally Tomlinson, *Hackney Downs: The School That Dared To Fight*, London, Cassell, 1999.

8   See, for example, M. Narayan, 'Schools of shame', *The Observer*, 3 March 1996; D. Blunkett, 'Damaging youngsters', *The Guardian*, 13 July 2000.

9   See, for example, C. Hymas and F. Nelson, 'Life at the bottom', *The Sunday Times*, 22 November 1992; 'Reprieved school heads A-level table', *The Independent*, 18 August 1995.

10 'Comprehensively catastrophic', *Times Educational Supplement*, 12 January 2001. See also Melanie Phillips, *All Must Have Prizes*, London, Warner Books, 1996.

11 'Tomlinson to kick off with good news', *Times Educational Supplement*, 19 January 2001.

12 For a full discussion of the development of secondary education in England during the nineteenth century, see John Roach's two-volume work, *A History of Secondary Education in England, 1800–1870*, London, Longman, 1986, and *Secondary Education in England 1870–1902: Public Activity and Private Enterprise*, London, Routledge, 1991.

13 Royal Commission on Secondary Education, *Report of the Commissioners* (Bryce Report), London, HMSO, 1895, vol. 1, p. xxvi.

14 Ibid., p. 1.

15 Ibid., p. 2.

16 Ibid., p. 136.

17 Ibid.

18 Ibid., p. 257.

19 David Reeder, 'The reconstruction of secondary education in England, 1869–1920', in D. Muller, F. Ringer and B. Simon (eds) *The Rise of the Educational System*, Cambridge, Cambridge University Press, 1987, p. 150. For further details on these developments see N. Daglish, *Education Policy-Making In England and Wales: The Crucible Years, 1895–1911*, London, Woburn Press, 1996.

20 Board of Education, Prefatory memorandum to the Regulations for Secondary Schools, 1904 [Cd. 2128].

21 See B. Simon, *Education and the Labour Movement, 1870–1920*, London, Lawrence and Wishart, 1974, especially p. 246.

22 M. Vlaeminke, *The Higher Grade Schools: A Lost Opportunity?*, London, Woburn Press, 2000.

23 W.B. Stephens, *Education in Britain 1750–1914*, London, Macmillan, 1998, p. 104.

24 B. Simon, *Education and the Labour Movement, 1870–1920*, London, Lawrence and Wishart, 1974, p. 273.

25 J.H. Brittain to Albert Mansbridge, 28 April 1907 (Mansbridge papers, British Library Add. Mss. 65346).

26 Labour Party, *Secondary Education For All: A Policy For Labour*, London, Labour Party, 1922, p. 7.
27 Ibid., p. 11.
28 Ibid., p. 29.
29 Board of Education, *Report of the Consultative Committee on the Education of the Adolescent* (Hadow Report), London, HMSO, 1926, p. xxi.
30 Ibid., pp. xxi–xxii.
31 Ibid., p. xxii.
32 Ibid., p. xxiii.
33 Cyril Norwood, memo, The School Certificate (n.d.; January 1928?) (Board of Education papers, Public Record Office, ED.12/255). See also, for example, C. Norwood and A. Hope (eds) *The Higher Education of Boys in England*, London, John Murray, 1909; and C. Norwood, *The English Tradition of Education*, London, John Murray, 1929.
34 M. Sadler, *The Outlook in Secondary Education*, New York, Teachers College, Columbia University, 1930, pp. 8, 16.
35 Board of Education, *Secondary Education With Special Reference To Grammar Schools And Technical High Schools* (Spens Report), London, HMSO, 1938, p. 293.
36 Ibid., p. 314.
37 See G. McCulloch, 'The power of three: "parity of esteem" and the social history of tripartism', in E. Jenkins (ed.) *Studies in the History of Education*, Leeds, University of Leeds Press, 1995, pp. 113–32.
38 R.H. Tawney to F. Clarke, 30 September 1940 (Tawney papers, Institute of Education, London).
39 Board of Education, *Educational Reconstruction*, [Cmd. 6458], London, HMSO, 1942, para. 2.
40 Ibid., para. 27.
41 Ibid., para. 28.
42 Board of Education, *Curriculum and Examinations in Secondary Schools* (Norwood Report), London, HMSO, 1943, p. 2.
43 Ibid., pp. 2–4.
44 Ibid., p. 24.
45 See G. McCulloch, *Philosophers and Kings: Education for Leadership in Modern England*, Cambridge, Cambridge University Press, 1991, especially chapters 2–3.
46 See, for example, T.C. Worsley, *Barbarians and Philistines: Democracy and the Public Schools*, London, Robert Hale Ltd, 1940, and T.C. Worsley, *The End Of The 'Old School Tie'*, London, Secker and Warburg, 1941; also E.C. Mack, *Public Schools and British Opinion since 1860: The Relationship between Contemporary Ideas and the Evolution of an English Institution*, New York, Columbia University Press, 1941.
47 Education Act, 1944, Section 8 (1) (b).
48 Ministry of Education, *The New Secondary Education*, London, HMSO, 1947, p. 8.
49 Ibid., p. 7.
50 R.H. Charles, memorandum, 12 September 1945 (Ministry of Education papers, Public Record Office, ED.146/13).
51 Ministry of Education, *School and Life*, London, HMSO, 1947. See also G. McCulloch, *Failing the Ordinary Child? The Theory and Practice of Working Class Secondary Education*, Buckingham, Open University Press, 1998, pp. 66–71.

52 Incorporated Association of Head Masters, *The Threat to the Grammar Schools*, London, IAHM, 1946.
53 E. James, *Education and Leadership*, London, George Harrap and Co., 1951.
54 M. Young, *The Rise of the Meritocracy, 1870–2033: An Essay on Education and Equality*, Harmondsworth, Penguin, 1958. See also G. McCulloch, *Philosophers and Kings: Education for Leadership in Modern England*, Cambridge, Cambridge University Press, 1991, chapter 5.
55 H. Rée, *The Essential Grammar School*, London, Harrap, 1956, p. 84. See also F. Stevens, *The Living Tradition: The Social and Educational Assumptions of the Grammar School*, London, Hutchinson, 1960.
56 T.R. Weaver, note, 'Secondary technical schools', 14 January 1955 (Ministry of Education papers, Public Record Office, ED.147/207).
57 See G. McCulloch, *The Secondary Technical School: A Usable Past?*, London, Falmer, 1989, especially chapter 4, and R. Edwards, *The Secondary Technical School*, London, University of London Press, 1960.
58 Ministry of Education, *15 to 18* (Crowther Report), London, HMSO, p. 391.
59 M.P. Carter, *Home, School and Work*, Oxford, Pergamon Press, 1962, p. 4.
60 J.B. Mays, *Education and the Urban Child*, Liverpool, Liverpool University Press, 1962, pp. 155–6.
61 For further details on the SMS, see G. McCulloch, *Failing the Ordinary Child? The Theory and Practice of Working Class Secondary Education*, Buckingham, Open University Press, 1998; W. Taylor, *The Secondary Modern School*, London, Faber and Faber, 1963; H. Dent, *Secondary Modern Schools: An Interim Report*, London, Routledge and Kegan Paul, 1958.
62 Sir David Eccles to Sir Anthony Eden, 14 April 1955 (Ministry of Education papers, Public Record Office, ED.136/861).
63 Ministry of Education, *Half our Future* (Newsom Report), London, HMSO, 1963.
64 Department of Education and Science, 'The organisation of secondary education', (Circular 10/65), 12 July 1965. See also McCulloch, op. cit. 1998, chapter 9.
65 McCulloch, op. cit., 1998, p. 1.
66 See, for example, B. Simon, 'The politics of comprehensive reorganisation: a retrospective analysis', *History of Education*, 1992, vol. 21, no. 4, pp. 355–62.
67 Public Schools Commission, *First Report* (Newsom Report), London, HMSO, 1968.
68 C. Benn and B. Simon, *Half Way There*, Harmondsworth, Penguin, 2nd edn, 1972, p. 101.
69 See C. Benn and C. Chitty, *Thirty Years On: Is Comprehensive Education Alive and Well or Struggling to Survive?*, London, Penguin, 1997.
70 *Hansard*, House of Commons, 27 November 1965, col. 1781.
71 Miss W. Harte, 'Comments on Secretary of State's draft paper on comprehensive education dated 29.12.64' (Department of Education and Science papers, Public Record Office, ED.147/827A).
72 A. Kerckhoff, K. Fogelman, D. Crook, and D. Reeder, *Going Comprehensive in England and Wales: A Study of Uneven Change*, London, Woburn Press, 1996, p. 210.
73 I. Goodson, *The Making of Curriculum*, London, Falmer, 2nd edn, 1992, pp. 140–1.
74 S. Ball, *Beachside Comprehensive*, Cambridge, Cambridge University Press, 1981, p. 34.
75 'What the PM said', *Times Educational Supplement*, 22 October 1976.

76 J.R.G. Tomlinson, Chairman's Address, Schools Council Convocation, Wembley Conference Centre, report of 1st meeting, 14 November 1978 (Schools Council papers, Public Record Office, EJ13/4).
77 See, for example, G. McCulloch, 'History and policy: the politics of the TVEI', in D. Gleeson (ed.) *TVEI and Secondary Education*, Milton Keynes, Open University Press, 1987, pp. 13–37.
78 See G. McCulloch, 'City technology colleges: an old choice of school?', *British Journal of Educational Studies*, 1989, vol. 37, no. 1, pp. 30–43.
79 Department for Education, *Choice and Diversity: A New Framework for Schools* [Cm. 2021], London, HMSO, 1992.
80 'Schools have failed says Blunkett: Labour to rewrite its comprehensive policy', *The Independent*, 28 February 1996.
81 See, for example, R. Pring and G. Walford (eds) *Affirming the Comprehensive Ideal*, London, Falmer, 1997.
82 T. Blair, 'Don't give idealism a bad name', *Times Educational Supplement*, 14 June 1996.
83 '"Go grammar" lure for schools', *The Independent*, 14 April 1997.
84 Department for Education and Employment, *Building on Success*, London, The Stationery Office, 2001; 'Are you a bog-standard secondary?' *Times Educational Supplement*, 16 February 2001.

Chapter 3

Further education

Bill Bailey

The situation in 2000

English further education (FE) is difficult to describe in terms of its purpose and scope. It stands as a distinctive sector of post-compulsory education, separate from the universities, but its work ranges from courses forming part of the official definition of higher education to courses over-lapping with the work of secondary schools. Traditionally its main focus has been vocational courses for students aiming at, or already in, employ-ment in local industry and commerce. However, since the first official use of the term 'further education', in the Regulations published in 1926, it has also included a wide range of evening classes in cultural and recre-ational subjects for adults.

After 1902 technical colleges and adult education centres were part of the public education service maintained and developed by the local educa-tion authorities (LEAs) through which they received their funding. This remained the case until April 1993 when the colleges became independent, self-governing institutions under the terms of the Further and Higher Education Act of the previous year. In England and Wales national Funding Councils for Further Education were established to channel public finance to the colleges. The government's aims were to increase post-16 participa-tion, to improve efficiency in the use of resources and to raise attainment, through the new funding methodology and national education and training 'targets'. This emphasis on achievement, measured by the proportion of the population possessing vocational and other qualifications at different levels, led government to leave responsibility for the funding of adult education which did not lead to a qualification with the LEAs.

The incorporated colleges, responsible (after 1993) for their budgets, staffing and physical resources, were no longer 'simple', single-purpose technical institutions. In part because of official policy, partly in its absence, they had become multi-purpose institutions of education and training for young people and adults. To their vocational 'core' work many colleges had added, mainly since 1970, the offer of GCSE and GCE 'A' level courses which duplicate those courses in schools' sixth forms.

More recently colleges have established and expanded their provision for students with learning difficulties/disabilities and that for adults whose skills of literacy and numeracy are inadequate (such basic skills education can also include, where necessary, the teaching of English as a Second Language). A further development during the last two decades of the century is that of programmes providing 'access' to higher education courses for adults without conventional entry qualifications.

The policy of increasing adult participation in higher education has been extended in many colleges through arrangements with local universities whereby college staff undertake the teaching of the early years of part-time degree courses in the colleges. A further important strand of provision is that associated with schemes for the unemployed, or for those returning to the labour market. This can include basic skills, and the skills of applying for jobs as well as training in an occupational area which can lead to a National Vocational Qualification (NVQ).

By 2000, the further education sector in England was serving a wide range of students with diverse needs and ambitions. This in turn was the reason for the diverse course-offer (the curriculum?) of the colleges – the breadth of which surprised and confused those who assumed that FE colleges existed only for courses leading to vocational qualifications. In fact they were serving the needs of many in the community at all levels: from degrees to basic communication and number skills; for recent school-leavers to pensioners; for those in full-time and part-time attendance, and by supplying bespoke short courses for local employers.

In 1997–8 there were almost four million students enrolled in the further education sector. Of these, one million (26%) were in full-time attendance, and almost three million (74%) were part-time (52% day students: 22% evening only). Of this total, 19% were aged under 19, and 81% were adults.

The situation in 1900

In 1900 post-school education was principally a 'night school' affair. Attendance at evening classes provided by recently established local authorities for education had increased greatly during the 1890s. From the 1870s the school boards, after their early concentration on providing places in elementary schools for working-class children, began to provide evening continuation schools for school-leavers and for adults. Initially, the curriculum of these remained 'elementary' in that it was aimed at the consolidation of the basic education of the students.

During the 1890s, especially after the introduction of new Regulations in 1898, the numbers of students had increased, and particularly those studying advanced, post-elementary subjects. These were mainly attending classes in the science, art, and technical subjects of the two examination bodies of the time: the government's Department of Science and Art (DSA) and the body established by the corporation and some of the livery companies of London, the City and Guilds of London Institute (CGLI). In the case of both these examining bodies students could attend classes from September to May, when the examinations were held; those successful received certificates showing the grade of their pass. The instruction and written assessment of these single subject courses was very theoretical and any connection to their occupations had to be made by the students themselves. Attendance after a day's work was the voluntary decision of the student, of course, and many did not complete the course and take the examination.

The second local authority in the field of further education were the county and borough councils set up by the Local Government Act of 1888. The Technical Instruction Act of 1889 empowered councils to raise a penny rate for technical education and to establish technical instruction committees to supervise this provision. From the following year the sums of money available for this purpose were much increased when the Local Taxation (Customs and Excise) Act allotted some three-quarters of a million pounds to councils with a strong hint that this could be spent on technical and secondary education. This money, the so-called 'Whiskey Money', the product of an additional duty on beer and spirits, prompted many councils to establish technical instruction committees.[1] The spending in secondary education went mainly on scholarships for elementary pupils to transfer to secondary schools where, again, Science and Art Department subjects were taught. Technical classes were mainly by evening attendance, in some cases in the premises of technical colleges recently opened in urban centres. These included the polytechnics in London (which also offered social and recreational activities for local people) and university colleges in provincial cities like Birmingham, Leeds and Sheffield.

While these developments reflected a small change from *laissez-faire* to government interest and action, prompted by evidence that foreign countries were building systems of general and technical education and that these were an important factor in their economic development and increasing competitiveness in world markets, initiative in this sector in the United Kingdom remained voluntary. In the absence of a national plan or policy, the provision of technical or other classes for young or adult workers remained a local decision, taken by the school board, the town or county council or other agency. Similarly, attendance was voluntary on the part of the young person after long hours of work during the day; it was often sporadic and many students did not complete the course by taking the end-of-year examination. The British tradition of the 'night class' was established at this time. Like the students, most teachers had come to the class after a day's work, while the small number of full-time teachers taught most evenings in the week, giving rise to the comment that 'Tired Tims are teaching Weary Willies'.

In 1900 concern about the 'educational muddle' – the low level of educational development resulting from divided responsibilities at the central and local levels and the consequences of this for national efficiency – was at its height. In that year the Board of Education, the first single central education authority for education in England and Wales, came into being. This was to take over the functions of the (elementary) Education Department, the Department of Science and Art, and the educational responsibilities of the Charity Commissioners.

Changes and continuities

Consolidation and stasis, 1900–40

The decades following the 1902 Education Act did not see a continuation of the expansion of technical and further education of the 1890s. After the abolition of the school boards, there was necessarily a period when the new local authorities adjusted to their responsibilities for all types of schools and colleges. At the same time the Board of Education was reorganized to draw together the hitherto separate offices and functions of the Education Department, the Science and Art Department and the Charity Commission. The relationship between the single local and central education authorities developed during these years, when the educational priorities were seen to be the establishing of the dual 'system' of voluntary and maintained elementary schools and the growth of secondary schools on the grammar school model. Political and official interest and resources were focused on these sectors up to the declaration of war in 1939. Though there were proposals for the development of post-school education at the time, these were not seen through to implementation, and opportunities for further education remained patchy and variable between the areas of the local authorities. An important reason for this variability was that the provision of education other than elementary (including further education) was a permissive power, not a duty, of the LEAs.

The Board of Education's principal means of achieving educational reorganization and development was its Regulations which stated the conditions on which the Board would pay grants to the local authorities. The Regulations for Technical Schools, etc. of 1904 were important in that they brought together the evening continuation schools and technical classes of the 1890s, and for the stipulation that grant was no longer payable only for single-subject classes of the DSA and CGLI. These were criticized by the Board's new Chief Inspector of Technological Education, Frank Pullinger, for their fragmentation and frequent lack of relevance to students' occupations. Supported by Robert Morant, Pullinger began to shift provision towards instruction in subjects relevant to industries' needs by 'grouping' subjects into courses, the successful completion of which over two or three years would result in the student being awarded a certificate. The course system, which became the basis of vocational curricula and qualifications, was based on developments in technical colleges in the industrial areas of Cheshire, Lancashire and Yorkshire. Pullinger determined to build on this progressive development by devolving responsibility for course content and assessment to colleges. In this he was again supported by Morant, who resented the influence of external examining bodies like the City and Guilds on technical courses and teachers. In 1911 the Board published Circular 776 which announced the decision of the Board to discontinue its own examinations, inherited from the DSA, and its wish to see these and those of other central examining bodies replaced by local grouped courses and certificates. These would reward continuous study and raise the prestige of technical teachers. The Circular brought the Board into direct conflict with the CGLI, already a major body and influence on technical education. There was no attempt to consult on the terms of the Circular before publication and, faced by this threat to its existence, the CGLI fought a rearguard action and refused to discontinue its examinations. This attempt to reform by diktat was doomed to fail, and not only because of the CGLI's opposition. Technical education was not ready for this kind of freedom. The Circular's proposals were educationally and politically impractical. The majority of teachers worked part-time in the evening and were not professionally trained to take on responsibility for course design and assessment and there was no evidence that their employers, the LEAs, were willing to allow that freedom. In 1918, after Morant's departure from the Board, the dispute was settled on terms that left the CGLI as a major national awarding body for craft level certificates while the Board's own examinations and certificates were replaced by those of regional examining bodies. Prominent among these were the Union of Lancashire and Cheshire Institutes (an old established body) and new bodies like the East Midlands Educational Union and the Northern Counties Technical Examinations Council. These were well placed to adapt courses to local and regional needs and circumstances.[2]

In fact, within the Board's Technological Branch, Pullinger, again with Morant's encouragement, was working on plans which reflected concern about the condition of the majority of young people who received no further education or training after leaving the elementary schools at an early age. Compulsory attendance at evening schools had been canvassed in the late nineteenth century by the Fabians and Liberal politicians, and bills introduced into Parliament annually between 1904 and 1907. The topic was referred to the Consultative Committee whose report in 1909 recommended compulsory attendance at evening classes, and where possible the release of young workers during the day. One of the members of the Committee was Michael Sadler, who had recently edited a landmark study of continuative provision.[3] Before the outbreak of the First World War the Board worked on draft regulations for continuation schools for all. The purpose was ambitious – to reform technical education in as significant a way as the Secondary Regulations of 1904. The period of adolescence was to be seen as the period of the formation of the future citizen, parent and worker; the continuation schools were to provide educational preparation for 'industrial citizenship' for working-class young people. The framework of this programme was published as revised draft Regulations in 1917, the same year as the Lewis Committee published its report which recommended compulsory attendance at day continuation schools. The view of the adolescent 'as primarily a little wage-earner' should be replaced, said the Report, by that of 'primarily the workman (sic) and citizen in training'.[4] Effect was given to these proposals in the 1918 Education Act, section 10 of which provided for the attendance of school-leavers at day continuation schools from the age of 14 until 18. Except in Rugby, this came to nothing, owing to a mixture of post-war financial stringency and employers' resistance.

A more successful initiative in course development on the part of the Board was the development from the 1920s of national and higher national certificates and diplomas. These built on the experience of grouped courses and were national qualifications in technology, awarded jointly by the Board of Education and professional bodies, for example in Chemistry, Building and Mechanical Engineering. Offered in major technical colleges with staffs of full-time specialist teachers, these schemes led to qualifications higher than those at craft level, and allowed the teachers some involvement in course design and delivery and in the assessment of students' achievements, with standards moderated by assessors appointed by the professional bodies. Some of these institutions were already preparing students for external degrees of the University of London.

Economic difficulties and depression, with consequent government 'economy' measures in public expenditure based on the principles of orthodox economics, made the 1920s and 1930s decades of little advance in further education. The Board's role became one of ensuring that the LEAs' spending was kept within Treasury allocations rather than that of promoting development in education as one of the 'locally administered "national" services'.[5] The 1917 draft Regulations had envisaged a fuller development of post-school education – for young workers and adults – as part of 'a complete and systematic plan of further education' in each area, a plan which would be formulated and carried out by the LEA.[6] These proposals, which contained the first official use of the term 'further education' to refer to vocational and continuation education post-school, anticipated the LEA development plans in the 1918 Education Act. In the post-war climate of 'economy' these, too, came to nothing. Instead, the

Board of Education retreated from a position in which it used its regulations as a basis and guide for progressive development of local education provision, to one where its 'dominant and exclusive concern' was the conditions for payment of central government's grant to LEAs. To this end, in 1926, revised regulations for elementary, secondary and further education were issued which were much reduced in length. Those for further education were reduced to five pages from 37, and they shared with the other regulations, in the words of Selby-Bigge in 1927, 'all the neatness of compressed tabloids ... their evaporation (having) dissipated their more liquid, volatile and aromatic components and left only a residue of financial solids'.[7]

This concern with the control and reduction of expenditure on education dominated the work of the Board and the LEAs through the crisis years of the 1930s, until the National Government began its preparations for the general election in 1935.[8] In February 1934, in a Cabinet memorandum, the President of the Board, Lord Halifax, stated that it would be necessary to defend the government's record since the emergency of 1931, and to offer plans for 'future policy in particular directions'.[9] This led to proposals, involving little additional financial commitment, for developments in nursery and secondary education, raising the school-leaving age to 15 with exemptions, the continuation of 'reorganization' of older classes in elementary schools, and an initiative in physical training, as well as a 'drive' in technical education. While many of these proposals, as a result of the increasing political priority given to preparations for war, were to come to very little, the Board's preparatory work for the 'T Drive' is revealing with regard to the state of technical education at the time.

In anticipation of a political commitment to development in this sector, the Board's Technological Branch conducted a general survey of technical education in England and Wales. Through the divisional inspectors in the various regions, data were collected in order to identify the volume and cost of additional accommodation and equipment needed to establish an 'adequate' level of service. The reports from the inspectors showed the patchy and underdeveloped state of technical education in their areas. While there were good examples in some LEAs, in many areas provision was minimal. In Durham, in the words of the reporting inspector, technical provision was 'simply NIL', while Leeds and Sheffield had no colleges and classes took place in schools. The Manchester College of Technology was one of the 'best buildings and one of the few places to which one can take a foreigner without a sense of shame at the squalor of our buildings'. There was a general North/South contrast. The London County Council had opened new colleges during the previous 15 years, as had the LEAs for Acton, Barking, Guildford, Twickenham and Walthamstow, always with the result of increased enrolments showing considerable unfulfilled demand. In many other areas poverty and apathy had led to little change, with classes taking place in the premises of elementary and secondary schools. In order to bring accommodation to an acceptable level, 320 'Projects' for new colleges and for substantial extensions to existing institutions were identified, at a cost of over £11 million.

By September 1939, progress had been made on no more than 20 of these projects. The Board could and did encourage LEAs to take action but, given that technical education was not mandatory and that the LEAs were required to meet 50 per cent of the cost, the decision to act rested at all times with the local councils and their officers. In many areas financial hardship was a real factor; in others indifference to the importance of technical education coupled with unwillingness to take on the financial commitment led to inaction. This meant that no system of technical education existed at the outbreak of war with an enemy much better provided for in this area of national life. The reasons for this failure lie chiefly in the continued adherence of government and industry to the principles of *laissez-faire* and voluntarism with regard to technical education. By 1939 there was little sign of any fundamental change in attitudes towards the training of workers. Given the permissive nature of the 1902 Education Act with regard to other than elementary education, the LEAs could decide on the level of provision, and the Board had no power to require development, as was shown in the fate of the 'T Drive'. Employers, whether individual or in their collective form, the Federation of British Industry, showed little serious interest, admittedly at a time of economic difficulties, although in the areas of the new industries, around suburban London, for example, some firms did support their local college. There was, though, no developed view that vocational or continuative education was a necessary sector in relation to the needs of an industrial economy. This, in turn, left the initiative with the voluntary decisions of individual students to enrol for classes in what often was officially admitted to be unattractive and squalid accommodation. Few young employees were granted 'time-off' during the day to attend classes, as is shown in Table 3.1. For the majority of students technical education was still, as it had been 40 years before, a matter of attendance at evening classes after the day's work.

Table 3.1 Students in grant-aided establishments for technical and commercial education (thousands)[10]

Year	Full-time students	Part-time day students	Evening students
1910–11	9	45	539
1920–21	14	63	733
1930–31	8	48	906
1937–8	14	51	1,179

Expansion and pragmatism, 1940–70

As in the First World War, the experience of the 1939–45 War gave rise to proposals for social reform, including proposals for educational development. The 1944 Education Act, for the first time, made the provision of 'adequate facilities' for further education a statutory requirement upon local education authorities, but the comprehensive schemes of the LEAs were not implemented in the ten years after the war. Instead, when attention turned to post-school education in 1956, it was focused on increasing provision for particular types of qualified manpower for clearly economic reasons. Nevertheless the period up to the early 1970s was one of growth in further education with significant increases in the numbers of students who attended during the day, either as full- or part-time students.

The Education Act, backed up by the new Ministry's Circular, 'Further Education', in 1947, laid out a comprehensive vision for post-war further education. Section 41 of the Act made it the duty of LEAs to 'secure' full- and part-time provision for those over the compulsory school age, and cultural and recreational activities for adults. The first of these included the proposal that young workers between the ages of 15 and 18 be required to attend county colleges on one day a week – a revival of the day continuation schools proposals contained in the 1918 Education Act. Further education was thus seen as possessing three 'aspects': the compulsory, continuative provision for all young workers; adult leisure-time education; and the vocational 'aspect', the traditional provision of courses in technical and commercial colleges. In the circulars issued by the Ministry to guide LEAs in the construction of their plans for development, the county college was seen as the compulsory springboard for voluntary advance. As local centres for community education they would shift attendance from evening classes to day-time courses for young people and provide a better foundation and a stimulus for continued study, whether vocational or non-vocational, either at the county college or at the local technical college.[11]

The local authorities submitted their plans to the Ministry but none received official approval for implementation. The worsening economic situation from 1947, and the competition for scarce building and other resources, undermined this comprehensive plan for post-school education. In the field of education the Ministry and LEAs were at this time allocating these resources to rebuilding war-damaged school premises and providing accommodation to meet the demands of raising the school-leaving age and of providing secondary school places for children.

This failure meant, therefore, that the institutional picture of further education remained very much the 'patchwork quilt' of the pre-war period. The amount and quality of places continued to vary between LEA areas according to the level of interest and willingness to spend of the LEAs. Nevertheless, despite the difficulties there was significant expansion in the

25 years up to 1970. Overall many more students enrolled at colleges, and within this larger student body a larger number and proportion attended during the day (full- or part-time). The willingness of more employers, as a rule the larger manufacturing and engineering companies, to release their apprentices and young trainees during the day accounted for this change. To accommodate these additional numbers, many new colleges were built during the 1950s and 1960s, filling the 'gaps' identified earlier in towns like Leeds and Sheffield, and in the form of extensions to existing colleges. As compared with 51,000 day-release students in 1938, there were 644,000 in 1968, while the numbers of full-time students increased from 20,000 to 244,000 (including sandwich courses) during the same period. Parallel to these figures of increased participation in colleges there were those young people who 'stayed on' at school; but the Crowther Report of 1959 pointed out that about 60 per cent of 15–17-year-olds were then receiving no day-time education or training.[12]

The growth in further education owed as much to the voluntary decisions of employers or the parents of the young people as to the policy decisions of politicians or officials. When the attention of the latter turned to post-compulsory education in the 1950s and 1960s it was driven by a narrower and more instrumental view than that which underpinned the generous and coherent vision of 1944. This is shown in the changes following the White Paper of 1956 on Technical Education, where the focus was on increasing the supply of technological manpower. This was achieved by raising the status and level of resourcing of ten technical colleges with substantial amounts of advanced course provision – the colleges of advanced technology (CATs).[13] This preoccupation with the higher reaches of the technical education sector was not new since the main lines of the proposals in 1956 were contained in the Percy Report of 1945.[14] Though not acted upon at the time, the need to increase the supply of technologists continued to be discussed during the 1950s, in the light of economic modernization and with reference to the performance of major competitors, including the USA and the USSR. The designated colleges of advanced technology were removed from the systems of their local authorities after 1956, and briefly formed a non-university sector of higher technological education before becoming universities consequent upon one of the recommendations of the Robbins Committee of 1963.

In 1965–6 the Labour government returned to the policy of identifying the highest technical institutions for use as providers of applied or vocational higher education when Secretary of State, Tony Crosland, announced the decision to revive a binary approach in higher education. The 30 'new' polytechnics in England and Wales were not removed from the control of their LEAs and were urged in policy briefings to supplement the supply of traditional university education by remaining true to their vocational history. In practice this was not always easy to achieve, given the swelling demand for places in the humanities and social sciences – from school-leavers and 'mature' adult students – during the 1970s and 1980s.

The decisions to select major technical institutions for a clear and prestigious national role were not mirrored for colleges lower down the further education ladder. Although the White Paper of 1956 contained sections referring to the grading of colleges below that of the CATs and the polytechnics, while that of 1966 was entitled *A Plan for Polytechnics and Other Colleges* – the same clarity of purpose and status was not given to the local colleges of further education.[15] Instead, official attention was given to the rationalization – or modernization – of the framework and content of vocational courses and qualifications. This took the form of national changes during the 1960s, each based on an assessment that the content and structure of qualifications should more clearly reflect industry's need for skilled manpower at various levels, and a view that a significant number of students failed to complete courses successfully. The White Paper of 1961, *Better Opportunities in Technical Education*, led to a new pattern of courses for technicians (a new category of worker), craftsmen and operatives in major industries. To reduce 'wastage' (non-completion) day-time attendance was to be further encouraged, diagnostic courses were to be introduced and the Ordinary National Certificate course reduced in duration from three to two years.[16]

A second intervention aimed at raising the volume and quality of training was the Industrial Training Act of 1964. While reflecting a general concern about the inadequacy of training, this Act showed the influence upon government of large companies who resented the 'poaching' by small employers of qualified workers trained at their expense. As a result Industrial Training Boards (ITBs) were established (30 by 1970) representative of both sides of their sectors and charged with the tasks of ensuring sufficient training for their industries and that the costs of training were fairly shared between firms. The latter objective was to be achieved by the imposition on all firms by ITBs of a compulsory levy which was repayable upon the delivery of satisfactory training. Progress by the ITBs was, again, patchy with the best work being done in areas like engineering which already had good records of training. In other industries, characteristically those with large numbers of small employers, there was opposition to the bureaucracy of the ITBs and, in particular, to the payment of the levy and the form-filling necessary for its repayment. The incoming Conservative government in 1970 was committed to reducing greatly the activities of the ITBs, thus bringing to an end a brief period when the freedom of employers to take no responsibility for the training of their employees was, at least in the industries for which ITBs were formed, compromised.[17]

At the end of the 1960s the Haslegrave Report on Technician Courses and Examinations recommended further changes in vocational courses for technicians in industry and across the range of courses in business and office studies. Responsibility for courses in these areas was given to two new statutory bodies. The Technician Education Council was established in 1973 and the Business Education Council in 1975, a delay reflecting resistance from some private examining and awarding bodies whose awards would be replaced by the new Councils. Following their merger the Business and Technician (later Technology) Education Council (BTEC) has become the major examining and awarding body in the field through its First, National and Higher Certificates and Diplomas and during the 1990s General National Vocational Qualifications (GNVQs). Its qualifications relate to all major areas of employment.

These initiatives made the 1950s and 1960s a period of significant growth and change within further education. Yet public policy did not account for all development. Clearly the decision to encourage the development of full-time advanced (higher education) courses in major institutions had a significant impact on the colleges affected, and on colleges lower down the pecking order. Some of these looked to develop their advanced work, at a time of growing student numbers, in order to be in line for promotion at a later date. Teachers and managers in colleges were also making the changes in course content, delivery, and assessment required by the examining and validating bodies. All this took place in the context outlined above; one in which student enrolments were increasing at a level which made further education colleges the fastest growing sector of education in the 1960s, despite the contemporary trend for more students to stay at school. In 1969 3.2 million students attended FE institutions, an increase of almost one-third since 1961. Many of these additional students were taking GCE 'O' and 'A' level courses. They included 16–18-year-olds from schools with no sixth-forms, students who were retaking courses failed at school, and those who preferred the more adult atmosphere in the college. No official policy decision underpinned the development of many FE colleges as alternative providers of GCE courses. Rather, with or without the approval of their LEAs, the teachers in colleges met and encouraged a flow of students which helped to raise their role and status locally.

The extent to which this diversification by the addition of general education to the vocational education function of the colleges took place varied between colleges, and from area to area. One crucial factor was the availability or otherwise of sixth-form courses in the local secondary school. In other places the presence of an enterprising head of department or group of teachers, keen to teach GCE classes, would also make the change more likely. The attitude of the LEA could also affect this development, a factor which influenced a second area of diversification during the 1950s and 1960s, that of non-vocational adult education. In some local areas, that of the London County Council (LCC) (later the Inner London

Education Authority (ILEA)) being the foremost example, the provision of adult education classes took place separately on school premises, while the colleges focused chiefly on vocational areas. In other areas technical colleges used their specialist accommodation and staff to broaden provision for adults by introducing practical classes, for example in car mechanics, house maintenance and decoration and personal finance. In such cases colleges were responding in a largely unplanned way to perceived needs, sometimes in competition with existing providers. In so doing it could be claimed that they were *de facto* stretching the definition of further education. The colleges were beginning to be multi-purpose institutions and providers of an increasingly wide range of courses for the communities they served.

Further education to lifelong learning, 1970–2000

After the expansion and optimism of the 1960s the latter decades of the century were characterized by economic difficulties, decline in traditional industries and, for the first time since the Second World War, significant numbers of unemployed school-leavers and adults. Changes in the economy, the shift from manufacturing to service industries, impacted on the course offer of colleges which experienced reductions in students in areas of engineering for example, and increases in business studies, health and community care, leisure and recreation and, later, in computing and information technologies. These changes in the labour market also stimulated interest in political circles in England in the 'recurring debate' on the relationship between education and industry. In turn this gave rise to a number of initiatives addressing the problems of preparing young and adult workers for the 'new economy'. These measures were aimed at modernizing the programmes of post-school education and training and involved the introduction of approaches drawn from private business aimed at changing the culture of the colleges which had diversified further as multi-purpose institutions.

Measures aimed at the unemployed began in 1973 funded by the Manpower Services Commission (MSC) which was formally established in that year. The MSC, in its original conception, was seen by the Conservative government of the time as a national agency within the Department of Employment responsible for manpower policies. Representative of both sides of industry, the Commission found that its attention and that of its executive branch, the Training Services Agency (TSA), was increasingly drawn to the provision of schemes for unemployed young people and adults, through the Youth Opportunities Programme (YOP) and Training Opportunities Scheme (TOPS) respectively. These work-experience schemes, whose names and conditions changed often up to 2000, took place mainly on employers' premises but provided for 'associated further education'. This brought into colleges people who would not normally have attended because they were in unskilled jobs for which no training was thought necessary. Programmes for these new students were arranged around basic and generic work skills relevant to a range of jobs which, it was hoped, would help in coping with the changing labour market. This work was taken on by many colleges whose recruitment in vocational areas was reduced. Additional MSC funding was welcome, and support for this work came from the LEAs whose expenditure was subjected frequently to 'cuts' during this period.

Other developments during the 1970s and 1980s brought in new groups of students and further diversified the colleges' range of work. The uncertainties in the labour markets for school leavers also strengthened the trend for more 16-year-olds to decide to continue in full-time education either at school or college. While many studied GCE subjects, an increasing number of these full-time students were not qualified for 'A' level courses, and for these students teachers and the awarding bodies developed one-year pre-employment courses which could lead to employment or to further study. A second source of new students was the result of the 1981 Education Act, which committed the government to the integration of young people with special educational needs as recommended by the report of the Warnock Committee, published in 1978.[18] While this focused mainly on mainstream schools, it led many LEAs to encourage their colleges to enable young people and adults with these special needs to join mainstream courses and to provide 'bridging' or 'gateway' courses for 16-year-olds to prepare them for employment or further study. The 1980s also saw the expansion of access courses which prepared older students without the traditional qualifications for entry to degree courses. Most colleges now offer this bridging route to higher education for adults for whom it is a second chance in education.

In these ways further education colleges were responding, in the absence of a national plan or policy defining their role, to some opportunities or needs in their local communities, and to some specific national initiatives. In so doing they replaced the vocational provision 'lost' as a result of change and decline in local industry. This was particularly the case where the decline of apprenticeship resulted in a significant reduction in the number of part-time day students on craft and technician courses. In some areas the LEAs decided on institutional reorganization as a response to their financial difficulties and to the demographic changes which reduced the number of school pupils. This involved the transfer of sixth-form courses and students from local schools to the further education college to form a tertiary college. The change resulted in increased staying-on rates and improved achievements by students, and a more efficient use of resources. Indeed, for a time in the 1970s it appeared that the tertiary change could become a national trend.[19] It slowed in the 1980s owing to opposition at the local and national levels, but in those areas where it was successfully implemented the tertiary college has become a local provider of a wide range of opportunities for people of all ages attending full- and part-time.

The Conservative governments of the 1980s were keen to reform vocational qualifications and the arrangements for skills training. These were the years of discussion of British 'economic decline', and of the place of education and training in its causes and remedies.[20] This analysis included comparisons of the provision of and participation in vocational training in the UK and its trading competitors, for example in the influential report, *Competence and Competition*, commissioned by the National Economic Development Office. The government's policy to improve this situation was to require employers to play a leading part in the redesign of vocational qualifications and in the promotion of training. First in 1986, the National Council for Vocational Qualifications (NCVQ) was established. Reporting to the Department of Employment, the NCVQ's brief was to create a framework of national vocational qualifications (NVQs) into which all vocational qualifications would be incorporated. In implementing this the NCVQ required that all qualifications be based on standards, or competences, for occupations, defined by industry-led bodies comprising employers, and that assessment should be in the workplace. The progress of this reform has been mixed; while qualifications now exist for occupations for which there were none previously, there is no single framework of qualifications.[21] This is because traditional qualifications remain popular with students and employers and because college-based students and trainees cannot normally be assessed in the workplace.

The second change based on the desirability of local, employer-led management was the introduction of Training and Enterprise Councils (TECs) in 1990.[22] After successive reductions in its status and role, the Manpower Services Commission was abolished in 1988 and 82 local TECs set up in England and Wales, with 22 Local Enterprise Councils (LECs) in Scotland. These had the task of identifying local needs for skills, training and enterprise development. They manage training programmes for young people, for the unemployed and for adult retraining by sub-contracting to local providers, which include colleges and private training organizations. Recently they have managed Modern Apprenticeships, introduced in an effort to restore a mode of training virtually lost by the decline of apprenticeship.[23]

While these reforms affected the colleges specifically with reference to their vocational training provision, their position with regard to the LEAs was affected by two major pieces of legislation. The first of these, the Education Act of 1988, though principally concerned with compulsory schooling, contained two provisions for further education. LEAs were required to draw up schemes for financial delegation to the colleges which were similar to the approach being introduced in schools. Colleges – now with an increased number of business representatives on their governing bodies – were to assume responsibility for their budgets. The second change was the 'incorporation' of the polytechnics. By giving them independent 'corporate' status financed via a new Polytechnics and Colleges Funding Council, polytechnics were removed from LEA control. These reforms were introduced by a government determined to 'change the culture' of educational institutions. As well as reducing the influence of LEAs, the introduction of competition between institutions at all levels, along with per capita funding and delegated budget management, was designed to raise levels of achievement and efficiency. The extension of the principles of the learning market was particularly successful in the case of the polytechnics in which recruitment of students increased, thus contributing to the participation rates in higher education and their income from the funding council.

These market principles and policies were extended to the further education colleges in England and Wales by the Further and Higher Education Act of 1992. Trailed by the White Paper of the previous year, and influenced by the poll tax crisis and the need to remove some expenditure from LEAs, responsibility for their management was given to corporations (governing bodies) with a majority of 'independent' (business) members. The new Further Education Funding Councils (FEFCs) were charged to fund colleges so that participation and achievement were increased in order to achieve the recently established national targets for qualifications in the labour force. A third aim was the more efficient use of the resources of further education colleges in the light of evidence of inefficiencies caused by some small teaching groups and low completion rates by students.[24] During the 1990s the colleges adapted to the complex demands of the new funding 'methodology' and were able to increase student numbers by 25 per cent while their income per student was reduced.[25] They were also able to draw funding from their local TECs for youth and adult training, but, because of the requirement to concentrate on programmes leading to qualifications, the funding of leisure and recreational adult education remained with the local authorities.

The election of the Labour government in 1997 made for some significant changes in the terms of the debate about the development of post-compulsory education while the emphasis on efficiency gains and the principle of 'something for something' remained. To the economic imperative was added the social aim of widening participation; that is, increasing the recruitment of people in society currently disproportionately underrepresented in post-school education (for example, some ethnic groups, adults in unskilled occupations, people with a background of failure in their schooling).[26] This also promoted the aims of the government's New Deal and the analysis of the Social Exclusion Unit which identified the still substantial number of 16–18-year-olds who were neither in employment nor in any form of education or training.[27]

The dual and complementary aims of social inclusion and economic development through enhanced participation in lifelong learning were the basis of the government's major piece of legislation, the Learning and Skills Act of 2000, implementation of which began in April 2001. The terms of this were summarized in the White Paper, *Learning to Succeed: A New Framework for Post 16 Learning*, 1999, and constituted a radical reform, in official terms the 'modernization' of all post-16 provision in England outside the university sector. From April 2001, a new national Learning and Skills Council (LSC) took over responsibility for the planning and funding of further education and government-supported training, thus replacing the FEFCs and TECs. It funds and plans post-16 education in schools (from 2003) and non-vocational adult education at present provided by LEAs. It works through a regional system in England of 47 local Learning and Skills Councils. In the words of the White Paper the LSC has responsibility for:

> strategic development, planning, funding and quality assurance of post-16 education and training (excluding higher education). The new Council's remit thus includes further education, community and adult learning, work-based learning for young people, workforce development, and information, advice and guidance support for adults.[28]

Conclusion

The history of English further education during the twentieth century has taken place in national and local contexts which failed to give the sector a clear purpose, focus or status. Until 1944 the provision of further education was permissive, and given the absence of a definition of 'adequate facilities', the commitment of local authorities to providing opportunities for young people and adults continued to vary. The comprehensive plans developed as a result of the legislation of 1918 and 1944 were not followed through to implementation, and for much of the century, when economic conditions allowed educational developments, there were alternative and competing priorities with regard to schools and higher education. Governments have acted in the belief that electoral advantage lay in these areas, with the result that the earlier plans for further education became 'dated'. An example of this was the decline in interest in compulsory day-release for young workers with the successive decisions to raise the school-leaving age and the increase in voluntary staying-on in education at 16.

The failure to establish a national pattern and strategy for further education and a legal requirement for attendance meant that voluntary initiative and decisions became important in the development of further education. Patchy provision in the areas of the LEAs has been referred to above, as has the unwillingness of many employers to support the training and education of their employees. The result has been that colleges have been forced to adapt to their local circumstances and have worked to meet the needs and ambitions of those young people and adults who have chosen to register with them, sometimes with their employers' support. This constant need to be responsive and entrepreneurial, in order to survive and grow, has led to the development of the FE college as the multi-purpose community institution which has been described above.

The changes of the 1990s, with the stated aims of increasing industry's competitiveness by increasing the qualifications held by the labour force, achieved a great deal, particularly in terms of increased participation and student retention and achievement. This also led to a national system of funding and inspection. Student numbers increased from 2.5 million in 1993–4 to 3.5 million in 1999–2000; the target of a 25 per cent increase in three years after 1993 was exceeded, all without a parallel increase in funding.[29] However, based as it was on a belief in the value of the learning market, the FEFC's funding system provided no strategic direction for the FE colleges in relation to national needs and also led to some colleges being in financial difficulties. Also apparent at the end of the 1990s, were the anomalies between the funding and quality assurance arrangements for FE and those for government-supported training (through the TECs) and in LEA provision for 16–19-year-olds and adults.

The merger of the Employment Department and the Department for Education to form the Department for Education and Employment in 1995 made possible the unification of responsibility for all post-16 education and training, outside the universities, enacted in the Learning and Skills Act 2000. This established the national Learning and Skills Council responsible for the strategic planning of previously disparate provision which had hitherto been subject to differing systems of management, funding and inspection by a range of local and regional bodies and authorities. The learning and skills sector – the largest in English education – currently has five million students and the LSC budget exceeds £6 billion. In the words of Secretary of State, David Blunkett, this 'new settlement' is as significant a change in post-compulsory education as was the 1944 Education Act for primary and secondary schooling.[30] The indications, in early 2001 as the LSC prepared to undertake its remit, were that the new post-16 settlement would be structured according to learners' ages, rather than by a division between vocational and other 'non-vocational' provision. The Council established two committees, one for 16–19-year-olds, the other for adults. A new, independent Adult Learning Inspectorate is inspecting provision for adults, while that for 16–19-year-olds is inspected by Ofsted. These inspectorates conduct joint 'area inspections' of all provision in a locality. The area reports, with their comments on value for money and the adequacy of provision, provide evidence for the local LSC in its decisions in relation to funding and possible institutional reorganization.

The government also declared its interest in providing for the needs of 16–19-year-olds through the linking of such provision in FE colleges with that in sixth-form colleges and centres and with sixth forms in schools.[31] This focus on the needs of 16–19 learners was also evident in the Curriculum 2000 changes to GCE A levels and GNVQs (now vocational A levels) introduced in September 2000. Qualifications for full-time students in this age group are now awarded by three unitary examining and awarding bodies, the result of mergers of academic and vocational bodies in 1999.[32] How these changes will impact upon colleges, whose work historically diversified through filling the gaps left by other institutions, remains to be seen. Finally, while there is the possibility of bringing about greater coherence and consistency to post-16 learning than has hitherto been the case, and government has given a commitment to finance additional numbers of learners, it is not clear how far the national LSC will make the learning market (with its implications for individual choice) compatible with the brief to plan in accordance with labour market needs as perceived by the local LSCs.

Key reading

A. Abbott (former Chief Technological Inspector) provides a good summary of the early period in *Education for Industry and Commerce in England*, Oxford, Oxford University Press, 1933. For official accounts, up to 1925 and 1950 respectively, see the Board of Education's *Annual Report* for 1926 and the Ministry's survey in *Education 1900–1950*, London, HMSO, 1951. The genesis of technical education is discussed at length in J.F. Donnelly, 'The origins of the technical curriculum during the nineteenth and early twentieth centuries', *Studies in Science Education*, 1989, vol. 16. The work and relationships of the relevant central authorities in the changing twentieth-century context are discussed in R. Aldrich *et al*, *Education and Employment: the DfEE and its Place in History*, London, Institute of Education, 2000.

E.J.R. Eaglesham's short study of the early years in *Foundations of 20th Century Education in England*, London, Routledge and Kegan Paul, 1967 is valuable, as is D.W. Thoms, 'The emergence of failure of the day continuation school experiment', *History of Education*, 1975, vol. 4, no. 1. L. Cantor and G. Mathews provide a study of a local technical college which rose to university status in *Loughborough: from College to University*, Loughborough, Loughborough University of Technology, 1977.

For adult education in its many forms during the century, *A History of*

Modern British Adult Education by Roger Fieldhouse and Associates, Leicester, NIACE, 1996, contains many useful contributions and sources, while developments in one, exceptional, local area are discussed in W.A. Devereux, *Adult Education in Inner London*, London, Shepheard-Walwyn and ILEA, 1982.

G. Fowler's 'Further education' in R. Bell, G. Fowler and K. Little (eds) *Education in Great Britain and Ireland*, London, Routledge and Kegan Paul, 1973, captures the characteristics and dynamic of further education in the 1960s, while changes in training policy since that time are examined in B. Evans, *The Politics of the Training Market: from MSC to TECS*, London, Routledge, 1992. The latter can be supplemented by P. Raggatt and S. Williams, *Government, Markets and Qualifications: An Anatomy of Policy*, London, Falmer, 1999.

Changes in vocational education and training 1990–2000 are discussed in G. Stanton and B. Bailey, 'VET under review: trends and developments', *European Journal of Education*, 2001, vol. 36, no. 1. For changes in further education after the Further and Higher Education Act 1992, see P. Ainley and B. Bailey, *The Business of Learning: Staff and Student Experiences of Further Education in the 1990s*, London, Cassell, 1997.

Notes

1 For the effects of this initiative in the country's largest local council see R. Floud and S. Glynn (eds) *London Higher: The Establishment of Higher Education in London*, London, Athlone, 1998, pp. 26–8.
2 E.J.R. Eaglesham, *The Foundations of 20th Century Education in England*, London, Routledge and Kegan Paul, 1967, pp. 62–72.
3 M.E. Sadler (ed.) *Continuation Schools in England and Elsewhere*, Manchester, Manchester University Press, 1907.
4 Board of Education, *Juvenile Education in Relation to Employment after the War* (Lewis Report), London HMSO, 1917, p. 5.
5 L. Selby-Bigge, *The Board of Education*, London, Putnam, 1927, p. 86.
6 Board of Education, Draft of Proposed Revised Regulations for Continuation, Technical and Art Classes in England and Wales 1917.
7 Selby-Bigge, op cit., p. 168.
8 B. Simon, *The Politics of Educational Reform, 1920–1940*, London, Lawrence and Wishart, 1974.
9 B. Bailey, 'The development of technical education, 1934–39', *History of Education*, 1987, vol. 16, no. 1, pp. 49–65. This is the source of comments and quotations in this and the following paragraphs.
10 Ministry of Education, *Education 1900–1950*, London, HMSO, 1951, Table 98 (adapted) p. 249.
11 Ministry of Education, *Further Education, the Scope and Content of its Opportunities under the Education Act, 1944*, Pamphlet No 8, London, HMSO, 1947.
12 Ministry of Education, *15 to 18*, a Report of the Central Advisory Council for Education (England), London, HMSO, 1959, vol. 1, p. 164.
13 Ministry of Education, *Technical Education*, [Cmd. 9703], London, HMSO, 1956.

14 Ministry of Education, *Higher Technological Education*, Report of a Special Committee appointed in April 1944.
15 Department of Education and Science, *A Plan for Polytechnics and Other Colleges*, [Cmd. 3006], London, HMSO, 1966.
16 Ministry of Education, *Better Opportunities in Technical Education*, [Cmd. 1254], London, HMSO, 1961.
17 B. Evans, *The Politics of the Training Market: from Manpower Services Commission to Training and Enterprise Councils*, London, Routledge, 1992, pp. 20–1.
18 Department of Education and Science (DES), *Special Educational Needs*, London, HMSO, 1978. See especially pp. 162–204.
19 A.B. Cotterell and E.W. Heley (eds) *Tertiary: A Radical Approach to Post Compulsory Education*, Cheltenham, Stanley Thornes, 1980.
20 R. Aldrich, D. Crook and D. Watson, *Education and Employment: the DfEE and its Place in History*, London, Institute of Education, 2000, pp. 160–3.
21 P. Robinson, *Rhetoric and Reality: Britain's New Vocational Qualifications*, London, Centre for Economic Performance, 1996.
22 Department of Employment, *Employment for the 1990s*, [Cmnd. 540], London, HMSO, 1988.
23 L. Unwin and J. Wellington, 'Reconstructing the work-based route: lessons from the modern apprenticeship', *Journal of Vocational Education and Training*, 1995, vol. 147, no. 4, pp. 337–52.
24 Audit Commission/Ofsted, *Unfinished Business: Full-time Educational Courses for 16–19 Year Olds*, London, HMSO, 1993.
25 P. Ainley and B. Bailey, *The Business of Learning: Staff and Student Experiences of Further Education in the 1990s*, London, Cassell, 1997.
26 A. Zera and T. Jupp, 'Widening participation', in A. Smithers and P. Robinson (eds) *Further Education Re-formed*, London, Falmer, 2000.
27 Social Exclusion Unit, *Bridging the Gap: New Opportunities for 16–18 Year Olds Not in Education, Employment or Training*, [Cm. 4405], London, HMSO, 1999.
28 Department for Education and Employment, *Learning to Succeed: a New Framework for Post-16 Learning*, [Cm. 4392], London, HMSO, 1999.
29 *Times Higher Educational Supplement*, 17 November 2000.
30 D. Blunkett, *Colleges for Excellence and Innovation: Statement by the Secretary of State for Education and Employment on the Future of Further Education in England*, London, DfEE, 2000, p. 7.
31 Ibid., p. 5.
32 Discussed in detail in G. Stanton and B. Bailey, 'VET under review: trends and developments', *European Journal of Education*, 2001, vol. 36, no. 1, pp. 7–22.

Chapter 4

Higher education

Roy Lowe

The situation in 2000

Higher education is generally understood to be that education which takes place either in, or under the auspices of, universities or colleges of higher education and which involves the students concerned, of whatever age, in doing work beyond GCE Advanced level. At the end of the twentieth century there are 114 university institutions in the United Kingdom, if the individual colleges of the federal institutions (the University of London and the University of Wales) are counted separately. These universities are given the power to award degrees by the Privy Council, which now uses the Quality Assurance Agency (QAA) to ensure standards of teaching in these institutions. Alongside the universities are the higher education colleges, which vary enormously in size, in function and in their histories, although those which had been established by and were under the control of LEAs were made independent by the 1988 Education Reform Act so that all such colleges are now self-governing. The key distinction between universities and colleges of higher education is that universities have been granted the power to award their own degrees, whereas colleges of higher education are obliged to have their degree qualifications validated either by a university or some other accrediting body.

The scale of higher education in the United Kingdom is such that it comprises a significant element in the national economy. About one third of the population now goes forward to pursue full-time higher education beyond the age of 18. Although most students go to university either directly from school or sixth-form college (or immediately after a 'gap' year, which is increasingly popular) there are a growing number of mature students within higher education using university or college to facilitate a redirection of career. The various higher education institutions employ, in total, about 120,000 academic staff. The total revenue for higher education in the United Kingdom is about £12 billion per annum and about two thirds of this comes either from the UK government or from the European Union. Devolution has resulted in the appearance of separate funding bodies for England, Northern Ireland, Scotland and Wales. These higher education funding councils operate in radically different contexts in each country. The result is that at the start of the twenty-first century the unit of funding resource for each full-time student is significantly different in each country. At the commencement of the 2000–1 academic year, the support given by central government to universities in England per student per annum is £5,360, in Wales £5,138 and in Scotland £6,744. This inequality originates in historical differences in spending patterns in each country and also from the Barnett formula which was introduced in 1978.[1] Attempts over recent years to 'iron out' these significant disparities have so far failed. Indeed, funding cuts imposed differentially in England and Wales in 2000 seem likely to widen these disparities. Since 1998–9 all residents of the European Union studying on full-time higher education courses in England and Wales have contributed to the cost of their courses to the tune of £1,000 per year. However, a strong stand by the Scottish Assembly, backed by the Student Award Agency for Scotland, resulted in these fees not being payable in Scotland, thus heightening the financial disparities between Scotland and the rest of the United Kingdom. The impact of these 'top up' fees has also distorted patterns of recruitment, with a growing percentage of students choosing to study closer to their family homes. This is of particular economic significance in those rural areas where the existence of a local university has a significant impact on the local economy and local employment patterns.

The majority of students are embarked on first degree courses and these range from Bachelors Degree schemes, to Higher National Diplomas, Higher National Certificates and Diplomas in Higher Education, some of which can be completed over a briefer period than the typical three-year undergraduate degree. Increasingly, British universities are switching to semesterization and offering their courses on a modular basis. This brings them more closely into line with developments in mainland Europe and enables freer movement of students between one institution and another than was the case in the past. At the same time, the drift from 'end on' assessment through three-hour unseen examination papers towards continuous assessment is under way on undergraduate courses but remains contested and is patchy in its implementation. The postgraduate courses available within higher education also vary enormously. Some are vocationally orientated Diplomas and Certificates such as the Post-Graduate Certificate in Education (PGCE), although many students are embarked on Masters Degrees (some of which are also vocational in nature) and the tradition of several years' intensive individual research towards a doctoral degree remains intact. The Quality Assurance Agency, which emerged from one of the recommendations of the 1997 Dearing Report,[2] is increasingly overseeing all aspects of teaching within higher education.

Universities in Britain have a long-standing commitment to research and still consider themselves to be research institutions. The total funding which is made available to support research in British universities is around £2,500 million per annum, although this is not evenly distributed. The 'Russell' Group of universities (so called from a preliminary meeting which took place in the Russell Hotel in London) claim to be those with the strongest commitment to research and this is reflected in the disproportionate amounts of support they receive. Much of this funding is directed to individual institutions and particular projects through the six Research Councils. These are the Biotechnology and Biological Sciences Research Council, the Engineering and Physical Sciences Research Council, the Economic and Social Research Council, the Medical Research Council, the Natural Environment Research Council and the Particle Physics and Astronomy Research Council. There is also a new Arts and Humanities Research Board, established in 1998, which performs similar functions in respect of Arts and Humanities subjects. There are also more than 50 science parks in the United Kingdom adjacent to university institutions where collaboration takes place between higher education and local industries. These contain more than 1,300 small companies and employ over 25,000 people. The quality of this research within institutions of higher education is monitored through a quinquennial research assessment exercise and the judgements made by the 70 specialist subject panels of the RAE are used to inform the pattern of funding and support offered by these government quangos.

Further, the Institute for Learning and Teaching, established in 1999, is seeking to establish patterns of accreditation for teachers within higher education analogous to the Qualified Teacher status enjoyed by schoolteachers. There is variable resistance to this organization within higher education and it remains to be seen whether it will survive and flourish or perish on the vine. There are numerous agencies responsible for strategic planning within higher education, but perhaps the most significant of them was the Committee of Vice-Chancellors and Principals (CVCP) which, in December 2000, changed its title to Universities UK.[3]

The situation in 1900

Possibly the greatest parallel between the situation in 1900 and that in 2000 was that higher education in the United Kingdom found itself, at both times, in the midst of a dramatic expansion. In almost all other respects the situation could hardly have been more contrasting. The universities in 1900 were fewer, smaller and quite different in function from what they became during the twentieth century. In England there were only the Universities of Oxford, Cambridge, Durham and London in existence before 1900. In Scotland Aberdeen, Edinburgh, Glasgow and

St Andrews had existed as universities in their own right for over 300 years. The small University College at Dundee, founded in 1881, was affiliated to St Andrews and there existed two small prototype technological universities, one at Glasgow and one at Edinburgh. These were the Anderson's Institution in Glasgow, founded in 1796 and known since 1828 as Anderson's University and the Watt Institution in Edinburgh which had emerged during the nineteenth century from the 1821 Edinburgh School of Arts and Mechanics Institute. In Wales, the Federal University was taking on its modern shape by the start of the twentieth century. University colleges were already in existence at Aberystwyth (1872), Bangor (1884) and Cardiff (1883) and in 1892 the University, with its registry at Cardiff, was granted power to award degrees. As in Scotland there already existed the prototype of a technological university in the 1866 Cardiff School of Science and Art, known since 1890 as the Technical School. Apart from this, there were, across England in particular (although not unknown in both Scotland and Wales), numerous local mechanics institutions of varying degrees of educational efficiency and also a considerable number of university extension centres, at which tutors from the established universities gave evening lectures to students who had no other access to higher education.

These institutions had all undergone expansion during the late-nineteenth century but they remained minute by modern day standards. For example, Oxford and Cambridge each catered for about 3,000 students in 1900, London less than 1,000 and Durham 250.[4] The university colleges which had appeared in several of the English industrial cities during the second half of the nineteenth century had larger enrolments, but the vast majority of these students were part-time and few were involved in degree level teaching. At Mason College, Birmingham, for example, in 1892 only 14 of the 700 students received University of London degrees and this pattern was replicated elsewhere. Interestingly, although of relatively low status, these provincial colleges were, from the outset open to female students. In 1901, Birmingham had registered more female than male students (381 to 368). Although this was exceptional, other university colleges had significant cohorts of female students at this time.

In this situation the seeds of some of the key issues of the twentieth century were already germinating. The existing universities remained, at the start of the century, largely wedded to the pre-eminence of a Classical education. The newer institutions had all been established on the grounds that they would teach one or other version of the new knowledge of the age. The second industrial revolution, involving petrochemical, electrical and engineering industries, called for a more highly trained labour force than had been the case previously in industry, and the university colleges and technical institutes which appeared up and down Britain set out to provide appropriate training. Meanwhile, the major professions and to a lesser degree management of these new industries all came under the ambit of the universities and sustained the primacy of a Classical education. By the end of the nineteenth century, the senior ranks of the Civil Service and most of the major professions were recruiting from the long-established faculties of the ancient universities.[5] This resulted in a two-fold tension within higher education which was felt throughout the twentieth century. First, particular subjects and particular curricular routes became seen as the ways into some of the more powerful professional positions and thus perceptions of a hierarchy of knowledge developed and were clearly evident at the start of the twentieth century. Alongside this was the tension which necessarily resulted over the extent to which higher education should be vocational, offering a training and particular skills for employment in identified locations within the expanding economy, or, on the other hand, should be pursued for its own sake or for the transferable skills of analysis and reason which some claimed could be derived from any general education.[6]

A second major issue which was already becoming evident by the start of the century was the extent to which this expanding system of higher education was offering opportunities to women.[7] The appearance of women's colleges at Oxford and Cambridge before the turn of the century, together with the appearance of a larger cohort of female students at the new civic university colleges, might be taken to suggest that higher education was to be the agency by which females were given real opportunities for full involvement in social, economic and political life in the twentieth century. Conversely, the continuing monopolization of the more prestigious routes through higher education by males would suggest that the universities themselves were to become one of the key factors by which the 'glass ceiling' remained so powerful throughout the century.

Finally, as we go on to chart the shifts between 1900 and 2000 from minority, elite higher education towards the 'multiversity' and towards a mass system of higher education, it is important to ask which of the elements of a highly-stratified society, acutely conscious of social class can be attributed to the effects of higher education during the twentieth century.[8] At the end of the twentieth century, poverty had still not been eliminated; there remained significant inequalities between social classes and between men and women. Regional contrasts in Britain remained as great, if not greater, than they were in 1900. Contrasts in health, in life expectancy and in lifestyle persist. How far has our developing system of higher education worked to address these chronic problems and how far has it sustained them in one way or another? These are the intriguing questions at the heart of this account of its development during the twentieth century.

Changes and continuities

The significant expansion of higher education which took place between 1900 and 1939 was largely the result of accretion. New universities were added to the list of those already recognized by the Privy Council and new subjects were taught at both these and at the pre-existing universities. Also, there was the first appearance during these years of agencies to oversee (and eventually plan) the growth of the sector as a whole.

The most dramatic sign of this accretion was the upgrading of the university colleges. By the outbreak of the First World War, Birmingham (1900), Liverpool (1903), Manchester (1903), Leeds (1904), Sheffield (1905) and Bristol (1909) had all become fully-fledged universities ('the Redbricks'). Also, new university colleges had been recognized at Newcastle, Reading and Southampton.[9] This resulted in an immediate transformation of these institutions. They grew in size; they shifted towards courses at degree level at the same time that the numbers of full-time students rose. In each case university status meant a swift growth of the Arts faculty as, ironically, they drifted away from their original purpose of supplying the local employment market towards one of looking as much as possible like a 'proper' university. These Arts faculties enabled significant female participation and ensured that one key function of these institutions was to act as regional centres of teacher education, especially for the growing number of secondary schools, with a three-year under-graduate course followed by one year of teacher training in a department of education.

Meanwhile, the ongoing demand for technical training at local level was met not just by the expansion of the applied science faculties of these new universities but also through the establishment of technical colleges by the new local education authorities. In these the local traditions of evening work as a kind of ancillary apprenticeship for a variety of crafts and trades persisted at just the moment that the new universities were moving away from this kind of provision. What enabled these colleges to become increasingly academically ambitious was the existence of the University of London external degree which resulted in London becoming far and away the biggest degree-awarding body in the United Kingdom prior to the establishment of the Council for National Academic Awards (CNAA). They also became a 'safety valve' for the expansion in the number of students embarked on vocational degree schemes of one kind or another, soaking up the demand which the universities could not or would not meet. Thus, this particular facet of the expansion of the system enabled academic hierarchies to be built in from the start and sustained for much of the twentieth century. Those involved in the planning of the system became well aware of these hierarchies and were not averse to sustaining them. For example the 1945 Percy Report on higher technological education, one of the numerous documents which planned the pattern of post-war expansion, observed that 'industry must look mainly to universities for the training of scientists, both for research and development; it must look mainly to Technical Colleges for technical assistants and craftsmen'. Thus fast-track higher education was to link with fast-track employment. This proved very largely to be the case as the universities came to occupy a pivotal role during the twentieth century as arbiters of a stratified employment market.

This expansion of higher education, which saw 50,000 students in full-time post-school education by 1939, came at a price. The funding of higher education in the United Kingdom by central government had begun in 1889 with the introduction of an annual Treasury grant to the universities and university colleges. An Advisory Committee on Grants was set up in 1906 to administer this growing burden. This was the forerunner of the University Grants Committee (UGC) which came into being in 1919 and which, for half a century, afforded the universities the now scarcely remembered luxury of quinquennial planning.

Governmental and local authority munificence enabled further steady expansion during the inter-war years, despite the effects of the slump. Exeter, Hull and Leicester were recognized as university colleges and student numbers continued their inexorable rise, although more slowly than had been the case during the relatively prosperous Edwardian period. But it was the aftermath of the Second World War which fomented a major soul-searching about the nature and curriculum of the university, and about the structure of the system of higher education. This was also the historical moment when planning was the order of the day in all aspects of public life. In 1946, significantly, the terms of reference of the UGC were widened to allow it to 'advise Government on the application of grants'. Thus, the pattern of post-war expansion was to be planned, not accidental. With the introduction of universal secondary schooling in the 1944 Education Act and the coming of affluence during the 1950s, growing numbers could aspire to full-time higher education. The outcome was little short of a revolution so kaleidoscopic in its nature that it may yet be too early to offer any meaningful historical judgements (a consideration which has not deterred numerous commentators and which will not long delay the present author).

Following the Percy Report, the 1946 Barlow Report on scientific manpower foresaw a significant expansion as well as some experimentation in the role of the universities. Barlow echoed the demand of the Percy Report for a few technical colleges developing into 'major university institutions' and went on to call for institutes of technology which could take their students to the level of doctoral research. This near revolutionary recommendation, coming at the same time as a major debate on the purposes and methods of universities, culminating in 1949 with Walter Moberly's, *The Crisis in the University*, was to prove almost prophetic.

In brief, what actually happened after the Second World War was that the unanticipated and continuing steady rise in demand for university places forced, first, another major expansion of some existing institutions, second, a series of waves of new foundations, and, third, further upgrading of other existing institutions.[10] The pre-existing universities benefited from the growing availability of local authority maintenance grants for students and widened their catchment areas, thus becoming, for the first time, national institutions in their own right rather than regional colleges. At the same time they continued to become steadily larger. One interesting point is that these civic universities never completely lost sight of the ideal of a collegiate institution on the Oxbridge model, placing enormous pressure on the Treasury during the 1950s and 1960s to support massive expansion of their halls of residence, so that they could continue to exercise a pastoral function. This may go far to explain why the American model of universities of 30 and 40,000 students, never came under serious consideration in Britain as a way of coping with growing demand. It also explains why a whole variety of new foundations came to appear necessary quite soon after the war.

The first response to this crisis was the new universities movement. By the early 1960s Keele, Sussex, East Anglia, Lancaster, Warwick, York, Kent, Essex and Stirling were all setting about the redrafting of the map of learning, although the fact that, collectively, they sound like a cast list of Shakespearian dukes is hardly suggestive of revolution and does betray the value system which was at work. Each sought to respond to the debate on over-specialization in higher education, which had preoccupied many good minds during the post-war years with novel curricular arrangements involving previously untried subject combinations and, in some cases, the collapsing of discrete disciplinary boundaries. The fact that the pioneering Keele foundation year survived for almost 50 years reflects the extent to which these new institutions marked an irreversible sea change in popular understandings of university study. Equally, its eventual demise illustrates how susceptible in the long run these innovations were to the dead hand of academic conformity. But, by any measure, these 'plate glass' universities facilitated the post-war expansion of higher education capacity.

It quickly became apparent that this, too, was nowhere near enough to satisfy demand. The technical colleges were increasingly using the external examinations of the University of London to soak up excess demand in most of the metropolitan centres. One catalyst for this was the further education and training grants available to demobilized ex-servicemen. The outcome was both an expansion in numbers and a shift towards degree-level work as these local colleges, mostly LEA funded, proved far more adaptable to swift changes in student demand than the centrally-funded universities. In this almost accidental process lay the origins of what was soon to be labelled the 'binary system' with two competing and differing sectors offering different versions of higher education. In 1956 the government of the day went some way to recognize this in its White Paper on technical education which identified technical colleges for designation as Colleges of Advanced Technology (CATs). Also, at this time, the National Council for Technological Awards (NCTA) was set up, with the power to award diplomas in technology but not degrees in these institutions.

The longer-term governmental response to this situation, anticipated by the Robbins Report of 1963, seems in retrospect to smack as much of panic as of measured strategic planning. What emerged was a threefold strategy. The demands of the economy for a more highly trained labour force were to be met through the 'Robbins principle', that any 18-year-old who was qualified to enter higher education and wished to do so should be given the opportunity. This chimed with the evidence given to the Robbins Committee by Jean Floud and the Fabian Society which suggested that, despite the expansion that had already taken place since the war, there remained a vast pool of 'untapped ability'. This expansion was to be facilitated in two ways: first, the kinds of higher education institution available were to be further proliferated and, secondly, a new degree awarding body, the Council for National Academic Awards (CNAA), was to give recognition to work done in non-university institutions.[11] This replaced the NCTA and the fact that it could award degrees as well as diplomas enabled higher education courses offered outside the universities to receive due recognition. The Robbins Committee also prophetically called for a single augmented grants commission to oversee the development of higher education as a whole. This would replace the University Grants Committee whose writ did not run further than the universities. The Robbins Report has been described as the first attempt to co-ordinate the development of a system of higher education in modern Britain, and as such it stands as a high water mark of post-war planning.[12]

In its rush to respond to the Robbins Report, and to deliver on its election promise of a 'white hot technological revolution', Harold Wilson's Labour government immediately converted several of the new colleges of advanced technology at Aston, Bath, Bradford, Brunel, Heriot-Watt, Loughborough, Salford and Strathclyde into technological universities. At the same time scientific and technological institutes were recognized in Cardiff, Edinburgh and Manchester. This *de facto* redefinition of the nature of a university appeared to some civil servants, such as Toby Weaver, to hold out the prospect of an almost limitless expansion of the university sector with potentially dire consequences for the public purse. Newly appointed to the Education Ministry, Tony Crosland was despatched to Woolwich on 25 April 1965, with journalists judiciously within earshot, to enunciate the 'binary policy' as a new template for any further growth.[13] Henceforth, expansion was to be achieved through the development of existing technical colleges as polytechnics. In May 1966 a White Paper put hard edges to this policy by designating some 30 polytechnics. These began work in the autumn of 1970, and, so, for a while at least, expansion was able to proceed on a lower per capita funding rate at the expense of local taxpayers rather than the national government. On such economic exigencies are high political principles founded.

What was particularly interesting about these polytechnics was the fact that no sooner were they at work than they began to replicate the processes which had taken place within the civic universities at the start of the century. Just as the Edwardian civic universities had been founded with the intention of concentrating on a technological education but quickly came to look strangely like Oxford and Cambridge, with fast expanding Arts faculties, so, too, the polytechnics discovered during the 1970s that the route to expansion was to mop up the excess demand for arts and humanities courses which was still overwhelming the existing universities. The first ever edition of the *Times Higher Education Supplement* in September 1971 showed that there were, across the United Kingdom that autumn, in total 1,240 applications for the 1,962 Engineering places available; 2,700 applications for the 3,571 Science places on offer; but over 10,000 applicants for the 2,200 Arts and Social Science vacancies. Doubtless the newly-installed principals of the polytechnics read this piece and licked their lips.

One further effort to soak up excessive demand for higher education during the 1960s was the establishment of the Open University, the brainchild of Jennie Lee, which received a Royal Charter in 1969 and enrolled its first students in 1971. It quickly became one of the most significant degree-awarding bodies, with over 60,000 students by 1980.

Thus, in the main during the 1960s, policy developments in higher education reflected the 'Butskellism'[14] which typified much of the politics of the decade, despite the almost kaleidoscopic rate of growth of higher education. One demurring voice at the end of the 1960s was that of Harry Ferns, who, in 1969, enlisted Max Beloff and the Institute of Economic Affairs to lobby for the creation of a free university. Although perceived by many observers as a maverick idea, this proposal took hold among some elements of the Conservative Right, and culminated in the establishment of a University College at Buckingham in 1972. Beloff became Principal Designate and, under the aegis of an Independent University Planning Board, efforts were made to demonstrate the viability of a university institution which was to remain completely outside and independent of the now familiar apparatus of state planning which was determining the growth patterns of all other areas of higher education. Although degree recognition was pointedly refused in 1974, forcing Buckingham to award its own degrees, Margaret Thatcher, as Prime Minister, was determined to give recognition to this embodiment of free market principles and, in 1982, it was duly incorporated by Royal Charter as the University of Buckingham.

Earlier periods of growth within higher education had given way to at least a few years of retrenchment and consolidation. What is perhaps most remarkable about the frenzied developments of the 1960s is that they were to prove only the forerunner of ongoing ferment which has continued unabated down to the present time. At the end of the twentieth century we can look back on a 40-year period of intense debate, kaleidoscopic policy change and ongoing transformation and growth in higher education which has persisted since the then Labour government's knee-jerk reactions to the Robbins Report.

One of the most disingenuous documents, which signalled at the time that more change was still to come, was *Education: a Framework for Expansion*, introduced by Margaret Thatcher in 1972, during her tenure of the Education office. This document foresaw 22 per cent of the age group (circa 200,000 new entrants per year) participating in higher educa- tion by 1981. Reflecting views which may not have been entirely her own, she told the House of Commons that:

> opportunities for higher education are not to be determined primarily by reference to broad estimates of the country's future needs for highly qualified people ... the Government consider higher education valu- able for its contribution to the personal development of those who pursue it. At the same time they value its continued expansion as an investment in the nation's human talent in a time of rapid social change and technological development.[15]

This was to be one of the last public pronouncements, by politicians of any hue, which reflected the underlying ideology of the Robbins Report.

What followed in reality, and in very short order, was that through the 1970s the Department of Education and Science (DES) responded to the falling birth rate and to economic crisis by a series of downward revisions of the target numbers. Whereas in 1970 the plan had been to see in total 850,000 students in higher education by 1981, by 1977 the fifth of a succession of these downward revisions saw this target fall finally to 560,000. This did result in a brief check to the almost relentless growth of higher education. The percentage of the population entering full-time higher education reached an unprecedented 14.2 per cent in 1972, but had fallen back to 12.4 per cent by 1978.

But the numbers of young people gaining two or more GCE 'A' level passes continued to rise, as did their aspirations. Unable to hold this deep- seated social trend in check for long, government responded with reductions in funding which at least had the advantage of guaranteeing a limit to the demands which further growth would make of the public purse, but which also had the inevitable effect of transforming the economic situation of the universities. In 1975 the quinquennial financial planning which universities had enjoyed for half a century was ended and annual funding with strict cash limits introduced. In February 1978, the Minister for Higher Education, Gordon Oakes, produced a consultative document, *Higher Education into the 1990s*, which pointed to the falling birth rate and the economic situation as justifications for further trimming. Almost prophetically, the one model of development that this document offered which anticipated any growth at all foresaw that this would be done through the involvement of more working-class, mature and part-time students in higher education. Thus was the cry of 'access' first heard: it was to echo until the end of the century.

If the financial constraints of the 1970s seemed unpropitious to those working within higher education, they were as nothing to the severity of the cuts programme introduced by Margaret Thatcher's government after 1979. The Conservative election manifesto in that year had warned the electorate that 'the balance of our society has been increasingly tilted in favour of the State ... This election may be the last chance we have to reverse that process.' No sooner was Thatcher elected than the universities began to feel the sharp effect of these words translated into day by day policy. In October 1979 subsidies to overseas students fees were withdrawn, cutting off at a stroke one key source of students. In the following month a White Paper announced a £411 million cut per annum in governmental support for the universities. A further White Paper on expenditure detailed swingeing economies to be applied by the UGC. The UGC was instructed to act selectively, imposing the greatest cuts on those institutions with inferior employment rates for their graduates. In response the UGC wrote its own death warrant by imposing cuts of only five per cent on Oxbridge and up to 40 per cent on some of the new technological universities (Salford claimed that its reductions were at this level), despite the fact that these had, by and large, very impressive graduate employment statistics. This may have been the last moment at which those within the longer established cloisters of academia had the chance to impose their own value system on the planning process and to reflect a well-established pecking order.

All this meant fixed ceilings on student recruitment and the real prospect of compulsory redundancy for academic staff. Despite a major Association of University Teachers (AUT) demonstration at Westminster in November 1981 and a national petition in the spring of 1983, it was becoming clear that the Conservative government was determined to intensify its financial control of higher education. Among the inevitable consequences were a semi-permanent deterioration of staff–student ratios and a worsening of conditions of employment for those in higher education. The test case for these policies proved to be that of Edgar Page of the University of Hull, who, after a long fight against compulsory redundancy during the mid-1980s, eventually lost his claim for reinstatement. Although other universities drew back from such strong action, the case left the AUT weakened on a number of fronts.

By March 1985 it was clear that there was something approaching an impasse between the UGC and the government. Sir Peter Swinnerton-Dyer, chair of the UGC, warned his colleagues in the CVCP that his advice on the need for level funding had been rejected by ministers and that even closures of entire universities as well as individual departments were on the cards. In response Maurice Shock, chair of the CVCP, commented that 'compared with the sudden and traumatic cuts of 1981–1984, our future funding prospects are more like a lingering and painful terminal illness'.[16] The response of government was to replace the UGC by the Universities Funding Council (UFC) in 1989, thus making the funding of universities subject to far more direct governmental control than had ever previously been the case and less open to rhetorical comment of this kind. Then, in 1992, the polytechnics were reconstituted as university institutions in their own right, at a stroke doubling the number of universities and for the first time subjecting the whole system to the tight controls and financial constraints which had been worked towards during the 1980s.

Putting a more positive spin on these events, it is arguable that they generated the situation in which, by the end of the century, one third of the population could aspire to full-time higher education; the shift from an elite to a mass system of higher education was now affordable. But this was achieved at the cost of a transformation of what went on in higher education. There was a sharp increase in the proportion of fixed tenure and part-time academic staff within the universities, which became, if anything, less rather than more accessible to aspiring female academics. There remained a 'skewing' of the student intake towards social classes one and two, particularly since the value of the student grant (which had been made mandatory on LEAs in 1960) was steadily eroded and finally replaced by a loans system during the 1990s. Perhaps most significantly, the 1990s saw the universities becoming more accountable: accountable for their financial procedures; accountable for the quality and extent of their research; and accountable for the quality of their teaching. The coming of the Research Assessment Exercise (RAE) and of the Quality Assurance Agency meant, on the one hand, that the public (or the consumer, depending on how one construed it) could be reassured about what went on within the ivory tower but also that, on the other, what did go on was irreversibly transformed. This was one ironic outcome of the inexorable rise of state interest in and control of the universities in the twentieth century.

Conclusion

In summary, it is interesting to reflect on the deeper significance of these traumatic changes which were taking place over the whole century. Some commentators, such as Michael Sanderson, have depicted a growing rapprochement between the universities on the one hand and industry and commerce on the other. This has resulted in the universities at the start of the twenty-first century being well positioned to continue to influence and interact with Britain's economic development.[17] In one sense this is undeniable. The number of vocationally orientated courses has proliferated within British higher education, particularly since the Second World War. The development of a mass system of higher education has undoubtedly resulted in the acceptance and incorporation of a range of applied studies which would not have been thought appropriate earlier in the century. At the same time, arguments around the need for a broad liberal education, which were particularly fashionable in the immediate aftermath of the Holocaust and which shaped the curricula of the new universities, are less frequently heard in recent years. The old fears of the dangers of 'over-specialization' which obsessed A.D. Lindsay and his associates resulted in the development of Modern Greats at Oxbridge during the inter-war years and in the novel curricula of Keele, Sussex, York and to a lesser extent the other new universities. In recent years the imperative to prepare students for employment is seen necessarily to imply the need for a wide range of skills. But audits of the 'value added' by particular courses are far more likely to focus on the development of information technology (IT) skills than on an understanding of the dangers of totalitarianism or the threat posed to the world's ecosystem by global capitalism. Thus, in brief, it does seem that one implication of the rise of a mass system in the form I have described does involve a general acceptance that it is the job of higher education to prepare its beneficiaries for employment in a swiftly changing labour market rather than, as some argued earlier in the twentieth century, to offer a critique of social, economic and political developments.

Nevertheless, these changes have not involved a breakdown in the widely-recognized 'pecking order' of British universities and it remains almost as true at the end of the twentieth century as it was at the start that certain schools have little short of a stranglehold on access to those courses which lead towards the higher echelons of the Civil Service and towards the major professions. It remains the case, in 2000, that almost half of the entrants to Oxbridge are drawn from the private sector (which educates seven per cent of the school population). The defence made by Oxbridge admissions tutors that these figures reflect the pattern of applications received seems rather to beg the question of why whole populations of school leavers choose to behave in this way. An exploration of that issue might well reveal a deep-seated set of assumptions, attitudes and aspirations which have survived the sweeping social changes outlined in this chapter.

Similarly with gender, the picture is far from straightforward. It is true that women now have the opportunity, to a greater degree than ever before, to participate (both as students and tutors) in higher education. But a glance inside the common rooms or into the seminar rooms betrays at once that the pattern is an irregular one. Deeper investigation shows that there are still remarkably few females in the more senior positions in academia (two Vice-Chancellors in 2000) and that it is the courses which lead towards those employments still deemed in the popular mind as being more appropriate for females on which women students are predominantly to be found. Thus, for example, there are very few males (less than five per cent of the cohort) embarked on courses to teach at primary level in schools whilst males and females are more evenly distributed on courses leading to teaching at secondary level. These imbalances, which can be found in all parts of the higher education system, reflect the continuing significance of the 'glass ceiling' in the wider economy, and remind us that the patterns which can be discerned within higher education are in part inherited, but in part echoes of wider social trends.

This, in turn, leads to a wider reflection on the ways in which higher education has generated social mobility during the twentieth century. In contemporary Britain, poverty remains a chronic problem. Regional contrasts persist and are reflected in wide differentials in employment rates and income levels. The transformation of the economy from one with manufacturing industry at its heart to one focused on the service sector has been undergone without the complete levelling out of social class contrasts. Indeed, in some respects they have intensified during the period since the Second World War.

On the one hand the expansion and transformation of higher education has been one of the factors enabling these changes to take place. But such expansion of higher education seems to have had little impact on these chronic social problems. This seems to be the case, in brief, because higher education continues (as it did at the start of the century) to point a way out and a way up to many of its first generation students. The drift to the South-East, into the professions and into the tertiary sector of the economy has been one largely dependent on the geographical mobility of the graduate classes. By using the qualifications and skills they gained through higher education to facilitate their own career advancement they have also, unwittingly, contributed to the maintenance of these social class contrasts and social problems. It is also worth remarking that one implication of the entry of thousands of first generation graduates to the tertiary sector of the economy has been a massive expansion of the professions concerned. In every case, as they expanded, these established professions have themselves been transformed, becoming more hierarchical, with more clearly designated roles and career routes within them, and, in every case with their own internal 'pecking order' which gives precedence to the graduates of the older, better recognized universities. That remains, to this day, the central irony of the expansion of higher education in twentieth-century Britain. It has facilitated change, but, at one and the same time, those changes have had a side effect of reinforcing existing power hierarchies. The challenge ahead in the twenty-first century is to devise a system of higher education whose outcomes will be social inclusion and social cohesion rather than the exclusivity and competitiveness which have marked much of its growth during the twentieth century.

Key reading

For many years W.H.G. Armytage, *Civic Universities*, London, Benn, 1955, was the standard work on this topic, offering a vivid account of the ways in which the universities interacted with the modernization of the economy and society during the twentieth century. However, more recently there have been more systematic and co-ordinated attempts to survey the development of higher education and its impact from a variety of perspectives. First, the coming of the new universities after the Second World War generated its own critical historical literature. W.B. Gallie, *A New University: A.D. Lindsay and the Keele Experiment*, London, Chatto and Windus, 1960, was the first. Within a few years each of the new universities had its own house history, one of the more notable being A.E. Sloman, *A University in the Making*, London, British Broadcasting Corporation, 1964, an account of the foundation of the University of Essex. As the 1963 Robbins Report led to consideration of higher education as a system, the literature came to reflect this. First came a series of Penguin Education Specials focusing on particular themes. *The Impact of Robbins*, 1969, although brief, was insightful and influential on policy makers. Similarly, E. Robinson, *The New Polytechnics*, Harmondsworth, Penguin, 1968, surveyed the technological sector of higher education just at the moment that it came to be seen as a fully fledged part of a co-ordinated system. Other works have focused on particular aspects of the contribution of the universities. M. Sanderson, *The Universities and British Industry, 1850–1970*, London, Routledge and Kegan Paul, 1972, offers a detailed and authoritative account of the engagement of higher education with economic transformation. In an altogether more critical spirit, M.J. Wiener, *English Culture and the Decline of the Industrial Spirit, 1850–1980*, Cambridge, Cambridge University Press, 1981, although not strictly speaking a history of higher education or of the universities, stresses the retarding effect of established institutions on the modernization of Britain and should be read alongside Sanderson's work.

Other key themes have included the professionalization of society, with

H. Perkin, *The Rise of Professional Society: England since 1880*, London, Routledge, 1989, being particularly influential. Konrad Jarausch's symposium on *The Transformation of Higher Learning*, Chicago, Chicago University Press, 1983, is perhaps the most systematic attempt to consider the linkages between higher education and the professionalization of society, and several of the essays in that book relate to the United Kingdom. At the same time as that research was under way, an ambitious collaborative research project at the Ruhr University, Bochum, examined the linkages between higher education and the systematization of society. This attempt to work through some of the hypotheses in Fritz Ringer's enormously influential *Education and Society in Modern Europe*, Bloomington, Indiana University Press, 1979, resulted in *The Rise of the Modern Education System*, Cambridge, Cambridge University Press, 1987, edited by Muller, Ringer and Simon, with significant sections on the stratification of higher education in England during the twentieth century. All of this is brilliantly summarized in R.D. Anderson, *Universities and Elites in Britain since 1800*, Basingstoke, Macmillan, 1992. Other notable incursions into the field include W.A.C. Stewart's magisterial *Higher Education in Post-War Britain*, Basingstoke, Macmillan, 1989; Carol Dyhouse's excellent study of the ways in which higher education has contributed to ongoing gender distinctions, entitled *No Distinction of Sex? Women in British Universities, 1870–1939*, London, University College London Press, 1995; and, not least, A.H. Halsey, *The Decline of Donnish Dominion: The British Academic Professions in the Twentieth Century*, Oxford, Clarendon, 1995, an account of the changing role and status of the academic professions during the twentieth century.

Notes

1 The Barnett formula, named after the then Chief Secretary to the Treasury, Joel Barnett, was a population-based formula for allotting public expenditure between England, Scotland, Wales and Northern Ireland. The population ratios used to drive the formula were updated in 1992 and 1998.
2 *Higher Education in the Learning Society*, London, HMSO, 1997.
3 Further detail can be found at the Universities UK website: *http://-www.universitiesUK.ac.uk.*
4 R. Lowe, 'The expansion of higher education in England', in K. Jarausch (ed.) *The Transformation of Higher Learning, 1860–1930*, Stuttgart, Klett-Cotta, 1982, pp. 37–56.
5 R. Lowe, 'English elite education in the late-nineteenth and early-twentieth centuries', in W. Conze and J. Kocka (eds) *Bildungsbergertum in 19. Jahrhundert*, Stuttgart, Klett-Cotta, 1985.
6 R. Lowe, 'Structural change in English higher education, 1870–1920', in D.K. Muller, F. Ringer and B. Simon (eds) *The Rise of the Modern Educational System: Structural Change and Social Reproduction, 1870–1920*, Cambridge, Cambridge University Press, 1987.
7 On this see C. Dyhouse, *No Distinction of Sex? Women in British Universities, 1870–1939*, London, University College London Press, 1995.

8 On this see R.D. Anderson, *Universities and Elites in Britain since 1800*, Basingstoke, Macmillan, 1992.

9 For details see L. Jilek (ed.) *Historical Compendium of European Universities*, Geneva, Conference Permanent des Recteurs, Presidents et Vice-Chanceliers des Universités Européennes, 1984.

10 W.A.C. Stewart, *Higher Education in Post-War Britain*, Basingstoke, Macmillan, 1989.

11 H. Silver, *A Higher Education: the Council for National Academic Awards and British Higher Education, 1964–1989*, London, Falmer 1990.

12 Stewart, op. cit., pp. 96–9.

13 M. Kogan with D. Kogan, *The Attack on Higher Education*, London, Kogan Page, 1983, pp. 21–2.

14 'Butskellism' was a term used to describe the supposed common approach between the Labour Chancellor, Hugh Gaitskell and his Conservative successor at the Treasury, R.A. Butler.

15 Quoted in Kogan and Kogan, op. cit., p. 23.

16 Quoted in the *University of Birmingham Bulletin*, 26 March 1985.

17 M. Sanderson, *The Universities and British Industry, 1850–1970*, London, Routledge and Kegan Paul, 1972.

Chapter 5

Central and local government

Paul Sharp[1]

The situation in 2000

A different kind of partnership

Writing in 1927, a quarter of a century after the creation of the Board of Education (the first statutory central government education ministry) and local education authorities (LEAs), Sir Amherst Selby-Bigge, the Board's recently-retired second permanent secretary, described the administration of the national education system as one of 'active and constructive partnership between the Central and Local Authorities'.[2] Over 50 years later, a former permanent secretary of the Department of Education and Science (DES), Sir William Pile, could describe it in almost identical terms: 'the education service ... is operated as a partnership between the central authority and the LEAs'.[3] How were responsibilities shared between these 'partners'? Essentially, central government determined national policy, while the local authorities ran the schools. Twenty-one years later, the situation is very different.

The policies pursued by the Conservative governments of Margaret Thatcher between 1979 and 1990 (and, to a lesser extent, by her successor, John Major, until 1997) transformed Britain politically, economically and socially. Radical change took place in education, and the way it was administered, as much as in any other policy area. The effect of the Conservative education policies of the 1980s through, for example, the introduction of the national curriculum and associated assessment arrangements, was to 'increase central government activity and power'.[4] At the same time local management of schools (LMS), whereby governing bodies of all maintained schools were given control of their budgets and staffing, coupled with allowing those schools that chose to do so to opt out of LEA control and become grant maintained (GM) effected a 'tremendous transfer of power from democratically elected LEAs to the governing bodies of all schools'.[5] The partnership of central and local government in the organization of the national education service, in which Selby-Bigge took pride, and which existed until the 1980s, has been dissolved.

Major changes in the opposite direction might have been expected, following the election of a New Labour government in 1997; but this did not prove to be the case. The White Paper, *Excellence in Schools*, published shortly after the new government took office, made it plain that raising standards in schools was New Labour's educational priority, and that it was pragmatic about how this was achieved. Even support for comprehensive education was qualified by acceptance that: the search for 'equality of opportunity in some cases became a tendency to uniformity ... The pursuit of excellence was too often equated with elitism.' New Labour did not see revival of the old partnership of central and local government as being the route to improved educational standards. Instead it would be achieved through the creation of a partnership of a different kind, involving not just LEAs, but all bodies concerned with education, such as the churches and other foundations, and the governors of 'largely self-determining schools'.

Thus, *Excellence in Schools* offered little comfort to those seeking restoration of LEAs' traditional role. While LMS and the increased powers of maintained school governors were regarded as having helped to improve standards, 'Schools have thrived on the opportunities offered by delegation of budgets and managerial responsibilities', the White Paper issued a challenge to LEAs: they needed to 'earn their place in the new partnership, by showing that they can add real value'.[6] Although GM status was ended, and GM schools were brought back within the LEA fold, this was in the context of 'extending the previous government's policies on school autonomy';[7] in particular, by devolving more control over expenditure to them: 'an 85% target for 2001–02 ... The Government believes that 90% delegation is a potential average level.'[8]

If schools are to have such 'substantial responsibility for managing their own affairs, including budgets and staffing',[9] and the function of LEAs is not to be one of 'control and direction' of local schools and local educational administration, what is it to be?[10] How can they 'add real value' to the education system? The government's answer is that they can do so by carrying out those functions which 'cannot be undertaken satisfactorily at the level of the individual school': identifying children with special educational needs and ensuring appropriate provision for them; securing access to schools by making sure that there are enough school places, ensuring fair admissions policies and enforcing attendance, managing major expenditure on buildings and organizing transport; monitoring school performance and providing support where there are weaknesses; and making provision for excluded pupils and those unable to attend school.[11]

LEAs are no longer the only (not even the senior) partners at local level, but one of central government's many local partners in the development and improvement of the education system. However, their continued existence seems to be assured as central government considers that they still have definite, distinct and important functions to fulfil.

The situation in 1900

An end to the era of administrative muddle?

In 1900, with the implementation of the Board of Education Act, 1899, a start was made to ending the muddle which had characterized educational administration in the second half of the nineteenth century. This Act had finally created a unified central government department of education, the Board of Education, by bringing together the former Education Department, Science and Art Department and the Charity Commissioners' responsibilities for endowed schools. The Board, which never met, consisted of a President (in effect, the minister of education) and senior cabinet ministers. It was responsible for the 'superintendence of matters relating to education in England and Wales', and was to be advised on educational matters by a Consultative Committee, also set up by the Act, which was to contain expert educationists.[12] In 1900, little attempt was made to forge one united department from its two main predecessors. The former Education Department in Whitehall continued to operate much as it had done for many years and dealt with central government assistance to elementary schools. At the same time, the former Science and Art Department, which had been set up in the 1850s to promote aspects of technical education, remained located in South Kensington and separate from activities in Whitehall. It continued with its work in technical instruction, although, by the turn of the century, it also provided grants to a large number of secondary schools in some subject areas. It was not until Robert Morant was appointed as the first permanent secretary to the Board of Education in 1903 that it began to operate as the consolidated single central government department responsible for education. Yet the Board's functions, like those of both its predecessors and successors, remained much more limited than those of central government departments in many other countries. It did not own schools and it did not employ teachers. Throughout the twentieth century matters such as these were consistently viewed as outside the scope of central government. In 1900 at local level, moreover, the country still suffered from muddle in the government of education.

During the last third of the nineteenth century, there was recognition that educational provision did not match the needs of an industrial nation which was beginning to extend the franchise and to move towards democracy. State support for voluntary effort by the churches could not guarantee a sufficient supply and an even distribution of elementary schools across the country. There were fears that the nation was falling behind its industrial competitors, and that this was partly due to inadequate elementary, secondary and technical education. In 1870, Gladstone's Liberal government introduced the Elementary Education Act to 'fill up gaps' in the voluntary system.[13] The country was split into school districts.

In those with 'insufficient' elementary school places[14] and where voluntary bodies were unable to make good the shortfall, school boards were elected to establish rate-aided elementary schools. As well as closing the 'gaps' and extending the concept of elementary education, particularly in urban areas, the 1870 Act had two important consequences for the government of education: it had introduced, in the school boards, directly elected local education authorities of a sort, while, according to Selby-Bigge, their existence helped turn the Education Department into 'an active agency ... for the extension and improvement of elementary education'.[15] School boards did not change the position of the existing voluntary schools, but created a 'dual system' under which some elementary schools were provided by school boards and others by voluntary bodies. The board schools, which were permitted to give only non-denominational religious instruction,[16] were funded by central government grants and rates; the voluntary schools (most of which were Anglican) by government grants and subscriptions. This situation still prevailed in 1900.

Concern about the country's industrial competitiveness led to the 1889 Technical Instruction Act, which empowered county and borough councils to 'aid the supply of technical or manual instruction', and to set up their own technical instruction committees.[17] Soon secondary schools, as well as technical classes, were receiving aid from these committees. However, the technical instruction committees did not have the field to themselves. The larger school boards, taking a broad view of 'elementary education',[18] began to establish evening classes and higher grade schools for older, more able pupils.

There was increasing concern in the 1890s about the divisions and lack of co-ordination in educational administration at local level. School boards and technical instruction committees were often going their own, but not entirely separate ways; and there were governing bodies of hundreds of endowed secondary schools and boards of managers of thousands of voluntary elementary schools which had no relationship with either. In some areas there were overlaps between the school boards and the technical instruction committees, and yet neither had clear responsibilities for secondary education. It was not until the early twentieth century that an attempt was made to grapple with these problems.

Changes and continuities

Towards a national system locally administered, 1900–40

There were factors in the early years of the twentieth century which made administrative reform at local level probable. The voluntary elementary schools, despite additional central government grants, were finding it hard to manage without rate aid, and the Conservative government was anxious to help them, while higher grade work had become a matter of dispute between the London School Board (LSB) and the London County Council (LCC). In 1899, the government auditor, T.B. Cockerton, 'disallowed certain items of that Board's expenditure' on higher grade work. The courts upheld his decision, ruling that, although the concept of elementary education might 'shift with the growth of general instruction', it must be for children and meet the conditions of the Board of Education's Code for Elementary Schools.[19]

The 'Cockerton Judgment' added weight to the view of Sir John Gorst, the Conservative Vice-President for Education,[20] that if county councils had existed in 1870 school boards would not have been invented. They had become a 'modern anomaly' in local government.[21] Of unequal size, there were too many of them; yet they did not cover the whole country, they were limited to elementary education, and they were expensive. The county and county borough councils were multi-purpose local authorities, already involved in secondary education through their technical instruction committees. According to Morant, the logical step was legislation to give these councils responsibility for all branches of education, and to make rate aid for the voluntary elementary schools a central part of the reorganization.[22] This would end the administrative muddle, bring every part of the country under a local education authority, and give all elementary schools equal access to public funds.

The 1902 Education Act made the county and county borough councils LEAs for all types of education: elementary education under Part III of the Act, and secondary, or 'higher', under Part II of the Act, enabling these authorities to 'promote the general co-ordination of all forms of education' in their areas. However, local feeling demanded that the councils of non-county boroughs with populations of over 10,000 and urban districts of over 20,000, become LEAs for elementary education only. Councils were required to establish Education Committees, to which all matters relating to the exercise of their powers under the Act (except those of raising a rate or borrowing money) were to stand referred. In many cases, the secretaries to the county technical instruction committees, or school board clerks, became the new LEA secretaries for education.[23]

The Act substituted 'dual control' of voluntary schools for the dual system. LEAs were to be responsible for maintaining all 'necessary' public elementary schools in their areas, both former board (provided) schools and voluntary (non-provided) schools. The managers of the latter were to provide school buildings free of charge, and keep them in 'good repair'. LEAs were to meet all other costs, including damage to buildings from 'fair wear and tear'. However, the voluntary schools gave up a substantial measure of independence in exchange for rate support. One third of their managers were to be LEA appointees, the LEA had control of the secular curriculum, a say in teacher appointments and dismissals and powers of inspection. Issues arising between LEAs and the managers of voluntary schools were to be determined by the Board.[24]

Together, the 1899 and 1902 Acts represented a major improvement in the coherence of national educational administration. Instead of having to deal with 2,568 school boards and the managing bodies of 14,238 voluntary schools, a unified central authority, the Board of Education, would now work with 318 LEAs (145 counties and county boroughs and 173 boroughs and urban districts), while all elementary schools had access to rate support. However, there were imperfections in the new arrangements. Under the Act, Part III LEAs had no specific duties in relation to higher (post-elementary) education, and the Board no powers to insist on its provision. Indeed, the limitations of the Board's role of 'superintendence' of educational development was underlined by its lack of sanctions against LEAs. If an LEA failed to carry out its duties, the Board could, following a public enquiry, issue an order compelling it to do so, and enforce it in the courts,[25] but this was a cumbersome process. The Board's main sanction lay in control of grants, but the 1902 Act did not reform the grant system and the Board paid over 50 grants for different purposes. The absence of a unified system of educational finance until the passing of the 1918 Education Act was an obstacle to the development of full partnership between the Board and the LEAs. The existence of Part III LEAs detracted from the aim of ending administrative muddle; many county LEAs were not responsible for elementary education throughout their area. The relationship between county and Part III LEAs was likely to generate friction, as was dual control of voluntary schools, particularly as there was no definition of fair wear and tear and no guarantee that voluntary school managers had the resources to bring their buildings up to provided school standards. The issue of the 'management' of elementary schools was left in an unsatisfactory state. All non-provided schools were to have managing bodies, as were schools provided by county LEAs (to ensure minor authority representation), but other LEAs could decide whether or not to establish them for their provided schools; many chose not to do so.[26]

The Act was a controversial Conservative measure, opposed by the Liberals who favoured retention of the school boards, largely on the grounds that they were directly elected and in touch with the educational needs of their locality.[27] Many members of Nonconformist churches were outraged at rate support for Anglican and Roman Catholic voluntary schools. In Wales, where denominational feeling was strong, and the school boards popular, David Lloyd George, the Act's principal parliamentary opponent although he had privately acknowledged the logic of county councils becoming LEAs,[28] threatened non-co-operation. In the end, this did not amount to a great deal, but forced the government to take additional powers to deal with recalcitrant LEAs.[29] The Liberals proposed drastic changes, if re-elected, but, despite a landslide victory in 1906, their attempts to do so, including transfer of voluntary elementary schools to LEAs, which would have undermined the 1902 Act,[30] were thwarted by the Conservative majority in the House of Lords. Given the Act's weaknesses and the opposition to it, strong guidance from the Board would be essential for successful implementation. This might have been provided by its political head. However, although of cabinet rank, the Presidency of the Board of Education was a relatively junior appointment, not filled by the Churchills or Lloyd Georges. Instead, in the early years, the vital leadership came from a civil servant, Robert Morant.

Morant is a controversial but outstanding figure. Tutor to the Crown Prince of Siam for seven years, in 1895 he brought an outsider's view to the Education Department, while his vision of future developments was influenced by his own education at Winchester.[31] He shared Gorst's view of the inappropriateness of ad hoc educational bodies, and helped the LCC in its dispute with the London School Board. His work on the 1902 Act led to his appointment as the Board's first permanent secretary. He was convinced that the 1902 Act could deliver a 'well-organized' education system. It allowed for 'schools of different type … each reacting upon and supplementing the other', but the partnership of central and local government would 'prevent variety from degenerating into competition'.[32]

The Board was reorganized into three branches: elementary (also concerned with teacher training), secondary (which took over secondary school inspection and responsibility for educational endowments) and technological (technical institutions and evening classes). The branches were organized in geographical divisions, to 'identify the work of the office more closely with that of the Inspectorate', and to facilitate co-operation with LEAs. Within ten years, 'in all essentials the present administrative organ' of the central authority had been created.[33] New regulations were issued, defining the different types of school. For elementary schools, their task was to 'form' the character and 'develop the intelligence' of children, fitting them, 'practically as well as intellectually, for the work of life'.[34] With secondary education (elementary and secondary education were different types of education, not different stages in the educational process), Morant wanted Part II LEAs to establish grammar schools 'mirroring the great public school as he knew it', not patterned on the school board higher grade schools with their technical bias. Secondary schools had to offer 'an approved Course of general instruction extending over at least four years', covering Arts subjects, maths, science and foreign languages (including Latin), manual work and physical exercise. The old endowed grammar schools were brought into association with LEAs. Where the governing body of a grant-aided secondary school was not an LEA, it was required to have a majority of 'representative' governors, for example, members of local authorities. All secondary schools were required to offer 'free places', 'ordinarily' not less than a quarter of admissions, to children who had attended public elementary schools.[35]

Developments in the years before the First World War enlarged the role of LEAs in partnership with the Board. They included establishment of the Board's Medical Department under its Chief Medical Officer, George Newman, and the creation of LEA school medical services. LEAs also acquired powers to provide school meals under certain conditions and duties to make provision for 'educable' mentally handicapped children.[36] Constructive use was made of the Consultative Committee. Their investigation of secondary school examinations led to establishment of the Secondary School Examinations Council in 1917, and restriction of external examinations in grammar schools to the School and Higher School Certificate.[37]

However, even those who acknowledge Morant's achievements, recognize that it is possible to portray him as a 'destructive force', and accept that he 'played an important part in the deliberate destruction both of the system of school boards ... and of the cardinal ideas on which it was based'.[38] Board policy on secondary education under Morant was later severely criticized by the Spens Committee; by discouraging schools of a 'quasi-vocational type', it had failed to meet the needs of a modern industrial society.[39] Board attempts to insist that LEA provided grammar schools had their own governing bodies, on the same model as public and endowed grammar schools, brought it into conflict with some LEAs, particularly Leeds.[40] Thus, despite his achievements, Morant's perhaps rather abrasive and elitist approach did not endear him to parts of the educational world, and publication of a memorandum by a Chief HMI (Her/His Majesty's Inspectorate), setting out the limitations of LEA inspectors with an elementary school background, brought about his resignation in 1911.[41]

The First World War disrupted progress, but saw Lloyd George's imaginative appointment of the distinguished academic, H.A.L. Fisher, as President of the Board in 1916 and legislation for further development of the education system. To create 'a national system of public education available for all persons capable of profiting thereby', the 1918 Education Act required county and county borough LEAs to ensure 'progressive development and comprehensive organisation of education in respect of their area', and submission of schemes showing how they were going to do so. All LEAs were required to provide, by means of 'central' (sometimes called 'senior elementary', or later 'modern') schools or classes, courses of 'advanced instruction' for older pupils in the elementary sector. There was long overdue reform of the grant system. Instead of a multiplicity of separate education grants, the Board now put in place a central system of financial aid to LEAs. The Act removed exemptions from school attendance below 14, and provided for establishment of 'continuation' schools, which (with exceptions) all young people who left school at age 14 would ultimately have to attend, on a part-time basis, up to the age of 18.[42]

Unfortunately, post-war financial austerity led to 'administrative repeal' of the Act by Board circulars; LEAs were not permitted to spend the money necessary to carry out their schemes. Despite some easing of the economic situation in the mid 1920s, the problems of the early 1930s brought another clampdown on expenditure.[43] This is not to say that nothing was achieved. Following the Hadow Report on courses of study for older pupils, other than those at grammar schools, LEAs made considerable progress with the development of modern schools. However, plans for continuation schools had to be abandoned, while implementation of legislation raising the school-leaving age to 15 was overtaken by the Second World War.[44]

Full implementation of the 1918 Act would have brought about major educational developments; however, it omitted important reforms. The Hadow Committee stressed the extent to which the existence of Part III LEAs, the separate systems of elementary, secondary and technical education, and dual control of voluntary elementary schools were obstacles to efficient educational administration; in particular, to development of provision for older pupils. Grammar schools, which operated under the Board's Regulations for Secondary Schools, were the responsibility of Part II LEAs, but modern schools, although catering for the 'post-primary' age range, were elementary schools, and came under the Board's Elementary Code. This did not matter too much in the county boroughs, or in county areas where there were no Part III LEAs; but in county areas with them (in Lancashire, there were 27), one authority was responsible for grammar schools and another for modern schools. LEA efforts to provide 'secondary education for all' through separate modern schools were often frustrated by voluntary school managers, unwilling to allow their older pupils to attend them, but lacking the resources to establish their own. In fact, managers were finding it hard to maintain existing schools. In 1925, 541 of the 753 schools on the Board's 'Black List' (those with defective premises) were voluntary schools.[45] The 1918 Act had left the defects in the administrative framework created by the 1902 Act untouched.

An even more fundamental problem was that the 1918 Act had placed responsibility for educational development on the LEAs. As Selby-Bigge commented, 'the initiative … is assigned to the Local Authority',[46] but the Act did not give the Board of Education new powers to ensure that LEAs took the initiative. With a Morant in charge, this would not have mattered; he would have acted anyway. Under his successors, including

Selby-Bigge,[47] and with political leadership that was often weak, it did. As both senior Board officials and LEA administrators recognized:

> since 1902 the Board had been charged by statute with the supervision of the public education system and for some time it had fulfilled that role. But as time went on the Board's administration had come to develop from below, waiting for issues to arise before taking any action ... The attitude of some Presidents had not always been helpful ... his [Eustace Percy's] general policy was to belittle the powers and position of the department ... while the Board had the means of restraining LEAs it had no adequate machinery for getting them to move forward.[48]

The system of national educational administration was again crying out for reform at both central and local government levels.

Towards a state system locally governed, 1940–2000

The Second World War brought severe disruption of education, including evacuation and widespread school closures, but it was also a catalyst for change. At the Board of Education, the Permanent Secretary, Maurice Holmes, was adamant that 'the Board should lead rather than follow',[49] and in 1941 the Board circulated the memorandum, *Education After the War*, containing a range of proposals for reform. Its circulation coincided with Churchill's appointment of R.A. Butler, one of the few first rank politicians to head the education department during the twentieth century, as President of the Board of Education.[50] In marked contrast to the polarization of educational views which the 1902 Act had both reflected and inflamed, Butler sought consensus. Extensive discussions with all interested parties (LEAs, the churches and educational organizations) about the shape of the post-war education system were followed by a White Paper, *Educational Reconstruction*, in 1943. Its proposals to 'recast the national education service', included acceptance that LEAs should be the 'counties and county boroughs only'; alternatives, such as making county districts with a given population LEAs for all purposes, were rejected. It also recognized the need to 'preserve and stimulate local interest' in education; to bring all types of secondary school under a single set of regulations; to secure changes to the system of dual control of voluntary schools, and to ensure that 'religious education should be given a more defined place' in schools.[51] The Education Act, 1944 marked a fresh start; all existing educational law, most of which had been consolidated in the Education Act, 1921, was repealed.[52]

The fiction of the 'Board of Education' was discarded; the Act provided for appointment of a Minister of Education to promote:

the education of the people of England and Wales and the progressive development of institutions devoted to that purpose, and to secure the effective execution by local authorities, under his control and direction, of the national policy for providing a varied and comprehensive educational service in every area.

This was a long way from 'superintendence' of the education system. Two Central Advisory Councils (one for England and one for Wales) were to be appointed, which, unlike the Consultative Committee they replaced, were empowered to advise the Minister on such educational matters as they saw fit, as well on matters referred to them.[53]

LEAs (counties and county boroughs only) were to provide schools 'sufficient in number, character, and equipment to afford for all pupils opportunities for education offering such variety of instruction and training as may be desirable in view of their different ages, abilities and aptitudes'. Indeed, as befitted a major measure for post-war reconstruction, the Act's emphasis was on ensuring that the operation of the education system increased educational opportunities and made possible the 'spiritual, moral, mental, and physical development of the community'. In place of the three separate types of education – elementary, secondary and technical – educational provision would be organized in 'three progressive stages' – primary, secondary and further. Modern schools would now become secondary schools, and all children would receive secondary education. All fees in LEA maintained schools were abolished, the school-leaving age was raised to 15, and, when 'practicable' to 16. LEAs would be required to establish county colleges, providing 'practical and vocational training' for those who had left school to attend part-time. LEAs were also required to provide milk and meals for school pupils; and there was more flexible and inclusive provision for the 'special educational treatment' of pupils with 'any disability of mind or body'.[54]

Educational finance was simplified by the fact that there were no longer two types of LEA, and retained the 'principle of a percentage grant', consisting of a main grant and special grants for other educational services.[55] LEAs were required, following consultation with the governors and managers of voluntary schools, to prepare for the Minister's approval development plans showing how they intended to carry out their duties. To sustain 'local interest', the Act provided for county LEAs to delegate some of their functions to local representative committees.[56]

All former provided schools became county schools under the 1944 Act,[57] but voluntary schools had to make a choice. They could become 'aided', in which case they were in substantially the same position as under the Education Act, 1921, except that there were now 50 per cent 'maintenance contributions' for alterations or repairs to school buildings and premises available to their managers or governors.[58] However, where managers could not afford the other half of such costs, their schools became 'controlled', in which case the LEA met all costs, but appointed two-thirds of the managers.[59] This was not the only price of freedom from financial anxieties. Whereas religious education in aided schools continued to be in accordance with schools' trust deeds, denominational instruction in controlled schools could be given only if requested by parents.[60] However, in the major break with previous legislation, promised in *Educational Reconstruction*, county schools were required to start each day with an act of 'collective worship' and to provide non-denominational religious education.[61]

The Act addressed the issue of school government. All schools, county and voluntary, were to have managing (primary) or governing (secondary) bodies; their composition and powers depending on the type of school. The intention of these provisions was to try to ensure that each type of school had 'an individual life of its own as well as a place in the local system'. However, the Act did permit LEAs to group schools under a 'single governing body'.[62] Provision was also made for registration of independent schools, although no action was taken on the Fleming Committee's proposals for associating these schools more closely with the rest of the education system through state bursaries for pupils who had attended state primary schools.[63]

The 1944 Education Act resolved the three issues that the Hadow Committee had identified as major obstacles to educational progress. There were no longer two types of LEA, with all the administrative complications that had caused in so many county areas. Different types of post-primary school were no longer administered under different sets of regulations and all children over 11 would now attend secondary schools. The Act provided an imaginative solution to the problem of dual control, but not through transfer of voluntary schools to LEAs. Instead, it enabled LEAs to take responsibility for all the expenses of those voluntary schools which could not pay any part of alteration or repair costs, but allowed them to retain a measure of their denominational character, while it provided financial assistance for those which could, allowing them to retain their full denominational character. It is thus fair to say that the 1944 settlement marked the end of religious controversy as a major issue in educational administration. The Act resolved these issues within a new administrative framework which created the potential for a much more fruitful partnership between local and central government. LEAs now had the powers to develop educational provision in a way which would enable all the children in their areas to take full advantage of the increased opportunities the Act offered; central government had a clear responsibility to ensure that they did so.

Indeed, local and central government set about turning the provisions of the 1944 Act into reality with vigour. By the end of 1947, 126 of the more than 140 LEAs had submitted development plans; by 1949, 46 had been approved.[64] Despite post-war problems caused by 'shortage of building materials ... complicated by the raising of the school-leaving age and the "bulge" [the rise in the birthrate]', every means, including widespread use of prefabricated classrooms, was made to provide necessary school accommodation. Nor did the pace slacken:

> The quarter of a century since 1944 has seen expansion and development of the educational system on a scale unprecedented in the nation's history ... By 1969 over 8,500 new Primary and Secondary schools had been built, housing over one-quarter of the 7.5 million children in maintained schools.[65]

But there were disappointments. County colleges proved as elusive as the continuation schools of the 1918 Act. An important report of 1959 by the Central Advisory Committee on Education (England) argued that raising the school-leaving age to 16 should be given 'priority in time over the introduction of compulsory county colleges',[66] but the school-leaving age was not raised until 1972. There were administrative problems, too. Divisional executives, designed to maintain local interest in education, 'introduced another tier' into administration and offered 'opportunities for friction'.[67] Local government reorganization in the 1970s swept them away, but, by reducing the number of LEAs, made the administration of local education services even more remote from local communities.[68] From 1958, the specific central government education grant to LEAs was replaced by a general grant for all local services. This gave local authorities 'greater autonomy in operating their services as a whole'[69] but also 'served to feed the notion that education was simply a local service like any other rather than a national service'. As the apparently prosperous 1960s became the unambiguously impecunious 1970s, central government pressure on 'local authority budgets really became significant', making it hard for LEAs to maintain adequate services.[70] Even more fundamental was the issue of the central government department's ability to lead educational development. Despite his impressive powers under the 1944 Act, and elevation to Secretary of State for Education and Science in 1964, what did the minister's 'control and direction' of national policy amount to, when he did not run any schools, employ any teachers, or even determine the content of the curriculum? The minister seemed to preside over a department that was 'little more than a post-box' between the LEAs and the teacher unions.[71]

Disappointments and administrative difficulties acquired greater significance as post-war educational consensus broke down. The great triumph of the 1944 Act had been delivery of 'secondary education for all'; but the view gained ground that although all post-primary schools were now 'secondary' the tripartite system afforded too many pupils the semblance, rather than the substance, of secondary education.[72] Ending selection at eleven-plus became Labour Party policy, leading, after Labour took office in 1964, to requests to LEAs for submission of 'plans for reorganising secondary education in their areas on comprehensive lines'.[73] This policy was generally opposed by the Conservatives, especially where grammar school closures were involved, and educational debate became politicized and embittered in a way that it had not been since the religious controversies of 60 years earlier.[74] As the secondary system entered a period of upheaval with comprehensive reorganization, there was also concern about the effects of the Plowden Report and of 'progressive' approaches to teaching on standards in primary schools. Events at the William Tyndale School in London seemed to justify these concerns.[75] In the *Black Papers*, Conservative-leaning educationists and academics condemned all these developments: 'Our notion that "progressive education" might be in some part to blame for lack of knowledge or for naïve and destructive political attitudes in its victims has been seen as common sense by many people.'[76] While the authors of the *Black Papers* might be dismissed as right-wing reactionaries, this could not be said of Prime Minister, James Callaghan. Launching his Great Debate on education in a speech at Ruskin College, Oxford in 1976, he called for 'a basic curriculum with universal standards', and expressed anxiety that 'school-leavers appeared to be inadequately equipped to enter work'.[77]

The feeling that the 'partnership' of central and local government was operating an education system insufficiently geared to meeting the needs of society and the wishes of pupils and parents manifested itself in the interest taken in school governing and managing bodies. Despite the intentions and provisions of the 1944 Act, research in the 1960s made clear the extent to which some LEAs which were responsible for determining the membership of county managing and governing bodies[78] used their powers under the Act to group governing bodies and deny them more than nominal responsibility for the conduct of their schools: 'There are many authorities, especially county boroughs, in which managing and governing bodies are mere formalities ... schools are grouped together in large numbers ... membership is restricted as closely as possible to members of the council'.[79] However, in the late 1960s, a number of LEAs, including some such as Sheffield where grouping had been common, began to develop managing and governing bodies as a means of ensuring 'the widest participation in the running of schools by parents, teachers, trade unionists, people from all walks of life'.[80] Such initiatives helped to bring about the appointment of the Taylor Committee in 1975 to review school management and government in England and Wales.

The Taylor Report of 1977 proposed that four groups, the LEA, parents, staff and the local community, all those with a 'common interest in the welfare of the school', should be equally represented on the governing bodies of all county schools. The term managers should be dropped. To be effective these governing bodies 'must operate in relation to individual schools', and LEA powers to group schools should be repealed. Taylor saw governing bodies as more than talking shops; they should have definite responsibilities, including a role in setting the aims of their schools, in finance and in staff appointments. Although the Taylor Report wanted as much delegation as possible by LEAs to governing bodies, it did not seek to undermine the ultimate responsibility of LEAs for running their schools; rather, governing bodies should stand 'in the direct line of formal responsibility between the local education authority and the head'.[81]

Although the Taylor proposals for a 'new partnership' now seem modest, at the time they appeared radical and, to some LEAs, unwelcome. The view of both the Labour-controlled Association of Metropolitan Authorities and the Conservative-controlled Association of County Councils was that the Report's 'challenging suggestions ... should not obscure the unique position of the democratically elected LEA'. They wondered whether invigorated governing bodies, with LEA appointees in the minority, could be 'called to account' if they chose to go their own way.[82] The Callaghan government was slow to act on Taylor; its White Paper proposed changes to grouping but only a guaranteed minimum level of representation for parents and teachers, while it was silent on governing body powers.[83] Labour lost office before it could legislate, but in 1980 the newly-elected Thatcher government secured an Act which gave all schools governing bodies and required the Secretary of State's approval for grouping unless only two primary schools were involved. It also stipulated that all county and controlled schools must have at least two elected parent governors and all aided schools at least one; and that all LEA maintained schools with fewer than 300 pupils must have at least one elected teacher governor and if larger at least two.[84]

The Thatcher government was critical of standards in the state system and the 1980 Act created the Assisted Places scheme to enable pupils, otherwise unable to so, 'to benefit from education at independent schools' at state expense.[85] Following Sir Keith Joseph's appointment as Secretary of State for Education in 1981, determined efforts were made to address perceived weaknesses in the education system. Although there were examples of 'high standards achieved in schools ... by pupils of all abilities', the government's view was that: 'in the light of what is being achieved in other countries, the standards now generally attained by our pupils are neither as good as they can be, nor as good as they need to be'. Individual school governing bodies (along Taylor lines) could be a catalyst for improvement: 'If a school is to succeed in all its tasks, it needs to have an identity and a sense of purpose of its own.'[86]

The 1986 Education Act essentially enacted Taylor. A new statutory basis was provided for the composition (along the lines of the 'four equal shares' principle for county, controlled and maintained special schools) and functions of all LEA maintained school governing bodies.[87] The Act provided for 'the conduct of the school to be under the direction of the governing body', and gave governing bodies a specific role in formulating the 'aims of the secular curriculum' and responsibilities in relation to discipline, finance, and staff appointments and dismissals.[88] As well as following the letter of the Taylor recommendations, the 1986 Act also embodied its spirit. Taken together, its provisions established individual governing bodies, representing the main groups concerned with the school, to which the LEA was required to delegate a strictly limited range of functions. While the Act enabled a school 'to recognise itself as more than an agency of the LEA', the LEA remained very much the senior partner in the 'new partnership' created by the Act.[89]

However, the next piece of Conservative legislation substantially increased governing body powers at the expense of LEAs. The 1988 Education Reform Act (ERA) required LEAs to delegate management of a school's 'budget share' to governing bodies. Governing bodies were also given responsibility for determining their schools' staff complement, and for controlling appointments and dismissals. Further, in order to increase parental choice, LEAs were no longer permitted to 'set aside parents' wishes' for a particular school for their child on the grounds of 'efficiency or economy'.[90] Instead the Act introduced open enrolment: schools could admit pupils up to their maximum capacity. It also struck at LEAs' role as the maintainer of the schools in their areas, by making it possible for the governing bodies of maintained schools, following a ballot of parents, to opt out of LEA control and to become grant maintained (GM) schools, receiving their maintenance grants direct from central government.[91] ERA also tackled the issues of the content of the school curriculum and where decisions about it were to be made. In future, these were to be matters for central government.[92]

In other areas, too, the role of LEAs was reduced during the 1980s. The Manpower Services Commission (MSC), operating under the Department of Employment not the Department of Education and Science, was set up in 1973 to run training services for adults and school leavers. Its importance increased as unemployment rose, and it was given the task of developing the Youth Training Scheme (YTS). During the 1980s, under the Conservative government, MSC-financed courses 'permeated LEA Work-Related Non-Advanced Further Education (WRNAFE) to a considerable extent', as a substantial proportion of the funding of WRNAFE courses was channelled through the MSC. It was argued that this approach made further education courses more responsive to the needs of employers. The MSC also came into contact with secondary education through its responsibility for the Technical and Vocational Education Initiative (TVEI) for 14–18-year-olds. While LEAs did not welcome these developments, as TVEI was 'the most important innovation in the secondary curriculum during the 1980s' they could neither ignore it nor the funding that came with it. [93]

In the late 1980s, the MSC became the Training Commission but was then abolished, following the Trades Union Congress's (TUC) refusal to co-operate with the government's training programme, and the Department of Employment became directly responsible for carrying out its functions. At local level, Training and Enterprise Councils (TECs), their membership dominated by local employers, were set up to supervise local training programmes.[94] The process of bringing to an end LEAs' involvement in training and, indeed, in a vast area of post-16 education, was carried further by the 1992 Further and Higher Education Act, under which 'all further education and sixth form colleges were removed from local authority control and became incorporated institutions funded directly by the Further Education Funding Council (FEFC)'.[95] At the very end of the twentieth century, the Blair government planned to replace the TECs and the FEFC by a new national Learning and Skills Council which was to be assisted by 47 such local councils. These reforms are now being implemented and the responsibilities for post-16 education and training (excluding higher education) are being transferred to the new learning and skills councils.

ERA went well beyond Taylor. It did not merely require delegation of responsibilities from LEAs to governing bodies, but enacted a major transfer of powers from LEAs to them, making the governing body, not the LEA, the senior partner in relation to the individual school. At the same time, in the provisions for a national curriculum and national assessment arrangements, central government had finally asserted its control over what was taught in schools, something it had not done since the days of Robert Morant. The reasons underlying the passing of ERA are complex, but it is certainly possible to see LMS, open enrolment and GM schools as 'consistent ... with the more market-led, free-enterprise approach to society and the economy which characterized the premiership of Margaret Thatcher' and as part of an attempt to make state schools 'more like independent schools': all at the expense of LEAs' role. National curriculum and testing can be interpreted not only as a means of 'ensuring basic product quality' and providing parents with more information about schools, but also as a 'mechanism for increasing central control'.[96] In addition to the reduction of their role as maintainers of local schools, the position of LEAs was further diminished by the creation of the TECs and by the loss of control over further education and sixth form colleges. While, in the 1980s, the expanding activities of the MSC seemed to be reducing the role of the DES as well as of LEAs, since 1995 the merger of the Department for Education with the Employment Department has created a powerful and influential central government department with responsibility for the whole field of education and training: 'the [Education and Employment] Department has got an economic arm ... a place at Cabinet Committee which Education never had access to'.[97]

Conclusion

A unified central government education department and local education authorities were established at the beginning of the twentieth century because there was a definite job for them to do. The existing 'system' of educational administration was a muddle; but the Board of Education and LEAs, in partnership, created a national system of education. Indeed, the onus of responsibility for doing so lay with the LEAs; the role of the Board was to 'superintend' their work, to spur on, or in times of austerity to rein back, their efforts.

Much was achieved under the administrative arrangements created by the 1899, 1902 and 1918 Acts, but they were far from satisfactory. A major overhaul was needed, and the 1944 Act created a new administrative framework to meet the challenges of the post-war world. Again, in what some would see as a golden age of central and local government partnership, a great deal was accomplished. By the late 1960s, however, there was mounting dissatisfaction with the education system, which was represented, at local level, by LEAs. The feeling had grown that it did not meet the needs of society, nor match the aspirations of parents for their children. James Callaghan acknowledged the justice of this dissatisfaction in his 1976 Ruskin College speech, and it was reflected in the appointment of the Taylor Committee and in the legislation of the 1980s.

That legislation dissolved the old partnership of central government and LEAs, and has led to its replacement by a 'new partnership'. It is not the one envisaged by the Taylor Committee, with LEAs as the senior partners at local level; but it is one in which LEAs have their part to play. Developments in educational administration in the 1980s and 1990s may have 'paved the way for the return of the system of over a century ago in which there were two tiers – a central government department and individual school governing bodies with little or nothing in between';[98] but this no longer seems to be quite the ultimate outcome. LEAs are a much-diminished feature of the educational landscape, but, unlike school boards and Part III authorities, it appears that they will remain a feature because central government considers that there is still a job for them to do.

The fact that there are still LEAs with essential functions to perform does not silence the objections that the changes in educational administration which took place in the 1980s and 1990s concentrate too much power at the centre while, at local level, they create a 'democratic deficit' and 'atomize' the education service. However, it is difficult to deny their value in devolving so much local educational decision making to the level of the school at which its effects will be felt, thus enabling schools to be more responsive to the needs of pupils and parents.

Key reading

R. Aldrich, D. Crook and D. Watson, *Education and Employment: the DfEE and its Place in History*, London, Institute of Education, University of London, 2000 provides an account of the creation of the Department for Education and Employment with historical background and analysis of its possible future role.

B.M. Allen, *Sir Robert Morant*, London, Macmillan, 1934 is still the standard work on Morant, but lacks a balanced treatment of his career and achievements. The Board of Education, Report of the Consultative Committee (Hadow), *The Education of the Adolescent*, London, HMSO, 1926, made clear the extent to which the existing system of educational administration was impeding necessary educational reforms, while the White Paper, Board of Education, *Educational Reconstruction*, London, HMSO, 1943, set out the Coalition government's proposals for far-reaching reform of the national education system. G.V. Cooke and P.H.J.H. Gosden, *Education Committees*, Harlow, Councils and Education Press, 1986, gives a historical account of the development of education committees and an analysis of their position in the mid-1980s. The White Paper, Department for Education and Employment, *Excellence in Schools*, London, HMSO, 1997, set out New Labour's education policies after its election victory. Department for Education and Employment, *The Role of the Local Education Authority in School Education*, Nottingham, DfEE Publications, 2000, contains the government's views on the future role of LEAs. The DES Report of the Committee of Enquiry appointed jointly by the Secretary of State for Education and Science, and the Secretary of State for Wales under the chairmanship of Mr Tom Taylor CBE, *A New Partnership for Our Schools*, London, HMSO, 1977, proposed major changes in the composition and powers of maintained sector school governing bodies.

P.H.J.H. Gosden, *The Development of Educational Administration in England and Wales*, Oxford, Basil Blackwell, 1966, gives an account and analysis of the development of educational administration, at central and local government level, up to the mid-1960s; J.S. Maclure, *Education Reformed*, London, Hodder and Stoughton, 2nd edn, 1989 gives a brief examination of the provisions of the 1988 Education Reform Act with some background information. L.A. Selby-Bigge, *The Board of Education*, London, Putnam, 1927, is an account by a former permanent secretary of the role and work of the Board of Education as it had evolved by the mid-

1920s. W. Pile, *The Department of Education and Science*, London, Allen and Unwin, 1979 is an account by one of his successors of the role and work of the DES as it had evolved by the late 1970s. P.R. Sharp and J.R. Dunford, *The Education System in England and Wales,* London, Longman, 1990, is an analysis of the administration of education in England and Wales as it was at the end of the 1980s which covers its historical evolution; P.R. Sharp, *School Governing Bodies in the English Education System: An Historical Perspective*, Educational Administration and History Monographs No. 19, Leeds, University of Leeds School of Education, 1995, provides an examination of the changing role of school governing bodies in local educational administration up to the mid 1990s.

Notes

1 I am grateful to David Mills Daniel who has researched and produced a draft of this chapter.
2 L.A. Selby-Bigge, *The Board of Education*, London, Putnam, 1927, p. 20.
3 W. Pile, *The Department of Education and Science*, London, Allen and Unwin, 1979, p. 24.
4 R. Aldrich, 'Educational legislation of the 1980s in England: an historical analysis', *History of Education*, 1992, vol. 21, no. 1, p. 68.
5 P.R. Sharp and J.R. Dunford, 'From local governance to LEA and from LEA to local governance: a study of the management and government of schools in England and Wales from 1839 to 1994', in E.W. Jenkins (ed.) *Studies in the History of Education: Essays Presented to Peter Gosden*, Leeds, Leeds University Press, 1995, p. 191.
6 Department for Education and Employment, *Excellence in Schools*, London, HMSO, 1997, pp. 11, 66–72.
7 M. Barber and J. Sebba, 'Reflections on progress towards a world class education system', *Cambridge Journal of Education*, 1999, vol. 29, no. 2, p. 185.
8 Department for Education and Employment, *The Role of the Local Education Authority in School Education*, Nottingham, DfEE Publications, 2000, p. 10.
9 Barber and Sebba, op. cit., p. 185.
10 Department for Education and Employment, op. cit., 1997, p. 69.
11 Department for Education and Employment, op. cit., 2000, pp. 7–9.
12 *Board of Education Act, 1899*, Sections 1–5. See also P.H.J.H. Gosden, 'The Board of Education Act, 1899', *British Journal of Educational Studies*, 1962, vol. XI, no. 1, pp. 44–60.
13 This was how W.E. Forster, Gladstone's Vice-President for Education, described the purpose of the Act to the House of Commons in 1870.
14 *Elementary Education Act, 1870*, Section 5.
15 Selby-Bigge, op. cit., p. 7.
16 *Elementary Education Act, 1870*, Section 14.
17 *Technical Instruction Act, 1889*, Section 1.
18 The 1870 Act (Section 3) defined an 'elementary school' as one 'at which elementary education is the principal part of the education there given'.
19 P.H.J.H. Gosden, *The Development of Educational Administration in England and Wales*, Oxford, Basil Blackwell, 1966, pp. 172–3.
20 As there was no statutory central government department for education until the creation of the Board of Education, the Education and Science and Art Departments operated under a committee of the Privy Council, headed by the

Lord President of the Council (who sat in the House of Lords) and a Vice-President for Education (who was always a member of the House of Commons).

21 From a minute to the Duke of Devonshire, quoted in G.V. Cooke and P.H.J.H. Gosden, *Education Committees*, Harlow, Councils and Education Press, 1986, pp. 11–12.

22 See Gosden, op. cit., 1966, pp. 175–8.

23 *Education Act, 1902*, Sections 1, 2, 5, 17, 22, First Schedule. Education Committees were to include persons with 'experience in education' and 'women as well as men'.

24 *Education Act, 1902*, Sections 6–9, 11.

25 *Education Act, 1902*, Section 16.

26 *Education Act, 1902*, Section 6. Until 1980, elementary (later primary) schools had managers; only secondary schools had governors. For discussion of the issues of elementary school management under the 1902 Act, see P.R. Sharp, *School Governing Bodies in the English Education System: An Historical Perspective*, Educational Administration and History Monographs No. 19, Leeds, University of Leeds School of Education, 1995, pp. 24–8.

27 Cooke and Gosden, op. cit., pp. 24–5.

28 In March 1902, he described the Bill as 'a very great improvement'. See K.O. Morgan (ed.) *Lloyd George, Family Letters 1885–1936*, Cardiff, University of Wales Press and London, Oxford University Press, 1973, pp. 131–2.

29 See E.J.R. Eaglesham, 'Implementing the Education Act of 1902', *British Journal of Educational Studies*, 1962, vol. X, no. 2, pp. 162–75.

30 See P. Gordon, R. Aldrich and D. Dean, *Education and Policy in England in the Twentieth Century*, London, Woburn Press, 1991, pp. 19–20.

31 For an account of Morant's early life and career, see B.M. Allen, *Sir Robert Morant*, London, Macmillan, 1934, pp. 3–137.

32 Allen, op. cit., p. 201.

33 Gosden, op. cit., 1966, pp. 100–5.

34 Board of Education, *Code of Regulations for Public Elementary Schools, 1904*, London, HMSO, 1904, 'Introduction'.

35 E.J.R. Eaglesham, 'The Centenary of Sir Robert Morant', *British Journal of Educational Studies*, 1963, vol. XII, no. 1, p. 12; Board of Education, *Regulations for Secondary Schools, 1904–05*, London, HMSO, 1904, Prefatory Memorandum, Articles 1, 4, *Regulations for Secondary Schools 1907–08*, London, HMSO, 1907, Prefatory Memorandum, Articles 24, 20. See also Sharp, op. cit., pp. 28–31.

36 From 1908, the Board published Annual Reports of the Chief Medical Officer, which cover development of the school medical service and educational provision for handicapped children.

37 See Board of Education, Report of the Consultative Committee (Acland), *Examinations in Secondary Schools*, London, HMSO, 1911, pp. 102–41.

38 Eaglesham, op. cit., 1963, p. 5.

39 Board of Education, Report of the Consultative Committee (Spens), *Secondary Education with Special Reference to Grammar Schools and Technical High Schools*, London, HMSO, 1938, pp. 72–3.

40 See L. Connell, 'Administration of secondary schools: Leeds v. Board of Education, 1905–11', *Journal of Educational Administration and History*, 1973, vol. V, no. 2, pp. 25–32.

41 See Allen, op. cit., pp. 255–63. Lloyd George appointed Morant Chairman of the National Insurance Commission in 1911. He became the first permanent secretary of the new Ministry of Health in 1919. He died in 1920.

42 *Education Act, 1918*, Sections 1–5, 8, 10–12, 44.
43 See, for example, Board of Education, *Circular 1185*, 17 December 1920, *Circular 1413*, 11 September 1931; J. Vaizey, *The Costs of Education*, London, Allen and Unwin, 1958, pp. 28–32, 57–8.
44 See *Education Act, 1936*, Sections 1–7, 15, 16.
45 Board of Education, Report of the Consultative Committee (Hadow), *The Education of the Adolescent*, London, HMSO, 1926, pp. 155–71, *Educational Reconstruction*, London, HMSO, 1943, p. 13. The 1936 Act enabled LEAs to assist with the costs of building new non-provided schools for 'senior children'; 519 proposals were submitted, but only 37 had 'materialised' by the outbreak of war. See *Education Act, 1936*, Sections 8–14; Board of Education, op. cit., 1943, p. 14.
46 Selby-Bigge, op. cit., p. 187.
47 The following poem on Selby-Bigge's retirement was found among one of his colleague's papers: 'Adieu, farewell, goodbye, dear Selby B, The faithful servant of the NUT, For years of blameless assiduity, Fitly created Bart, and KCB'. See G. Sherington, *English Education, Social Change and War 1911–20*, Manchester, Manchester University Press, 1981, p. 39.
48 P.H.J.H. Gosden, 'From Board to Ministry: the impact of the War on the education department', *History of Education*, 1989, vol. 18, no. 3, pp. 188–9. These were the views of R.S. Wood, Deputy Secretary of the Board of Education and A.L. Binns, Director of Education, West Riding of Yorkshire. Lord Eustace Percy was President of the Board of Education, 1924–9.
49 Ibid. An account of the education system during the war is contained in P.H.J.H. Gosden, *Education in the Second World War*, London, Methuen, 1976.
50 Board of Education memorandum, *Education After the War*, June 1941. The full text of the memorandum appears as an appendix to N. Middleton and S. Weitzman, *A Place for Everyone*, London, Gollancz, 1976.
51 Board of Education, *Educational Reconstruction*, London, HMSO, 1943, pp. 1–18, 28–30. The Hadow Committee had suggested four possible ways in which local educational administration could be reformed. See Board of Education, *The Education of the Adolescent*, London, HMSO, 1926, p. 164.
52 This had brought together all unrepealed educational legislation from 1870, including the major Education Acts of 1902 and 1918.
53 *Education Act, 1944*, Sections 1–5.
54 *Education Act, 1944*, Sections 6–8, 61, 35, 43–46, 49, 33, 34. Secondary education was defined as that for 'senior pupils': those who had attained 'the age of twelve years but ... not ... the age of nineteen years'.
55 *Education Act, 1944*, Section 100; W. Pile, op. cit., p. 46.
56 *Education Act, 1944*, Sections 6, 11, First Schedule. These were known as divisional executives. LEAs were also now under a statutory obligation to appoint a chief education officer, after consulting the minister. See Section 88.
57 *Education Act, 1944*, Section 9.
58 *Education Act, 1944*, Sections 13, 15, 18, 102. Maintenance contributions were increased: to 85 per cent of costs by 1975. The provisions applied to voluntary secondary as well as voluntary primary schools, putting voluntary grammar schools, which had been 'aided' by LEAs under Part II of the 1902 Act (Part VI of the Education Act, 1921), on the same footing as voluntary primary schools. If they became voluntary schools under the 1944 Act, LEAs would have a duty to maintain them.

59 *Education Act, 1944*, Sections 15, 18, 19. There were also, following the provisions of the 1936 Education Act, 'special agreement' schools, which were a 'half-way house' between aided and controlled schools. Only one-third of their governing body were LEA appointees, but appointment of staff was 'under the control' of the LEA. See Section 24.

60 *Education Act, 1944*, Section 27. In special agreement schools, religious education was in accordance with the trust deed. See Section 28.

61 *Education Act, 1944*, Sections 25, 26.

62 *Education Act, 1944*, Sections 17–21; Board of Education, *Principles of Government in Maintained Secondary Schools*, London, HMSO, 1944, p. 3. Voluntary schools could only be grouped with the consent of their managers or governors.

63 *Education Act, 1944*, Sections 70–75; Board of Education, Report of the Committee on Public Schools (Fleming), *The Public Schools and the General Educational System*, London, HMSO, 1944, pp. 60–9.

64 Ministry of Education, *Annual Report and the Statistics of Public Education, for England and Wales, 1947*, London, HMSO, 1948, p. 14, *Annual Report and the Statistics of Public Education, for England and Wales, 1949*, London, HMSO, 1950, p. 15.

65 S.J. Curtis, *History of Education in Great Britain*, London, University Tutorial Press, 1963, 5th edn, p. 397; H.C. Dent, *The Educational System of England and Wales*, London, University Press, 1969, 4th edn, p. 34.

66 Ministry of Education, Report of the Central Advisory Council for Education (England) (Crowther), *15 to 18*, London, HMSO, 1959, p. 107.

67 Gosden, op. cit., 1966, p. 204.

68 *Local Government Act, 1972*, Section 192.

69 Pile, op. cit., p. 46.

70 Cooke and Gosden, op. cit., p.76.

71 B. Donoghue, *Prime Minister*, London, Jonathan Cape, 1987, p. 110. The remark is attributed to Harold Wilson.

72 As well as being the established pattern, the tripartite post-primary system had been endorsed in an important report by a committee of the Secondary School Examinations Council. See Board of Education, Report of the Committee of the Secondary School Examinations Council Appointed by the President of the Board of Education (Norwood), *Curriculum and Examinations in Secondary Schools*, London, HMSO, 1943, pp. 1–6.

73 See Department for Education and Science, *Circular 10/65*, 12 July 1965.

74 See R. Davis, *The Grammar School*, Harmondsworth, Pelican, 1967, pp. 93–119 and C. Benn and B. Simon, *Half Way There*, Harmondsworth, Penguin, 1972, 2nd edn, pp. 38–98 for contemporary accounts of political attitudes towards comprehensive reorganization from very different perspectives.

75 Department of Education and Science, Report of the Central Advisory Council for Education (England) (Plowden), *Children and their Primary Schools*, London, HMSO, 1967, vol. 1, p. 187. For many critics of 'progressive' educational methods, the Plowden Report came to symbolize the developments in the education system which they deplored. For the William Tyndale School, see Sharp, op. cit., p. 52.

76 C.B. Cox and A.E. Dyson, 'Letter to Members of Parliament', in C.B. Cox and A.E. Dyson (eds), *Black Paper Two*, London, The Critical Quarterly Society, p. 15.

77 Gordon *et al.*, op. cit., p. 95.

78 The composition of the managing and governing bodies of voluntary schools was specified in the Act. See above.

79 G. Baron and D.A. Howell, *School Management and Government*, Research Studies 6, Royal Commission on Local Government in England, London, HMSO, 1968, p. 139.

80 See Sharp, op. cit., pp. 50–1.

81 Department of Education and Science, Report of the Committee of Enquiry appointed jointly by the Secretary of State for Education and Science and the Secretary of State for Wales under the chairmanship of Mr Tom Taylor CBE, *A New Partnership for Our Schools*, London, HMSO, 1977, pp. 21–35, 17–18, 47–75, 16.

82 Sharp, op. cit., p. 54.

83 Sharp, op. cit., pp. 54–5. See also Department of Education and Science, *The Composition of School Governing Bodies*, London, HMSO, 1978.

84 *Education Act, 1980*, Sections 1–5. The parent governor provisions applying to aided schools also applied to special agreement schools.

85 *Education Act, 1980*, Section 17.

86 Department of Education and Science, *Better Schools*, London, HMSO, 1985, pp. 3, 63.

87 *Education (No. 2) Act, 1986*, Sections 3–7.

88 *Education (No. 2) Act, 1986*, Sections 16–18, 22–4, 29, 34–41. The governing bodies of aided and special agreement schools had more extensive responsibilities than those of county, controlled and maintained special schools. See Sections 19, 25.

89 Department of Education and Science, *Better Schools*, p. 63.

90 J.S. Maclure, *Education Re-formed*, London, Hodder and Stoughton, 2nd edn, 1989, p. 33.

91 *Education Reform Act, 1988*, Sections 33–51, 26–32, 52–104.

92 *Education Reform Act, 1988*, Sections 1–25.

93 P.R. Sharp and J.R. Dunford, *The Education System in England and Wales*, London, Longman, 1990, p. 88.

94 Sharp and Dunford, op. cit., 1990, pp. 87–9, 99–103. Three of the MSC's ten commissioners were TUC representatives.

95 J.J.S. Higham, P.R. Sharp and D.J. Yeomans, *The Emerging 16–19 Curriculum: Policy and Provision*, London, David Fulton Publishers, 1996, p. 14. The 1988 Education Reform Act had removed the polytechnics from LEA control.

96 Aldrich, op. cit., pp. 59, 61.

97 R. Aldrich, D. Crook and D. Watson, *Education and Employment: the DfEE and its Place in History*, London, Institute of Education, University of London, 2000, p. 206.

98 Sharp and Dunford, op. cit., 1995, p. 191.

Chapter 6

Teachers

Philip Gardner

> We do well to let our minds linger now and then over the thought of the
> many obscure men and women who have in their day served the
> commonwealth by training its children, doing work for small reward in
> money or fame, such as could never have been undertaken in the spirit
> of the mere hireling.[1]

Sustained and systematic schooling constituted one of the great common
experiences for the citizens of Britain in the twentieth century.[2] To a degree
unmatched in the nineteenth century – and, for all that we know, possibly
also in the twenty-first – formal schooling was accepted as the unchallenged
expectation and the natural condition for all the nation's children. And
when they reflect upon the meaning or significance of this universal experience, each of the twentieth century's citizens will easily bring to mind a
constellation of names responsible for investing that experience with its
particular recollected qualities, whether positive, negative or neutral. At the
forefront of this list of long-remembered names will always stand the
teachers. Strangely, teachers have been overlooked in most histories of
education in favour of the larger public narrative of the legislative, administrative and institutional advance of the machinery of schooling itself.[3] But
for most citizens, the practical meaning of the history of education is
inscribed not in these things, but more intimately, in the names of their
former teachers.[4] In recognizing this, we would do well to consider the
implications it carries for the ways in which we set about trying to design,
interpret and relate the research we undertake on the history of teachers and
teaching. In particular, we might turn towards accounts attuned to the day-
to-day concerns of teachers themselves, rather than to the broader strategic
interests of those who trained, employed, inspected or represented them.

The situation in 2000

A century of schooling has demanded in increasing numbers the service of
large numbers of men and women, many of them unrecorded, few of them

quite forgotten. On the eve of the twenty-first century, the population of England and Wales stood at 52,689,900.[5] The teaching force in aided or maintained primary and secondary schools – accounting for the overwhelming majority of the available school provision – was 423,520 strong.[6] Within the secondary sector – leaving on one side the important issue of differences in promotion patterns – there was an even balance of the sexes, with women teachers (at 53 per cent of the total) marginally the more numerous. In the case of the primary sector, differentiation by sex remained quite as strong as it had done nearly a century before, with 83 per cent of posts filled by women.[7] These numbers do not, however, comprehend the true extent within the nation of what, a hundred years before, would have been referred to as its 'teaching power'. At the end of the century, in addition to those in post, the pool of trained but professionally inactive teachers amounted to an additional 382,000 individuals.[8]

As the process of schooling developed over the century, the image of the trained and professionally disciplined teacher came to stand both as an index of its progressive success and as a symbolic figurehead of its lofty goals for a better society, at once more just and more efficient. At its end, professional training, together with graduate status – a cherished ambition from the earliest days of the National Union of Teachers (NUT) – were virtually universal.[9] There was one trained teacher (if we include the pool of inactive teachers) for every 65 members of the general population.

In 1999, the average annual salary received by women classroom teachers was £22,520; for men, the figure was £24,360.[10] More informative than these bald statistics, of course, is their comparative relation to the incomes of other occupational groups. The nature of such broad comparisons is always problematical and the results of such exercises must always be crude. They do indicate, however, that a century of systematic schooling has not led to any relative increase in the levels of remuneration which have been seen as appropriate for the nation's teachers. In 1993, the average income of a general practitioner was 80 per cent greater than that of a male teacher; the incomes of a police officer and face-working coalminer were broadly equivalent to it; a labourer received approximately 50 per cent of the teacher's salary.[11]

Responding to the last of the twentieth century's cyclical recruitment crises attributable, in some degree, to the enduringly modest remuneration of teachers, the final government of the century declared its goal as the 'rewarding our leading professionals properly'. Such a strategy – 'the modernisation of the teaching profession' – was envisaged as part of a larger ambition to reform the effectiveness of the nation's entire system of education.[12] 'In the process', it was averred, 'we hope to create a new and positive culture of excellence and improvement within the profession, and to restore teaching to the status it deserves.' The invocation of the idea of 'restoration' is a significant and intriguing one. To the degree that 'modernization' became the guiding theme of late-twentieth-century policy formulation, historical perspectives tended to inform political strategy very much less than they did in the early years of the century. Nevertheless, the allusion to the restoration of a professional status which was lost somewhere, somehow, in the course of the century raises important questions for any review of the modern history of teachers and teaching.

The situation in 1900

In 1901, with the population of England and Wales at about 31,000,000, there were 149,804 teachers at work in the inspected elementary day schools which then comprised the educational provision for the great bulk of the nation's children.[13] The great majority of these, some 76 per cent, were women. Trained teachers were still relatively few, with scarcely one such teacher for every one hundred pupils on the rolls of the nation's schools.[14]

At the start of the twentieth century, the average remuneration of a certificated male teacher was just over £107 per annum, the equivalent figure for a female being about £78.[15] In comparative terms, the average income of a general practitioner was, as it remained at the end of the century, 80 per cent greater than that of a male trained teacher. In terms of relative standing to other workers, however, the position of the teacher showed a clear advantage. A face-working coalminer received about two-thirds of the teacher's salary, a police constable close to one-half and a labourer about one-third.[16] Nevertheless, Frank Roscoe's plaintive observation of 1913 that teachers' labours were 'for small reward in money' has stood the test of time far better than he would have hoped.

In reflecting on the differences between teachers and the practice of teaching in the first and last years of the century, our most convenient and accessible starting points will always be with those quantifiable demarcations resting upon comprehensive statistical data of the sort considered above. Generalizations about the characteristic ambience and experience of teaching regimes at either end of the century will be much harder to advance. We might, however, seek to achieve an initial orientation by briefly identifying some of the areas in which, nearly a hundred years earlier, teachers and teaching would have appeared very different in the eyes of their modern counterparts.

As the century turned, those earlier teachers were celebrating a swing in the educational pendulum which saw the easing of a long period of central control of the curriculum and a particularly noisome regime of school inspection. This was about to be followed by the beginning of a series of policy shifts which would nudge the traditional focus for initial training policy away from the classroom and towards the training college. Most teachers from this early period would have been more likely, by comparison with their successors, to have had no former occupation other than teaching and no expectation of such in the future. Teaching was characteristically a life-long career, though women were routinely required to resign their posts on marriage.[17] Teachers were more likely to work in schools that were smaller in terms of staffing, pupil numbers and physical appearance but notably larger in terms of average class size. They were also likely to be far more formal in their dealings with their pupils and with their colleagues. In the same vein, they would hope to maintain a degree of elevated local status by seeking social separation from the neighbourhood culture of parents with whom they had minimal formal contact.[18] Though often originating from the same working-class backgrounds as their pupils, teachers would probably be remote from the social and familial lives led by their pupils when they were away from school.[19] Within the classroom, they were likely to be less prepared to tolerate pupil noise and movement; they were more likely to be severe over infractions of school rules and conventions; and they – especially males – would be routinely familiar, either directly or indirectly, with the practice of corporal punishment. Teachers, particularly those in elementary schools, were inured to the close regulation of their professional autonomy, though this was likely to be felt more directly from local sources, the church or the local authority, than from central government. To take an example, an unexceptional advertisement of 1900 in *The Schoolmaster*, the journal of the National Union of Teachers, gave details of the expectations for a teaching appointment 'in Girls' Department ... Assistant. Communicant. Disciplinarian. Good Needlewoman. Salary £50 – Apply, The Vicar.'[20]

Changes and continuities

If we were to search for a powerful dramatization of some of those differences to which we have alluded, we might turn to the visual images which decorate the endpapers of a valuable commemorative volume published by the Department of Education and Science in 1990.[21] Here we see two contemporary photographs of idealized classroom settings, the first from the early years of the century, the second towards its end. The images share a common purpose in that each is artfully composed in the service of a set of officially approved pedagogical messages. The first shows a large class of boys, traditionally and uniformly organized and earnestly engaged in the improving task at hand, under the close and watchful direction of its attentive teacher. The second is a much closer and more intimate composition, presenting a small group of students of mixed sex and race, sharing a relaxed and evidently joyful learning moment, not under the control of their teacher, but in her company. Despite their artifice, these are representations which signal real and important changes across this century of schooling. Teachers have been well aware, from the years of the Revised

Code and first national curriculum of 1862, of the power which officially sanctioned pedagogical discourses may wield. But, where it has been possible, teachers have frequently proved adept in conforming to the letter, rather than to the law, of prescription from above.[22] It is certainly the case, to give an example, that in the second half of the century, primary teachers began to embrace the philosophies of progressivism with a warmth that had not been matched in the first. And yet, as the work of Galton, Simon and Croll, amongst others, has shown, educational philosophy and classroom practice did not come together in any straightforward way.[23] Teachers who visualized their professional approach broadly within a progressivist discourse might in practice utilize teaching and organizational strategies which drew strongly upon more traditional pedagogical forms.

There has sometimes been an element of cynicism in such strategies, but this has not generally been so. More usually, allegiance to the thrust of successive educational reforms has been honest in intent, but simply more difficult to match in practice. Here, the key factors have always been the enduring situational constraints of daily classroom life, together with the influence of an associated and enduring occupational culture. Of these we will hear more later. For the moment, in listening to the evocative words of F.H. Spencer – an experienced and highly perceptive classroom teacher from the turn of the century – we might simply note that such constraints and such a culture have been, to a greater or lesser degree, recognizable parts of the pedagogical experience of each one of the teachers of the twentieth century.[24]

> I had to teach more than fifty boys and girls every subject of the curriculum ... I was condemned to hold them down by an iron discipline, with no backing from the head ... I began to fear failure: certainly I lost self-confidence ... I set my teeth and tried violently to master the situation. But my spiritual condition grew worse. I succeeded only in part. In many things I could interest the pupils. One or two boys, however, could torture me with silent insolence, and one or two girls could sail off with an indefinable impertinence; for they were by instinct past masters in the art of knowing how far they could go without being culpably and provably wrong ... The last half-hour of the afternoon often saw me dead tired. And ... the sympathy ... of most of the staff ... could (not) free me from my forebodings or salve my shattered pride.[25]

A century ago, teaching was a career with many entrenched divisions. Yet these were not commonly fed by active disputes between hostile groups. Rather, they were the more straightforward product of historical and, often, geographical separation. Such distinctions included, for example, those resting upon the divergent experiences of male and female teachers, of rural and urban teachers, of public and private teachers, of elementary/primary and secondary teachers, of unionized and non-union-ized teachers, of more 'progressive' and more 'traditional' teachers, and so on. The distinctiveness and the relative isolation of the work of each of these groups of teachers meant that they did not often feel themselves to be part of a single profession, united in fulfilling complementary roles in the service of the educational interests of the nation. Despite a record of considerable periodic public disagreement and fragmentation both within and between their professional associations over the course of the twen-tieth century, it would be much easier for teachers at its end to see the profession as, in some elemental sense, a unitary one than it was for their forebears a century earlier.

There are a number of reasons for this. In the first place, it was a consequence of the move, particularly in the second half of the century, towards physically bigger schools with larger concentrations of staff.[26] In the early years, many schools employed only a handful of teachers and, in combination with the prevailing emphasis upon professional formality, this meant that day-to-day contact between colleagues could be surpris-ingly abbreviated and perfunctory.[27] In this earlier period too, the profession remained sundered by the residual effects of the stark class and gender divisions in educational provision which were the legacy of the nineteenth century to the twentieth. By the close of the latter, though such divisions were still powerfully felt in the differential patterns of experi-ences and opportunities available to individual pupils, they had long since ceased to be officially endorsed by the State through administrative arrangements explicitly designed to maintain a segregated schooling provi-sion. With the incremental fusion of the elementary and secondary sectors to produce a universal sequential progression across both phases, the teachers of schools previously marooned from each other could begin to perceive themselves – in principle if not always immediately in practice – as being engaged in a joint task of co-operative professional endeavour. As the century came to its close, this accelerating process was further accentu-ated by the elevation of education to a central place in national policy formulation and media attention.[28] That same category of teachers who, at one end of the century, were famously castigated as 'uncultured and imperfectly educated ... creatures of tradition and routine' were celebrated at the other as part of 'a profession that is recognised and valued by the wider community'.[29]

Statistics offer particularly convenient and conducive sources for broad historical comparisons. No other data are able to dramatize change with similar economy and power. But as our earlier illustrations have already indicated, in the case of the history of the teaching profes-sion, even the statistical record has two stories to tell. The first gives an optimistic account of progressive growth and improvement in the manner conventionally approved by successive presidents, ministers and secretaries of state holding political responsibility for education; incremental increases in teacher numbers and academic qualifications would exemplify this approach. The second story belies the idea of progress in any straightforward or unequivocal sense. It speaks instead to a recognition of fundamental continuities or similarities across time. It adduces statistics primarily to show that *plus ça change, plus c'est la même chose.* In the terms of this type of account, which commends itself more readily to classroom practitioners than to politicians, it is the comparative statistics of teachers' salary levels across the century that are more likely to be emphasized.

When we turn from statistics to another stalwart of factual history, chronology, we find a similar disjunction between the measures which commend themselves to the policy maker or the commentator, on the one hand, and the practitioner on the other. For the greater part of the twentieth century, we can make no assumption that the key dates from which we might seek to hang a general historical account of the development of teaching would be those which classroom teachers themselves would choose or recognize with any great warmth. It is not difficult to construct a list of such dates. Among many other possible contenders we might cite the establishment of the London County Council's Day Training College in 1902; the teacher training regulations of 1904 and 1907; the 1905 *Handbook of Suggestions for Teachers*; the 1918 Teachers' Superannuation Act; the 1919 Burnham scales and subsequent secessions from the NUT; the 1925 Departmental Committee on the Training of Teachers for Public Elementary Schools; the McNair Report of 1944; the 1963 Robbins Report; the 1972 James Report; the 'Ruskin speech' of 1976; the 1983 White Paper on *Teacher Quality*; the 1988 Education Reform Act and its subsequent legislation; the establishment of Ofsted in 1993 and the Teacher Training Agency in 1994; the Teaching and Higher Education Act of 1997; the 1999 Green Paper, *Teachers: Meeting the Challenge of Change.*

These and many others are of great importance in constructing any historical narrative of the modern teaching profession. Cumulatively, they have set the organizational limits within which the work of teachers throughout the century has been done. And yet they are seldom the turning points upon which the history of the classroom has turned; they are not the historical markers which the majority of teachers themselves have used when they reflect upon their own experience of teaching.[30] Characteristically, such reflections, most powerfully and sensitively heard in the valedictories offered to their colleagues by long-serving teachers on their retirement, answer to a timeframe of local rather than national events. Their periodization depends on the personal and the idiosyncratic – the arrival of a new head teacher; a school reorganization; a particularly troublesome pupil; an outstanding social event. The national issues which are incorporated into such intimate accounts are those which impinge in some notably direct way upon the essential interiority of daily school life – events such as the raising of the school-leaving age in 1972; the Houghton pay award of 1974; the teachers' strikes of the 1980s. Paradoxically, as the direction of government policy at the start of the twenty-first century moves towards an emphasis on diversity in schooling, the closer oversight of teachers' work by the State operates towards the nationalization of teachers' professional memory. For a previous generation of teachers, even the landmark 1944 Education Act often appears as a marginal moment against the more intimate rhythms of daily life in schools. But for any teacher at work in the last two decades of the century, the 1988 Act and its subsequent shoal of legislative activity will always be likely to be accorded a central place in relating or explaining the course of their subsequent professional lives.

One of the most striking features of the history of the modern teaching profession is the pattern of recurrent themes by which it is marked. The close of the twentieth century was, to take one example, marked by professional anxieties about a 'return' to 'payment by results', a policy of which, at the close of the nineteenth, classroom teachers believed they had seen the last.[31] To illustrate this tendency towards recurrence in another way, we might turn to the columns of *The Schoolmaster* in its first issue of the twentieth century. In reviewing the state of public education at this momentous juncture, the journal sought to epitomize the present and to predict the future. Taking the unfolding South African conflict as its guiding metaphor, *The Schoolmaster* warned that in the new century, 'the fighters against the beginnings of crime, vice and incapacity, the battalions of the teachers in the war against ignorance will be *thinned*, not augmented'.

In seeking to validate this prediction, the journal went on to adumbrate a series of concerns which, saving stylistic convention, would not have been much out of place in the pages of its successor publication, one hundred years later.

> If there be a dearth of teachers the nation suffering from it will have itself alone to blame; and the only way to swell the ranks of the certificated will be to offer a better "Queen's Shilling", a fuller ration, a safer berth, a higher public estimation, and a larger pension at the end. But these are terms at which the Chancellor of the Exchequer will look awry. We may see expedients adopted for the staffing of the schools; a few more of those side-doors to the profession through which hardly anybody enters may be thrown open; yet it will not avail. The English parent knows pretty well in these days how ill-rewarded, lowly-esteemed, anxious, toilsome, and subject to petty tyrannies is the

career of the teacher in many a public elementary school; he will enter his son for anything rather than that.[32]

That the modern history of public sector teaching should be so amenable to readings which highlight insistent circulating themes should not surprise us. Over the course of the century, many individual teachers have been endlessly industrious, flexible and ingenious in seeking to develop or extend their professional capacities. But the constraints upon their endeavours have always been severe. These have derived, above all else, from the dominance, both real and symbolic, of the irreducible importance of the classroom in shaping and organizing the day-to-day labour of most teachers.[33]

For policy-makers, the limits of what might be expected from teachers' labour have been set principally by the scope of legislative and electoral ambition. For teachers themselves, such limits have always been imposed much more locally, by the pressures of the immediate physical spaces in which they have worked.[34] Minimal floor space, large class sizes, poor heating, fixed or inflexible fixtures and fittings, insufficient teaching materials, all these have set their own discipline upon what it may be possible, week in, week out, to achieve within the classroom. In one way or another, such practical limitations have been part of the collective experience of the modern teaching profession from its inception. For many occupations, the form, organization and characteristic patterns of daily labour have been transformed during the twentieth century. Teaching has not notably been among these.[35] The corresponding structural transformation of teaching, it might be argued, had substantially taken place earlier, in the nineteenth century, under the intense pressure of a process of urbanization which, by the beginning of the twentieth century, had rendered England and Wales nations of city-dwellers. The schools which served such populations had already taken on that characteristic form which, in an American context, Lortie has described as 'the "cellular" pattern ... of multiple self-contained classrooms'.[36]

Unarguably, teaching would see many great changes in the course of the twentieth century, some of which, especially in the primary sector, would offer significant challenges to the cellular pattern. And yet the fundamental structure of teaching under such a pattern has remained, at least until the very end of the century, remarkably constant. A visit to a late Victorian museum school is both evocative and striking for the degree of its ambient similarity to the classrooms of our own childhood, and much less for its significant differences. A visit to a modern secondary school is evocative and striking in just the same way, and for the same reason. As Philip Jackson so tellingly wrote, 'In a fundamental sense, school is school, no matter where it happens ... a classroom (is) a classroom'.[37] It has been this relative endurance of form over time which has resulted in the sedimentation of many conventional strategies for class-room management within what might be seen as the dominant occupational culture of the profession.

This was a culture in which essentially contradictory goals were neces-sarily resolved into a tradition which could respond simultaneously to notions of teaching as both high calling and low cunning. This complex and subtle combination is nowhere better expressed than in Edward Blishen's memory of the emergency training college where, in 1949, he was a student. Blishen remembers the interaction between Mr Trellis, the prin-cipal, 'tall, grey-haired, with the sort of gentle, sonorous voice that proclaims a desire to *ennoble* everything', and Mr Jepp, the head of Education, 'I've seen thousands of you in my time. I'm here to nip your idealism in the bud.'

> 'What we have to learn to do,' said Mr Trellis on the second morning, 'is to open windows in the souls of the children we teach' ... A shy smile was instantly corrected by an expression of total gravity. 'We must bring sweetness and light into their lives.'
>
> He was followed by Mr Jepp, who merely wished to say that he'd been short of one or two persons in his optional tutorial the day before, and that if they did not appear that afternoon he would take them apart in a very slow and cruel manner.
>
> 'Do you think they work this out together?' Bing whispered. That seemed unlikely; but the perfectly amiable contradiction of Trellis by Jepp, and the other way round (their good relations were evident from the smiles they exchanged, a friendly swopping of the gentle for the fierce), was to become the mark of the whole of that year of training.[38]

The culture of which such an exchange was a product evolved as a complex amalgam of the expressive and the instrumental. It did not merely operate to maintain and transmit recipe knowledge.[39] Over the course of the century it also played an important part in the defence and promotion of a self-assigned professional status which took the classroom as its prin-cipal symbolic representation. Here, the classroom stood for the mystery, the artfulness and the essential unknowability of the skills of teaching to those who did not participate directly in them. For the teachers of the twentieth century, the image of the recondite classroom was at once a powerful resource and a profound weakness. It enabled them to stake out a ground upon which, despite the ambivalent nature of their formal professional status, persuasive claims to specialist expertise and autonomy could nevertheless be realistically built.[40] At the same time, however, it rendered the teachers open to public misunderstanding and suspicion and often perplexed those who were temperamentally disposed to be their friends or allies. With the replacement of a separate elementary sector by a universal primary phase, with the progressive raising of the school leaving age, with the spread of external examinations and with the relentless acceleration in the level of political expectation attaching to public education, the teachers came under increasing pressure to cede the ground upon which the symbolic classroom stood.[41] One way of understanding the complex and often painful development of the public teaching profession in the later decades of the century is as a slow and difficult retreat from territory which it had always understood, and had been allowed to understand, as its own.

In 1921, Sir Henry Newbolt's committee on the teaching of English reminded teachers that they no longer laboured under close central control of the curriculum. Newbolt urged the teachers to seize professional responsibility for what went on in the classroom. 'Teachers' the report observed, 'seem, at times, to be unaware or afraid of their liberty, and to desire the restrictions that no longer bind them.'[42] Forty years later, in the very different political and social climate of the post-war period, it was no longer clear that governments were so relaxed about the notion of leaving the classroom in the hands of the teachers. The then Minister of Education, Sir David Eccles, notably identified the 'secret garden of the curriculum' as a renewed policy concern, signalling a series of new emphases, in the various names of efficiency, effectiveness, partnership, openness and accountability, about responsibility for teaching and learning in the classroom.[43] By the time of the passing of the 1988 Education Reform Act, such emphases had become hugely amplified. They were also irresistible. The old, informal culture of the classroom which had been built from the early years of the century and which carried an inherent unease about the involvement of non-teachers, such as parents, policy-makers, trainers, inspectors, in classroom matters, had to give ground. A culture which had learned to look inwards for its resources, standards and conventions now found its face being turned outwards, towards different professional models, towards the interests of stakeholders and towards the values of the market.

The pace of legislative and administrative change in education towards the end of the twentieth century has been very rapid.[44] Corresponding movement in teachers' professional culture has also been breathless though, in the way of cultural change, far more difficult to measure. Perhaps one way of doing so is to look in detail not at the current moment but at the past, in order to assess the extent of contemporary change. Where we are going is not for historians to say, but what we can do is to inform judgements about future directions by clarifying from whence we have come. In this exercise, therefore, we might seek to approach the cardinal constituent elements of what could be called the traditional expression of teachers' professional culture. Limiting our analysis to public sector teachers, we will seek to identify some of these elements at the height of their influence. If we take the second half of the century – in effect, the post-war period – as one in which traditional professional culture came under increasing and accelerating pressure to change, then it is to the mid-century that we should look to identify such a culture in its most developed and extensive form. Three contemporary sources serve as a guide. These are: the McNair Report, *Teachers and Youth Leaders* of 1944; *Teachers Made and Marred*, a slight but perceptive volume produced in 1943 by Maurice Harrison, director of education for Oldham; and Eric Partridge's enduring and entertaining linguistic reference book, *Usage and Abusage*, first published in 1947.[45]

In *Usage and Absuage*, Eric Partridge indulged in a kind of parlour game in which the object was to coin an appropriate collective term for this or that social or occupational group – thus, a 'scamper' of children, a 'collation' of scholars, an 'indifference' of politicians and so on. The exercise was a whimsical one, and the terms suggested were often trite. But one entry carries a resonance that is more challenging. In searching for a word to apply to contemporary schoolteachers, Partridge arrived at an 'unselfishness'. An 'unselfishness of schoolteachers': the term is an arresting one precisely because it seems to capture an elemental aspect of the enduring impulse and expectation of an organized teaching profession rooted in the Christian missionary vision of its most notable founder, James Kay-Shuttleworth.[46]

Despite its evocative force, Partridge's suggestion must, in its nature, be a partial one. Its suggestive power comes from the fact that the device of conceptual concentration always excludes other possible alternatives. If we are to make full use of its analytical potential, we will have to play Partridge's game a little more and see what other group names might commend themselves. And if we can achieve that, then we will be in a position to explore how these generalizing, common-sense categories might be explored and illuminated in the works of McNair and Harrison. For some clues to apposite alternative collective nouns we might turn once more to Frank Roscoe, certainly one of the most perceptive, engaged and sympathetic commentators on the teaching profession from the early years of the century. The words from Roscoe which serve as an epigraph for this chapter offer his telling summation, characteristically concise and insightful, of the principal common features of the nation's emergent teaching force.

Roscoe's informed and measured judgement endorses Partridge's more flippant observation. An 'unselfishness' of teachers is given to the service of the commonwealth, wittingly 'doing (such) work for small reward in money or fame'. But this is not the only characteristic signalled in Roscoe's words. He goes on to assert that in the face of the generally low level of formal regard, whether financial or civic, extended to them, teachers nevertheless maintain an orientation to their work 'such as could never have been undertaken in the spirit of the mere hireling'. The rejection of such a mean spirit speaks of that collective concern for the status of the profession, that thirst for public recognition which has so emphatically marked the consciousness of the teachers of the twentieth century. In the sense of Partridge's game, we might speak of this ambitious impulse in terms of an 'aspiration of teachers'.

Roscoe's assessment offers other possibilities. Above all, it is his use of the word 'obscure' that is so striking. The 'obscurity' of the teachers of the twentieth century is perhaps of a very particular kind. Teachers are never forgotten by those whom they teach, whether they go on to become paupers or prime ministers. Yet on leaving school, all former pupils inevitably move beyond the restricted worlds they shared with their teachers to a point where gratitude, respect and even affection are tempered by a kind of pity for those whose work, in its nature, must divorce them from the moment and consign them to a perpetual, circulating negotiation with the state of childhood. In the nineteenth century, this recognition was often expressed through the common association of teaching with personal failure, restriction or disability of one kind or another, enforcing disqualification from full engagement with the routines of adult life.[47] Such associations were considerably ameliorated with the progressive professionalization of teaching from the 1870s and by the early years of the twentieth century, teaching had begun to enjoy the degree of qualified popular respect that attended it thereafter. But the taint of 'obscurity' has been hard to escape. It has found expression in a number of ways, but two distinctive though associated strands particularly stand out.

The first is reflected in the physical space in which teachers' working lives have been typically lived out. This is a space which has been, for most of the twentieth century's teachers, defined by separation. Within the enclosed confines of his or her classroom, the teacher has been the sole representative of the remunerated world of work, with children as the nearest approximation to shop floor co-workers. But the focus of the teacher's whole endeavour has been precisely upon the preparation of these rising generations for life on the outside, for that adult working world of which the teacher himself or herself is never quite, in some sense, a full member. Clever, talented, qualified and worthy to a degree unlikely to be matched by the generality of his or her charges, the schoolteachers have nevertheless characteristically used their abilities to prepare others rather than to further themselves. And as successive cohorts depart the school for the world, it is the teachers who always remain, vicariousness written into the index of their own perceptions of success. It is in this respect that we may understand 'obscurity' to be a function both of physical separation and of that unworldliness which might be seen as its inevitable accompaniment. And the collective appellation, an 'isolation of teachers' does not seem inappropriate.

Across an entire career, isolation of this kind stimulated in many of the teachers of the twentieth century a second dimension of that which Roscoe sought to identify under the name of 'obscurity'. If the profession as a whole might be seen, across most of these years, to be enthused by an aspirational impulse, the cumulative experience of a lifetime's classroom teaching was, for many practitioners, ultimately a dispiriting one. For such, the balance sheet of public reward and recognition against personal industry, dedication and loyalty has failed to tally and, at its end, the zeal of early career has dissipated. This is a sensation known, if by a succession of different colloquialisms, throughout the teaching profession of the twentieth century. It has also been addressed by those who, though not having themselves given their lives to teaching, have sought to understand it. The departmental committee on teacher training in the early 1920s, for example, spoke of the teacher's 'comparative unadventurousness' – one of those numerous, striking and provoking observations, mixtures of insight and ignorance, which pepper the writings of educational commentators striving to seize upon some elemental characteristic of the teacher's life.[48] That which, in their different ways, Roscoe and the departmental committee were seeking to define might be loosely understood as a 'disappointment of teachers'.

Having reflected – more seriously than he would have wished – on Partridge's parlour game, we have noted the persuasive appeal of his 'unselfishness of teachers'. To these, after a consideration of the insights of Frank Roscoe, we have added three further suggestions: an 'aspiration of teachers'; an 'isolation of teachers'; and a 'disappointment of teachers'. Let us now turn to an examination of how these notions were handled by McNair and Harrison.

For each, the quality of unselfishness among teachers was recognized as a central, even a defining one. Such a spirit of self-sacrifice, as McNair indicates, carried a degree of nobility which commended itself to public opinion and which was recognized above all in the extent of the trust accorded to teachers by parents. Such confidence was, for example, the single most significant factor in assuring the government that the plans for wartime evacuation would be both feasible and acceptable to the parents of school-age children.[49] But teachers' unselfishness was far from unequivocally applauded. Both works ascribed to it a strongly negative and potentially corrosive capacity in its tendency to reflect and therefore to perpetuate the humble origins of the public teaching profession a century earlier. The political and social expectations according to which that teaching force was prepared were appropriate to the nineteenth century and not the twentieth. 'It would' said McNair, 'be foolish to rely upon this missionary spirit for maintaining the supply and the morale of ... teachers.

Teaching is indeed a form of social service but like other professions it is also a bread and butter affair.'[50] The ethos of missionary sacrifice with which the products of the early training colleges had been imbued was inextricably bound up with that 'tradition of cheapness' associated with a segregated tradition of schooling from which a modern teaching profession needed to be distanced. 'The truth is that we have not yet emancipated ourselves from the tradition of educating our children on the cheap.'[51] The strength of this analysis, by contrast with those elicited by government inquiries at the close of the century, we might note, was that it offered a case for professional reform which rested explicitly upon an awareness of history and not upon the force merely of assertion and insistence. 'We cannot emphasise too strongly the need that the public should recognise these historical facts, because in our opinion realization of them both affords explanation of so much that is unsatisfactory and suggests the remedy for its improvement.'[52]

Harrison noted that despite their history of altruism and self-effacement, the relatively modest salaries of teachers were increasingly 'at the root of discontent which shows itself in various forms'.[53] Moreover, as the extent of their personal and professional qualifications grew, as their higher education, previously segregated, became conjoined with the mainstream and as they mixed with others destined for more elevated careers, trainee teachers found it progressively harder to sustain a traditional ethos of service.[54]

> The teachers who have ... had a university education, who have lived among these others, are, with a few exceptions, destined for a lower position in terms of financial reward and social prestige. This fact accounts for the unwillingness of so many graduates to turn to teaching ... Teachers should not be expected to be more altruistic than other(s).[55]

If the toleration of modest material reward threatened a demoralization of teachers themselves, it also rendered them supine and unnaturally quiescent in the eyes of public opinion. This, in turn, raised the risk of further accentuating the social isolation of a professional group whose standing in local communities had always been ambivalent. If self-interest was the accepted yardstick in other professions, teachers should not be expected to adhere to a different measure. 'There is, indeed, a positive danger in such an expectation. It encourages people to treat teachers as a race apart, when the prime need is that they should be regarded as what in fact they are: ordinary people with a personal life to live.'[56]

Such an observation exposed an important paradox for teachers' professional self-perception. In pressing their case for greater material reward on the grounds of their 'ordinariness', teachers risked compromising a cherished professional status which depended precisely upon their symbolic separation, upon their isolation from the communities they served. Teachers' isolation was, as in so many aspects of their professional culture, both a major strength and a persistent weakness. Within their localities, the respect they evinced was achieved at the price of being seen as odd and as unworldly. Harrison noted that he was regularly asked, 'How do I get on with teachers? – as though it would be surprising if one could "get on" with them. Can I make any sense of them and their child-ishness?'[57] McNair, too, recognized that through their 'constant pre-occupation with the young', teachers were drawn, and perhaps more damagingly, seen to be drawn into a world that was in some way juvenile through and through.[58] 'I hear them called', reported Harrison, '"Men among boys and boys among men."'[59] The education, the training, the professional demeanour of teachers, all of these attracted popular respect, even admiration; the focus of their professional expertise – the child – did not. In consequence, the status that teaching attracted was a flawed one, a kind of counterfeit professionalism. Characteristically combining ambition and sensitivity, teachers felt this keenly, as a disappointment that was undeserved. 'Many teachers sense the attitude, and more than one has frankly admitted to me that he is careful to hide his calling when away from his home district or on holiday.'[60]

'The teacher is often said to lead a narrow life.'[61] McNair's trenchant comment encapsulated an official concern about the composition of the teaching force which had been strongly felt from the days of Robert Morant.[62] The narrowness was seen to consist particularly in a sufficiency of education credentials against a deficiency of what might be described as life credentials. Teachers had never escaped school and had therefore never developed a perspective from which fully to understand it. Following his or her course of training, the young teacher returns to 'an institution, the school, with its familiar shape and organisation ... an institution tending to mould its servants to the pattern of an institutional life'.[63]

For both McNair and Harrison, the alleviation of this professional narrowness was the most urgent of potential reforms. 'In no profession could incomplete normal development be more dangerous. The very essence of the teacher's work is that he should be wholly mature, worldly-wise, tolerant, and endowed with a width of interest and understanding.'[64] McNair explored possibilities for widening the profession by getting long-serving teachers periodically away from the deadening influence of the school and for ending the customary arrangements which barred from employment teachers who were wives and mothers, rendering teaching, 'for women, a celibate profession'.[65] A still more radical recommendation was that the profession be opened to those seeking to enter later in life, bringing with them the broadening influence of the world beyond the classroom.[66] This was easier said than done. Even supposing that such might be attracted to classroom life, the stringent requirements of professional training and, more, disastrously, the relatively poor levels of remuneration, militated against it.

> The system of salary calculation for teachers puts a premium on the limitation of teaching ability and the narrowing of the teacher's outlook. The teacher who has spent part of his life in industry, government, or commerce before or after his university or training college career is in a worse position financially than his colleague who has pursued the stereotyped sequestered course, school to college and back to school.[67]

In the face of the post-war challenge for the reconstruction of a modern, twentieth-century education system, McNair and Harrison perceived the nation's aspirations and those of its teachers to have fallen out of step. From the late nineteenth century, teaching had been a principal channel of upward social mobility for able working-class pupils. In this way, the expression of aspirational ambition within early twentieth-century schooling was locked into the figure of the teacher himself or herself. The narrow identification of educational success with the aspirational figure of the teacher in his or her local community was, by mid-century, appearing as an unexpected barrier to the realization of burgeoning national ambitions for the education system itself. The teacher had, in this sense, become the repository of working-class ambition, rather than the agent for its more general development. Within working-class communities, this produced complex tensions which highlighted the aspirational anxiety of the teachers themselves, the perceived pomposity of their local status claims and the general confusion of parents about what they might expect from the education system for their children. On the one hand, parents were ready to acknowledge the personal achievement of teachers and thereby to demonstrate 'the esteem in which the profession is held by the public'.[68] On the other:

> There may be a deep-seated and unconscious jealousy on the part of the manual worker. The majority of teachers are originally of his social class, he went to school with them and they were playmates in childhood. To him the teacher must seem a highly paid person with very short hours, an easy job and excessively long holidays. The fact that the teacher is his cousin or former playmate aggravates the point.[69]

An indication of this paradoxical perception was that 'parents may highly value what a particular ... teacher has done for their children and yet discourage one of those same children from entering the profession'.[70]

The school was not the only site where the aspirational status of teachers faced complex challenges. This was also the case at the other end of the educational hierarchy. Having glimpsed, as teachers in training, the intellectual – and sometimes, the social – delights of the world of higher education, many found the return to a lifetime of unadorned classroom toil a hard one. For those – still relatively few – whose professional training was gained at university rather than training college, the aspirational shock was yet greater, and further complicated by a general awareness of 'the poor regard in which Education has ... been held by some universities'.[71] It is a harsh irony that school teachers, the embodiments of ability, endeavour and advancement through learning, should find that the educational settings in which they trained and worked could bring great professional satisfaction but, at the same time, could be the source of intense and sustained personal disappointment.

Disappointment was, in a sense, written into teaching as it was experienced at mid-century. As we have seen, teachers' experience of professional training and of daily classroom life often served, in different ways, to belie the aspirational zeal that the prospect of teaching excited, both in terms of public service and personal advancement. Many individuals found consoling strategies but for others, disappointment was a significant part of their working lives, and one which characteristically became more pressing with the passage of time, as the age-gap between their pupils and themselves became harder to bridge. McNair, with some awareness of the risks of general demoralization rooted in private disappointment, was anxious to record a 'high appreciation of the profession', together with an injunction that, 'The life of teachers should be made more attractive'.[72] These are messages which have been easily incorporated into the standard repertoire of much subsequent policy thinking though, to the extent that teachers in the later twentieth century perceived such phrases as ultimately insubstantial, the degree of their underlying disappointment has sometimes been compounded rather than eased. Harrison was particularly perceptive in his assessment of the ways in which the complex combination of selflessness, service and status through which twentieth-century teachers approached their work could be frustrated and upset.

> The impression exists that teachers as a body are "different" and that they are difficult for the ordinary man to get on with. Such a difficult personality could arise from narrowness of outlook or interests, intolerance of the unusual, undue readiness to argue or to split hairs instead of getting on with the job, an unreadiness to compromise, suspicion of official action (not perhaps without cause), sense of exposure to improper and unjust treatment by employing bodies, a feeling of frustration in many due to unfitness for their work, or of being

thwarted or unjustly treated in respect of remuneration and social status.[73]

Conclusion

There were, in Harrison's view, 'grounds for believing that there is among teachers a feeling that they suffer under such injustices and that they cannot escape them ... and that they ... tend to regard themselves and to act as a group apart'.[74] This sense of pained but dutiful aloofness was characteristic of an informal professional culture that was at its height in the mid-twentieth century but which can be seen to have exercised an enormous influence across the whole period. It was a culture which offered support and consolation to its members at the same time as seeking to defend them from threats, real or imagined, from society and State. It was a culture held together by a common perception of being wilfully misunderstood by the society it sought to serve in the pursuit of noble aims for the good of all.

This has been a culture which, over the last three decades of the twentieth century and with varying degrees of irritation, governments sought to engage as a necessary condition for the dramatic structural reforms in education which were successively rolled out. And as the century came to its close there were signs that it was a culture that was indeed changing.[75] The rock upon which the traditional culture was built was a classroom which was innocent of the many technological advances which teachers now understand may transform it.[76] This was a place, moreover, which could be shielded from the enquiring gaze of the outside world to a degree which has now become quite impossible. The cement which held the culture together was a recognition among teachers of shared backgrounds, homogeneous educational experiences, similar career trajectories and common motivations. All of these are now – as a consequence of general cultural change as much as policy intent – incomparably more diverse. The claim that teachers could once make – that they were, in some complex way, different from any other group of workers – now seems an increasingly untenable one.

It is always easy to overestimate the significance of short-term change against long-term continuities. The twentieth-century record is littered with educational commentaries insisting on the epoch-making significance of reforms which, a decade or two later, were effectively forgotten. Nonetheless, it does not seem fanciful to suggest that, when they seek to understand the roots of their professional culture, the teachers of the mid-twenty-first century may look predominantly to the last quarter of the twentieth for their answers. As they do so, they may ponder on the comparative utility, for the twenty-first century, of those descriptors – an 'unselfishness' of teachers; an 'isolation' of teachers; an 'aspiration' of teachers; a 'disappointment' of teachers – which reflected so much of the life and work of school teachers over the greater part of the previous century.

Key reading

Issues relating to teaching as a burgeoning policy concern across the industrial world are highlighted in *The Teacher Today: Tasks, Conditions, Policies*, published in 1990 by the Organization for Economic Co-operation and Development. The focus for most of the published work on the history of teachers and teaching in England and Wales has been upon policies and structures for professional training and teachers' professional organizations. Though dated, the cited works by Tropp and Dent remain useful. To these can be added Lance Jones's important study of training reforms in the early years of the century, *The Training of Teachers in England and Wales*, Oxford, Oxford University Press, 1924 and, from the other end of the period, Martin Lawn, *Servants of the State: the Contested Control of Teaching 1900–1930*, Lewes, Falmer, 1987, together with Eric Hoyle and Peter John, *Professional Knowledge and Professional Practice*, London, Cassell, 1995. Also useful are the collections of essays edited by Martin Lawn and Gerald Grace, *Teachers: The Culture and Politics of Work*, Lewes, Falmer, 1987, and by Ivor Goodson and Andy Hargreaves, *Teachers' Professional Lives*, London, Falmer, 1996. Much of the most interesting recent work in the field has been concerned with the activities and experience of women teachers. Particularly valuable are Alison Oram, *Women Teachers and Feminist Politics, 1900–39*, Manchester, Manchester University Press, 1996, and Dina Copelman, *London's Women Teachers: Gender, Class and Feminism*, London, Routledge, 1996.

The voices of teachers can be heard more directly and extensively in Frank E. Huggett, *Teachers*, London, Weidenfeld and Nicolson, 1986 and Judith Bell, *Teachers Talk about Teaching*, Buckingham, Open University Press, 1995. An evocative memorial of the experience of elementary teaching at the start of the century is Philip Ballard, *Things I Cannot Forget*, London, University of London Press, 1937; and of the far more numerous recollections of teaching in the private sector, Ronald Gurner, *I Chose Teaching*, London, Dent, 1937. Locally published teacher memoirs are always rewarding; a good example is Norman Bridge, *My Liverpool Schools*, Portinscale, Kirkland Press, 1992.

The most significant starting points for policy history are undoubtedly the major official inquiries into the supply and training of teachers which have punctuated the twentieth century – the 1924 Report of the Departmental Committee, the 1944 McNair Report and the 1972 James Report, *Teacher Education and Training*. To these might be added the Board of Education's 1907 circular, *Memorandum on the History and*

Prospects of the Pupil-Teacher System, and two reports from 1939: the Joint Standing Committee of the Training College Association and Council of Principals, *Memorandum on the Training of Teachers*, London, University of London Press; and the NUT, *The Training of Teachers and Grants to Intending Teachers*.

Notes

1 Frank Roscoe, 'The teacher's inspiration', *The Teacher's World*, 1913, vol. x, no. 446, p. 1.
2 D. Wardle, *The Rise of the Schooled Society*, London, Routledge and Kegan Paul, 1974; D. Hamilton, *Learning about Education: An Unfinished Curriculum*, Milton Keynes, Open University Press, 1990, p. 69; P.W. Jackson, *Life in Classrooms*, New York, Holt Rinehart and Winston, Inc., 1968, p. 3.
3 H. Silver, *Education as History: Interpreting Nineteenth- and Twentieth-Century Education*, London, Methuen, 1983, p. 89; K. Rousmaniere, *City Teachers: Teaching and School Reform in Historical Perspective*, New York, Teachers College Press, 1997, pp. 5–7; G. Grace, *Teachers, Ideology and Control*, London, Routledge and Kegan Paul, 1978.
4 W. James, *The Teacher and His World*, London, Gollancz, 1962, p. 11.
5 Crown Copyright 2001, National Statistics.
6 DfEE, *Statistics of Education: Teachers, England and Wales*, London, The Stationery Office, 2000, p. 39.
7 Ibid., p. 49.
8 Ibid., pp. 106, 109.
9 PP 1924–25, xii, [Cmd.2409], *Report of the Departmental Committee on the Training of Teachers for Public Elementary Schools*, pp. 56, 77.
10 DfEE, op. cit., 2000, p. 73.
11 O. Newman and A. Foster, *The Value of a Pound: Prices and Incomes in Britain 1900–1993*, New York, Gale Research International Ltd, 1995, p. 269.
12 DfEE, *Teachers: Meeting the Challenge of Change*, London, The Stationery Office, 1999.
13 P. Clarke, *Hope and Glory: Britain 1900–1990*, London, Penguin, 1996, p. 8; PP 1902, lxxviii, [Cd.1139], *Statistics of Elementary Day Schools, Evening Continuation Schools and Training Colleges 1900–01*, p. 68; G.A.N. Lowndes, *The Silent Social Revolution: An Account of the Expansion of Public Education in England and Wales 1895–1965*, Oxford, Oxford University Press, 2nd edn, 1969, p. 32.
14 H.C. Dent, *The Training of Teachers in England and Wales 1800–1975*, London, Hodder and Stoughton, 1977, p. 51; Lowndes, op. cit., p. 17; A. Tropp, *The School Teachers: The Growth of the Teaching Profession in England and Wales from 1800 to the Present Day*, London, Heinemann, 1957, p. 114.
15 PP 1902, pp. 44–5.
16 Newman and Foster, op. cit., p. 4; Board of Education, *Teachers and Youth Leaders: Report of the Committee appointed by the President of the Board of Education to consider the Supply, Recruitment and Training of Teachers and Youth Leaders* (McNair), London, HMSO, 1944, p. 35.
17 McNair, op. cit., p. 23.
18 M. Harrison, *Teachers Made and Marred*, London, Pitman and Sons, 1943, p.10; Robert Roberts, *A Ragged Schooling: Growing Up in the Classic Slum*, Manchester, Manchester University Press, 1976.

19 A.M. Carr-Saunders, D. Caradog Jones and C.A. Moser, *A Survey of Social Conditions in England and Wales*, Oxford, Clarendon Press, 1958, pp. 121–5.

20 *The Schoolmaster*, 7 April 1900, vol. lvii, p. 645.

21 DES/HMI, *1839–1989: Public Education in England: 150th Anniversary*, London, HMSO, 1990.

22 Lowndes, op. cit., p. 11; G. Troman 'The rise of the new professionals? The restructuring of primary teachers' work and professionalism', *British Journal of Sociology of Education*, 1996, vol. 17, no. 4, pp. 473–87.

23 M. Galton, B. Simon and P. Croll, *Inside the Primary Classroom*, London, Routledge and Kegan Paul, 1980, pp. 155–65; M. Galton, 'An ORACLE Chronicle: a decade of classroom research', in S. Delamont (ed.) *The Primary School Teacher*, London, Falmer, 1987, pp. 21–44.

24 P. Gardner, 'Classroom teachers and educational change 1876–1996', *Journal of Education for Teaching*, 1998, vol. 24, no. 1, pp. 35–6.

25 F.H. Spencer, *An Inspector's Testament*, London, English Universities Press, 1938, pp. 159–60.

26 R. Lowe, *Education in the Post-War Years: A Social History*, London, Routledge, 1988; *Schooling and Social Change 1964–1990*, London, Routledge, 1997.

27 Gardner, op. cit., 1998, p. 39.

28 P. Cunningham, 'Teachers' professional image and the press, 1950–1990', *History of Education*, 1992, vol. 21, no. 1, pp. 37–56.

29 Holmes-Morant Circular, January 1910, reproduced in Tropp, op. cit., pp. 271–2; DfEE, *Excellence in Schools*, London, The Stationery Office, 1997, p. 46.

30 Jackson, op. cit., pp. 3–4.

31 Spencer, op. cit., pp. 86–99.

32 *The Schoolmaster*, 6 January 1900, vol. lvii, p. 26.

33 A. Pollard, P. Broadfoot, P. Croll, M. Osborn and D. Abbott, *Changing English Primary Schools? The Impact of the Education Reform Act at Key Stage One*, London, Cassell, 1994, pp. 15–16; S. Acker, *The Realities of Teachers' Work: Never a Dull Moment*, London, Cassell, 1999.

34 I. Grosvenor, M. Lawn and K. Rousmaniere, *Silences and Images*, New York, Peter Lang, 1999.

35 D. Lortie, *Schoolteacher*, Chicago, University of Chicago Press, 1975, p. 23.

36 Lortie, op. cit., p. 14; see also Jackson, op. cit., p. 5, who uses the term 'enclosure' to refer to organization by separate classrooms.

37 Jackson, op. cit., pp. vii, 6.

38 E. Blishen, *A Nest of Teachers*, London, Allison and Busby, 1978, pp. 8–9.

39 S.A. Sackmann, *Cultural Knowledge in Organizations*, Newbury Park, Sage, 1991, pp. 117–19.

40 E. Friedson, *Professionalism Reborn: Theory, Prophecy and Policy*, London, Polity, 1994.

41 M. Lawn, *Modern Times?: Work, Professionalism and Citizenship in Teaching*, London, Falmer, 1996.

42 Board of Education, *The Teaching of English in England*, London, HMSO, 1921, p. 57.

43 R. Brooks, *Contemporary Debates in Education: An Historical Perspective*, London, Longman, 1991, pp. 6, 63.

44 C. Chitty, 'The changing role of the state in educational provision', *History of Education*, 1992, vol. 21, no. 1, pp. 1–14; R. Aldrich, 'Educational legislation of the 1980s in England: an historical analysis', *History of Education*, 1992, vol. 21, no. 1, pp. 57–70; G. Welch and P. Mahony, 'The teaching profession',

in J. Docking (ed.) *New Labour's Policies for Schools: Raising the Standard*, London, David Fulton, 2000, pp. 139–57.
45 E. Partridge, *Usage and Abusage*, London, Hamish Hamilton, 1947.
46 Dent, op. cit., p. 13.
47 P. Gardner, *The Lost Elementary Schools of Victorian England*, London, Croom Helm, 1984, chapter 4.
48 PP 1924–25, p. 39.
49 McNair, op. cit., p. 29.
50 Ibid.
51 McNair, op. cit., pp. 30–1.
52 McNair, op. cit., p. 31.
53 Harrison, op. cit., p. 46.
54 Harrison, op. cit., p. 48.
55 Harrison, op. cit., p. 46.
56 McNair, op. cit., p. 29.
57 Harrison, op. cit., p. 8.
58 McNair, op. cit., p. 28.
59 Harrison, op. cit., p. 8.
60 Harrison, op. cit., p. 9.
61 McNair, op. cit., p. 25.
62 Board of Education, *Report of the Consultative Committee on the Education of the Adolescent*, London, HMSO, 1926, p.125.
63 McNair, op. cit., p. 25; Harrison, op. cit., pp. 24–5.
64 Harrison, op. cit., p. 13.
65 McNair, op. cit., pp. 25, 28, 26.
66 McNair, op. cit., p. 23.
67 Harrison, op. cit., p. 52.
68 McNair, op. cit., p. 29.
69 Harrison, op. cit., p. 10.
70 McNair, op. cit., p. 29.
71 McNair, op. cit., pp. 12–14.
72 McNair, op. cit., pp. 29, 28.
73 Harrison, op. cit., p. 13.
74 Ibid.
75 G.F. Riseborough and P. Poppleton, 'Veterans versus beginners: a study of teachers at a time of fundamental change in comprehensive schooling', *Educational Review*, 1991, vol. 43, no. 3, pp. 307–34.
76 W. Mach, 'All of these results at the touch of a button', *Teachers: the DfEE magazine for the teaching profession*, 1999, no. 2, p. 17.

Chapter 7

Pupils and students

Ruth Watts

To capture the diverse experiences of pupils and students over a century of enormous change in English education in one brief chapter is not easy. Since issues of equality of access and opportunity seem to this author to be the most significant factors in that diversity, this chapter will focus on these. Out of a range of inequalities, three outstanding ones – gender, ethnicity[1] and class, have been selected.[2] Even within these there are difficulties of over-generalization and stereotyping, so some telling examples and unique experiences have been chosen rather than any attempt to tell the 'whole story'. Those included as 'pupils' and 'students' will be those from the age of five onwards in formal education, including schools, further and higher education. The interrelationship of gender, 'race' and class will be shown to be crucial in our understanding of the changing history of education and highly significant for understanding of how a more just and equitable system could be achieved in the future.

The situation in 2000

Despite a hundred years of confronting inequalities in education, great diversity of experience remained at the end of the century. Two telling reports which appeared in 2000 were *Educational inequalities in mapping race, class and gender*, issued by Ofsted and a critique of this by the Commission for Racial Equality (CRE). Gurbux Singh, chair of the CRE, berated the contrast of the excellent start of black pupils in formal education with their low performance by 16, as 'a clear failure' of the education system.[3] Such a racial issue is international, as are those of inequalities between rich and poor, although 'class'[4] is more peculiar to England. That the question of elitism certainly, if not class, is still a divisive force in English education was seen in 1999 by the storm raised over Laura Spence and her non-admission to Magdalen College, Oxford. Arguments raged as to whether, given equal excellent A level results, students from state schools would be as likely to be accepted as those from private schools by presumed 'elite' higher education institutions.[5]

A different inequality also raised headlines. After a century of difficult, often acrimonious, struggle to obtain greater equality of opportunity for females in education, the fact that girls did better than boys at GCSE even in the so-called 'masculine' subjects of maths and science in 1997 sent shock-waves through the educational establishment. It was not the enormous progress in girls' academic achievements which made hearts race, however, but the under-achievement of boys. Furthermore the ensuing generalizations in the media about both boys and girls mostly overlooked the huge range of differences within each sex, differences attributable to class and other factors including ethnic identity. Yet, in reality, all these factors underpin many current educational controversies such as league tables, inspection, failing schools, the curriculum, social inclusion and student grants.

Perceptive participants and commentators have analysed how historical studies prove that ultimately good educational practice actually rests on good equal opportunities. All too often, however, pathological models can permeate perceptions of black people, females and the working classes.[6]

The situation in 1900

In 1900 'pathological models' commonly influenced the education of the vast majority of the population. From their seemingly secure cultural heights, nurtured in the public schools and Oxbridge, the men of the educational establishment looked down on the elementary system which state education comprised and sought to 'civilize' the masses. Although on the brink of transformation, state schooling nevertheless would remain dominated by the elite 'public' and independent school system. It had only recently become available, compulsory and free for all. The increasing numbers of elementary school children roused awareness not only of widespread depths of ignorance but also of equally prevalent physical under-development, a national 'deterioration' which was marked in the recruitment for the Boer War. Moves to aid the masses of malnourished and poverty-stricken children in the richest nation on earth and eugenicist ideas equally throve on such realizations.[7]

Superior attitudes were exemplified in those shown towards the significant minority of Irish–British children living in leading commercial and industrial areas. Despite the fact that they were by no means all unskilled or destitute and many gradually merged into the middle class, the Irish were problematized into an alien 'other' by the imperialist, racist ideology which fanned English nationalism. Fears of their social 'contamination' and 'lawlessness' were compounded by the allegiance of many of them to Roman Catholicism. This led in turn to Roman Catholics fighting for equality of opportunity in education, but against being absorbed into the board school system. This won them some religious and political allies among Anglicans and among Tories who abhorred the development of higher grade schools offering cheap 'secondary' education on the rates. Such schools, however, pleased those, mostly from the upper-working and lower-middle class and often Nonconformists or Labour supporters, desirous of greater educational opportunities for all.[8] Demands in education were virulently debated, therefore, in a cross-fire of conflicting racial, class, religious and political attitudes which sometimes united in strange alliances.

Gender differentiation was inherent throughout education, although generally subsumed under the ubiquitous 'he' of pupils and students. Amongst the middle classes, girls were increasingly attending the new high schools such as those of the Girls' Public Day School Trust (GPDST). Some of these offered liberal opportunities, but the resources and numbers of such schools still lagged far behind those of boys even though boys, too, lacked sufficient secondary schools. The steep ladder whereby scholarships enabled pupils to climb beyond elementary education was longer for girls, caught as they were in the traps of femininity and the glorification of motherhood. Yet for anyone from the working classes, schooling was liable to be brief, narrow in compass and more likely to control than enlarge the spirit.[9] This was even more likely if the child came from stock that was not 'pure' English.

Changes and continuities

Gender

On the surface the twentieth century dawned as a brave new world for girls. Not only were women now allowed to study at Oxford and Cambridge but they could also receive degrees at London and the new civic universities. High schools for girls were much increased when the 1902 Education Act placed local secondary education on the rates. Elementary education for all had at last enabled nearly full literacy for both girls and boys.[10]

The reality, however, was somewhat different. In education, as elsewhere, apparent growing equality between male and female masked differentiation of treatment and opportunity. In higher education, for example, Oxford withheld degrees from its women students until 1919 and Cambridge until 1948. Most women undergraduates actually attended London and the civic universities, but even here female students were just 25.6 per cent in 1920–1, rising to 29 per cent in 1934–5.[11] This was, nevertheless, a substantial growth and owed much to women wanting degrees prior to secondary teaching. This growth was class-based, female students, like most males, coming mostly from the middle and lower-middle classes, even among intending teachers. Women medical students, however, were more likely to be from affluent families since the course was longer and more expensive.[12]

Furthermore, female students only gradually integrated into the full life of the university, despite assertions to the contrary.[13] Supervised residence, countless rules and regulations sprang up to defend both the virtue of females and the spaces of male students. As Carol Dyhouse has pointed out, this worsened after the First World War with much reassertion of masculinity in the universities and sexual segregation in many university activities such as sport and debating societies. Women did gain near equality or even domination of numbers in arts courses in many instances, but this had to be counter-balanced by both their marginalization in scientific subjects and the perception of arts subjects as feminine.[14]

These issues were reflected in every level of education. Everywhere the fact that girls and women were being educated led to differentiation from the norm perceived as male – a fact often only revealed when educational reports and policies were seen in the context of people's lives. It was very obvious, however, in 'practical' education where girls did domestic subjects and boys the higher status manual instruction of carpentry and wood-work. The growing emphasis on domestic subjects for girls, fuelled by psychological, imperial, Social Darwinistic, eugenicist and political concerns in a rapidly changing world, meant that girls spent more time on their practical subjects even to the extent of domestic science replacing science and then maths for some.[15]

Domestic science, indeed, can be seen as a focal point for gendered education because so much ideology concerning 'womanliness', 'mother-hood' and the 'natural' role of females was invested in it. It also became a class issue since, on the whole, generally such teaching was advocated for girls in elementary schools or, at most, those in the bottom streams of secondary schools. Girls might actually find such lessons useless compared to what they learnt at home, but such a conception would not accord with official pejorative views of the working-class mother nor with those who saw teaching domestic subjects as opportunities for an expanded profes-sional role for women.[16] This domestic emphasis pervaded those few opportunities open for girls and women in technical and trade classes and evening schools in the early twentieth century. Women's skills were enhanced but within a very narrow range which would keep them largely within low-paid, low-status employment. As the National Union of Women Teachers cogently argued in 1939, women in such classes were thus denied the cultural capital or employment opportunities that they could earn at the more prestigious girls' independent and grammar schools.[17]

Yet even in the secondary schools there were tensions between the highly academic curriculum and snobbish attitudes against clerical and secretarial jobs and teacher training colleges on the one hand and the realities of middle-class girls' employment and family finance on the other.[18] Divided aims met girls' education at every turn, even where academic learning was gradually prized more for them. For example, the growth of public examinations, despite their flaws, usually helped girls since they were able to prove their intellectual ability. At the same time examinations could be biased against them as the introduction of the School Certificate at 16 plus in 1917 demonstrated. Subjects which were compulsory for or much taken by girls – domestic subjects, music and art respectively – did not count for an overall pass. Even when, in 1938 after a long struggle, the regulations were modified, these subjects did not win parity. The women teachers who had fought for this significantly wanted these to become status subjects for boys too, but such 'feminization' of the curriculum was not to be.[19]

The opportunities to share in any education after 12 (14 from 1918) depended greatly on parental income, aspirations and beliefs. Daisy Cowper remembered that in Liverpool at the turn of the century there were only about six scholarships for girls to the High School and just two more for boys. She pursued advanced elementary education through the pupil–teacher route, eventually borrowing the fees to reside and train at Edge Hill Training College. Kathleen Betterton, in London some 20 years later, won a rare scholarship to a public boarding school where, despite the rigid, irrational rules and forbidding atmosphere, she was given the where-withal to win a scholarship to Oxford. Vera Brittain, from a much higher social class, had to struggle against family prejudice to do the same, then only, like many men, to have her dreams and studies disrupted by the First World War.[20] It was possible for a girl to achieve high honours as Hilda Lloyd (later Rose, née Shufflebotham) in Birmingham exemplified. She was lucky enough to have parents who could afford and were willing for her to go to both the prestigious King Edward VI High School for Girls, unusual in its promotion of science education for girls, and the new University of Birmingham, all of whose courses were open to women and men alike. Hilda, a medical student from 1910 to 1916, was one of the first women to become a Fellow of the Royal College of Surgeons and the first woman professor of the University Medical School. Few girls, however, even if they had equal talent, had all Dame Hilda's chances and, even in her case, she has been almost written out of the University's history.[21]

Technological, economic, social and political changes in the 1930s to 1950s, which lessened both family size and household drudgery and widened employment opportunities and women's public role, dramatically altered life opportunities for women especially if they had appropriate educational qualifications. The reality was somewhat different, however, as society struggled psychologically to cope with the challenge to deeply held gendered perspectives. A widespread post-war longing to restore traditional family life was exacerbated by the influential writings of D.W.

Winnicott and John Bowlby on the absolute importance of mothers being with young children.[22]

The ambiguities of providing full educational opportunities to those deemed by many in power in education to be destined for a life of home-making always underwrote the realities of educational experience. The growing reliance on the work of psychologists led to the development of intelligence testing, which supposedly put all children on an equal footing. When, however, girls demonstrated their equal if not better ability than boys in the eleven-plus examinations usual for selection to the post-1944, nation-wide structure of free secondary schools, adjustments were made to ensure that boys were not disadvantaged in gaining grammar school places. Such practices lasted in many LEAs until the 1970s and even beyond. Since in many areas the single sex grammar schools had more places for boys anyway, it was in fact the girls who were disadvantaged. But, despite the fact that leading psychologists could find little innate mental differences between boys and girls, there was rarely any discussion that these practices might be unfair. 'Common-sense' attitudes decreed that girls simply matured earlier while educational and political reformers were exercised by the social, not the gender, iniquities of selection.[23]

This was important as for the majority of the population who did not attend private schooling, the quality and length of their education was decided by whether they passed the eleven-plus, albeit this was also affected by their own internalization of contemporary attitudes, their family background and where they lived. The overwhelming significance of this has been graphically conveyed by many. Ruth Kirkley's parents, for example, only just managed to pay the fees when she passed for the grammar school in the early 1940s, but at least passing separated her from the 75 per cent of her age group she had already been taught to think of as failures.[24] Mary Evans remembered vividly it was the major event in a child's life, marking the difference between those who wore expensive uniform and took publicly recognized exams and qualifications and those who would end up with virtually no qualifications at all. Nevertheless, believing that the education was weighted towards the middle class, racist, sexist, unchallenging intellectually and highly competitive, she concluded that many grammar school pupils were neither happy nor well educated. From the late 1950s, significant social changes challenged selective, elitist institutions, but Evans doubted that the old values were ever seriously undermined.[25]

Not all grammar schools were exclusively middle-class even if their ethos was, although, as Jackson and Marsden showed, working-class girls were even less likely than working-class boys to go from grammar school to university, especially a prestigious one. Nearly half of the girls they researched went to training college, however.[26] The needs of many working-class girls, indeed, were most sharply differentiated from those of boys. Girls received limited technical education, while in educational debate they were either ignored or, despite some acknowledgement of change, placed largely in a domestic, 'feminine' setting as a series of influential reports, Norwood in 1943, Crowther in 1959 and Newsom in 1963, stressed. Although, as Newsom's earlier criticism indicated, public policy and institutional practice had not always cohered, his conviction that 'females are uniquely fitted for a single social role' underlay official policy for secondary modern schooling for girls. [27]

It is not suggested here that women necessarily resisted the domestic role thrust upon them. Nevertheless, education, plus a changing economic and social situation in the 1950s and 1960s, increasingly made other roles possible, as Stephanie Spencer's analysis of the genre of the girls' career novel in the 1950s illustrates.[28] Changes in educational structure, however, did not necessarily overcome gendered attitudes in education.[29] Sue Sharpe's exploration of working-class girls' education in Ealing in the early 1970s showed that in comprehensive and secondary modern mixed schools alike, the girls largely accepted that they were destined for low status, boring jobs with marriage and children as the only likely relief. Thus they saw little relevance in school subjects. Learning to be 'feminine' socialized many girls into not competing with boys and distrusting intellectual ability, distrust reinforced by the lower expectations that schools might have of all working-class children. Gendered curriculum assumptions limited girls' later chances further as the more skilled, better-paid jobs went with 'boys' learning'. Furthermore, it was accepted that boys could and did succeed in the 'girls' subjects' in arts, but not that girls could in maths and science even when examination results proved the contrary. Many of these factors affected middle-class girls, too, but the possibility of greater parental support and guidance, the greater likelihood of being in selected schools or top streams, helped give the psychological confidence to succeed academically, stay in education longer and try a larger range of career options.[30]

Such findings were backed up by much research undertaken by feminist educationists and historians in and on the 1970s and 1980s. The Equal Pay Acts of 1970 and 1975 and the Sexual Discrimination Act of 1975 made the dream of gender equality seem nearer, but feminists increasingly wanted more than just approximating to a male 'norm'. They challenged alike traditional assumptions of male ownership of cultural capital and access to 'legitimate' knowledge and high status academic qualifications and the arbitrary assignment of gender to social characteristics and roles. They revealed the lack of a real freedom of choice in education and career for many youngsters and exposed school structures, pedagogy and teacher attitudes to a critique which uncovered ideas and practices inimical to the full development of potential, not only of girls but often of boys, too, and those disadvantaged by social or ethnic origin.[31]

These conclusions were verified by studies in the late 1970s and 1980s investigating how gender stereotypes affect curricula, teacher behaviour and the moral and social context of schools.[32] Equal opportunities provision led to a range of projects concerning anti-sexist and anti-racist curricula, pedagogy, and classroom practice, many of which were supported by the Equal Opportunities Commission (EOC) and some LEAs, notably the Inner London Education Authority (ILEA). They roused bitter political opposition and tabloid hysteria, as some highly involved participants have recalled. Nevertheless, pioneering ideas and projects, for example Girls into Science and Technology (GIST), not only raised the consciousness of many pupils and teachers in schools but taught many lessons about how to manage change for the future. Curricular initiatives of the 1980s and 1990s, however, proved to be more positive influences in promoting educational equality than changes in administration and organization.[33]

The debate over GCSE was an interesting example here. It has been seen as *the* positive reform for girls, allowing them to do new subjects and all the sciences and having a national comparison of standards by gender. Yet more boys still take the elite single science than the balanced science associated with state schools, while in those subjects which are tiered, teachers tend to enter girls more for the safe 'C' than the top levels which will secure them a brighter educational path. Coursework, to which female success at GCSE has widely been attributed, has been cut back and child-centred pedagogy, another assumed equalizer, attacked. In contrast, the greater likelihood of males to take subjects which led to higher paid jobs and to rise to the top in business and professional life (including education), is not taken to compensate for their lesser overall success at school. Similarly in vocational examinations and the various training schemes established in the 1970s and 1980s, not only were subjects still highly gendered, but also the more prestigious types which lead to skills and jobs of economic significance to the country were mostly taken by men. The National Curriculum gave equal entitlement to all pupils (within the state sector) to all subjects, but successive revisions have whittled this entitlement away, although chances have been given and taken for girls and boys to do subjects previously barely open to them.[34]

Research has revealed the complex patterns of identity which make it impossible to talk of gender without including class and/or ethnicity. Within the GCSE results, for example, the better results of girls against boys overall have masked the wide differences within both sexes. In 1995, for instance, although white middle-class girls did largely achieve superb results, they were bettered by Chinese girls in Berkshire. African, Caribbean and Asian girls did do better than their male counterparts but not in the professional and intermediate social classes. In August 2000, for the first time in England and Wales, girls achieved more A grades than their male counterparts but at both GCSE and GCE A levels the gender gap is very close and hardly compares with differences of class, the most significant factor for all candidates.[35] As Pete Maldeshap noted, 'A boy at a leafy private school is still likely to do far better than a girl in an inner-city comprehensive.'[36]

Despite such knowledge of the complexity of examination achievement, widespread anxiety was generated that *all* girls were doing better than *all* boys. That females are now attaining more in many areas of education is clear: for example, they now are present in equal numbers in further and higher education, albeit still overwhelmingly in courses deemed to be suitable for females.[37] Indeed, it could be said that female success, with all its qualifications, is the outstanding feat of twentieth-century education in England. Yet such a potentially revolutionary improvement is explained away, for instance attributed to girls' hard work not excellence, or seen as a problem.[38] Concern for boys' underachievement has rightly led to a plethora of projects but these are mainly to help boys only, despite the many problems still faced by working-class girls. Indeed, earlier initiatives on equal opportunities which were so hardly and briefly won and so berated by the media, are now being applied without difficulty in the case of boys.[39]

Furthermore, the differences between those from the more privileged educational establishments – the public, independent and selective schools, comprehensives in the leafier suburbs – and those from the more deprived areas, is not always spelt out. Worries about the predominance of boys in special educational needs units, or truanting or depressed, have led to crude psychological and sociological explanations. These tend to blame the female influence at home and school, to problematize working-class and some ethnic minority families, especially Afro-Caribbean, and to reinforce didactic, structured pedagogy at the expense of affective, reflective, language-rich teaching. Other solutions call for male role models in home and school, though rarely questioning which are really needed, and for more 'macho' literature in the classroom, with little regard for the harm already done by sexist and racist literature.[40] Furthermore, such nostrums do not always listen to the multiple voices there are among male pupils and students as there are among female. 'Billy Elliot' often still cannot find a voice. Some research which has listened to under-achieving boys suggests they are all too aware of the peer pressure culture which restrains them. They want positive images, challenging, sensitive teaching and respect for their differing situations, to help them forward.[41]

Images and role models of masculinity vary across the differing sections of society although this has not always been apparent in educational literature. One study which has demonstrated different views of masculinity according to social group and historical period, is Christine Heward's account of an independent Woodard boys' school from 1929 to 1950.

Here boys had to fit into a finely graded hierarchy, partly determined by their age and social class. Monastic toughening in a feminine-free space was supposed to train character and mind for future achievement. Such success was often at a personal price, especially for those in the C stream. Parents, however, obviously realizing that 'men were made not born', approved the social class and gender reproduction of such schools so much that when social class distinctions seemed under threat when grammar schools' fees were abolished in 1944, they turned to the independent schools in increasing numbers.[42]

Mairtin Mac an Ghaill similarly explored schooling as a masculinizing agency. His critical examination of how dominant definitions of masculinity become affirmed in school showed how this disadvantages both those males (including, but not only gays) who do not fit and all females. On the other hand he found that working-class and ethnic peer groups gave confidence even to those who 'failed' academically, although 'macho' lads formed only one such set. These groups cohered largely according to their aspirations and their varying positions in different sections of the working and new middle class and somewhat looser racial groups. Their self-awareness was counter-balanced by that of the girls who resented sexual harassment, ritual and privilege and yet admired those boys who challenged authority.[43] Other ethnographic research in the 1980s and 1990s in England revealed that girls do resist gendered practices towards them as they do class and ethnocentric attitudes, but their patterns of resistance, such as their games in the playground and 'silence' in the classroom, only reinforce the stereotypical attitudes shown towards them by teachers (and boys).[44]

Ethnicity

Class and gender therefore impact on those already differentiated by racial identity, but the latter is a factor affecting all pupils and students. The white majority is itself multi-ethnic, for Britain has always been a multiracial country, although this has not necessarily eased the immigration of successive groups of immigrants in the last 150 years, fleeing poverty and persecution in Europe and beyond. The way the Irish were problematized as an alien threat to English order and decency has been reiterated from the late 1940s for the increasing numbers of black immigrants from the dwindling empire and growing commonwealth. The latter, however, are even more easily stigmatized because of their colour.

Ian Grosvenor has ably demonstrated the widespread uncritical use of 'race' categories, despite the long proven exposition of 'race' as a social construct not a biological phenomenon. His researches show that an 'enduring commitment to assimilation' survived both the important shift to multi-culturalism in the 1970s and the greater cultural pluralism of many local education authorities after the Swann Report of 1985. Black families and culture were seen as inherently different and implicitly inferior to the dominant 'white', 'British' culture, always assumed to be a coherent whole. Even when the Interim Rampton Report of 1981 recognized that racist 'negative and patronizing attitudes' by teachers affected West Indian children badly, this made little impact. Indeed, right-wing politicians, rampaging against the 'subversion' of those in education who attacked British history and culture as racist, won favour with Margaret Thatcher's government. The right-wing media's systematic undermining of what they termed 'loony left' egalitarian policies, although later proved to have been mostly completely distorted, played into the hands of the 'think-tanks' who became so influential around 1990. The Education Reform Act of 1988, in trying to unify national culture could be seen as 'profoundly assimilationist', as was the 'Section 11' funding which had a mercurial fortune in the 1990s. Added to this were the market values of Thatcherism whereby equal opportunity policies were marginalized by parental choice, competition between schools and the decline of local government. It was not a time to challenge successfully institutional racism and power structures in English society. The Ofsted Report of 1996 showed that the gap between ethnic groups in education was actually widening, but 'Whiteness' as a racist problem still has to become part of widespread educational thinking despite the MacPherson Report of 1999 on the murder of the black teenager, Stephen Lawrence.[45]

Throughout the varying shifts of policy on racial concerns, pupils and students within the ethnic minorities have been affected equally by neglect and by misleading assumptions. One myth, for example, that young Afro-Caribbean women are more positively motivated than their brothers because theirs is a female-centred society, has been deconstructed by Heidi Mirza. She found, in very disadvantaged areas of south London, a historical situation of relative autonomy between the sexes. The differential achievement between males and females she attributed more to the racially and sexually segregated labour market.[46] Another prevailing attitude of white educationists has been that some groups of children fail because of a poor self-concept which in turn is often blamed on assumed poor parenting. Such beliefs have often ignored alike the poverty and insufficient resources of these communities and the positive resistance to patronizing attitudes from those who may not fit into school values but who build up their own instead. Maureen Stone's research on West Indian communities in 'depressed inner city areas of multiple deprivation', in London in the late 1970s, for example, depicted a range of Saturday schools, some officially funded, others painstakingly established by community groups themselves. Testifying to a longing for achievement in basic skills and a wish to know black history and culture, some of these schools had to turn children away.[47] Such projects were paralleled by those in Birmingham for instance, set up by West Indians, the Sikh community, Indians and others from the 1950s onwards. Their constructive efforts had some gradual success in the 1970s and 1980s in winning some teaching of Asian languages, employment of black teachers and funding for some of the desired multicultural and anti-racist developments. Above all they forced these issues into mainstream education, but they were contested all the way especially by the New Right agenda of the 1980s and 1990s.[48]

Such projects testify to the significant contribution of black communities themselves in education, but community initiatives in education, however dynamic, have rarely been sufficient to iron out the inequalities that beset English society and impact negatively on the disadvantaged. The black and Asian community groups who challenged racism in education from the 1960s were motivated partly by reactions against the high proportion of black children, especially Afro-Caribbean ones, who were put in schools for the educationally sub-normal. By 1998 it appeared that black children were likely to be excluded altogether from school up to six, or, in some areas, even 15 times as much as white children. This was at a time when the overall numbers of excluded children had risen to over 12,000. A market-driven educational system allowing the ghettoization of some schools and the undesirability of those children presumed likely to lower a school's ratings in the league tables, coupled with racist bullying, have further created black underachievement.[49]

That Afro-Caribbean pupils, especially boys, have underachieved over the years partly because of negative expectations from white teachers, has been well documented. The evidence given to the Swann Committee from university students of Caribbean and African origin made depressing reading. Even those who had 'made it' knew well the likelihood of low streaming, limited curriculum choices, a lack of correlation between cultures and poor teacher expectations and attitudes.[50] Eighteen-year-old Aaron Dixon explained why Britain's schools fail many black children, saying 'All my schools felt like white places where there happened to be black kids who had to fit in'.[51] This can feel so even in predominantly black schools if pupils think the curriculum seems irrelevant or denies or underrates black achievements. Students spoke bitterly to the Swann Committee about the 'whitening' of history and a suppression of dialect or patois, a resentment echoed by the 'Black Sisters' of Mac an Ghaill's studies. These aspects have been exacerbated since the advent of a National Curriculum which in its first years at least, was intended to stress 'English' history, language, and 'culture'.[52]

Similarly, language differences have been seen far more as language 'deficiency' than a chance to develop and capitalize on bilingualism. Initiatives from the 1960s to the mid-1970s, notably the Bullock Report of 1975, gradually tried to integrate second language pupils into normal classroom life. The desire of ethnic minority communities to have the fore-most languages of the South Asian communities in the curriculum was backed by the Swann Committee, but not by Kenneth Baker.[53] On the other hand, there are now increasing numbers of curriculum materials that recognize the diversity of experience and achievements which have made up British and other cultures. Similarly, the greater celebration of the black contribution to music, the arts, media and sport can help the development of Britain as a multi-ethnic society provided stereotypical notions of cultures do not prevail or black pupils and students are only channelled into those areas.[54]

Despite much stereotyping, not all ethnic minority pupils experience it in the same way. There is evidence that Asian pupils, despite encountering similar racist obstacles, have greater chances of achieving than Afro-Caribbeans because of white teachers' assumptions that they are well-disciplined, hard-working, highly motivated and have 'a valid civiliza-tion'.[55] Both the Swann Report of 1985 and the Ofsted report of 2000 illustrate differences in achievement between these two groups in 16-plus examinations. The reality, however, is even more subtle. ILEA data of 1985, for example, showed that in London Bangladeshi children had lower results than Caribbean while Turkish pupils had lower still. Indian and African-Asian youngsters, on the other hand, did markedly better than all other pupils. Such statistics are averages and differ further if class and gender are taken into account while there are always further variations according to region and area. Nevertheless, by 1999, taking figures from the two-thirds of local authorities who monitored ethnic minority pupils' achievement, nationally Indians were achieving better results than whites but Pakistani and Bangladeshi pupils, like the African-Caribbeans, were further behind than ten years previously. Equally worrying was the fact that in one large urban authority, African-Caribbean pupils began well ahead in tests on average at five but were well behind at 16.[56]

Class

The frustration and alienation which many black pupils and students have felt in education has been compounded by the fact that many, but not all of them, are working class. The huge gulf in the 1900s between the privi-leged Etonian and the elementary school child, perhaps from a poverty-stricken industrial area, has resonance throughout the changing structures of schooling in the twentieth century. Memoirs of life at preparatory, public or independent school are not always idyllic tales of comfortable privilege or stimulating intellectual activity. Nor are they free of gendered or racial inequalities even when they are open to both sexes and all who can pay. Nevertheless, attendance at such schools does bring valuable social and cultural capital. Pupils in them are more likely to succeed in both their education and career than others are, although, admittedly, they usually begin with economic and social advantages. Able to adapt sufficiently to overcome periodic bouts of severe public criticism of them, independent schools were helped financially to survive by the assisted places scheme in the 1980s and early 1990s, whereby pupils from state schools could win scholarships to some.[57]

At the beginning of the century the carrot for elementary pupils was to win a scholarship to a state secondary school. The huge expansion in these by 1930, however, was more open to boys than girls and places were sometimes declined because of the cost of the uniform or the cost to the family of the loss of children's earnings. Nor was the growth of central schools after 1911 and junior technical schools after 1913, sufficient to enable the average child (or any child in some areas) to receive more than an elementary education. Real mobility through education was so rare that when Lionel Elvin, for example, eventually won a scholarship to Cambridge, his old village elementary school at Buckhurst Hill had a half-day's holiday.[58]

There was, however, a huge increase in the physical care of children led by those such as Margaret McMillan in Bradford and London who emphasized that education is impossible unless pupils are healthy in the first place. The development of a schools meals system, of the schools medical department, child guidance clinics and better physical training in schools, all helped in different ways to foster healthy, well-balanced children. Increasingly, too, provision was made for the handicapped and mentally retarded.[59] Nevertheless, undernourishment and poor living conditions long impacted on many pupils at school.

In the inter-war years, campaigns to win secondary education for all asked that all pupils should receive an education according to their needs. The increasing influence of intelligence testing appeared to promise that this could be done 'scientifically' through selecting pupils by ability. In reality it led to a system of classifying pupils which conveniently largely fitted the limited availability of secondary schools, eugenicist ideas of hereditary ability and the class nature of English education. Its effect was streaming within the elementary system and selection, which allowed a few of the brightest of the working class to gain a grammar school education. Acceptance of the predictive power of 'intelligence' tests fed into the Education Act of 1944 and the subsequent tripartite system, although some distinguished psychologists had long argued that environmental factors largely determined intelligence at any given time. Selection and streaming, indeed, survived the gradual implementation of comprehensive schooling from the 1960s and have returned in various guises since.[60]

Such practices have also furthered gender and ethnic inequalities. Common assumptions of the inferior intelligence of West Indian children have themselves probably partly caused their disproportionate presence in the lower streams of secondary schools.[61] The Swann Committee investigating this, subsequently argued forcefully that most of the differences between West Indian and 'indigenous' children seemed to be related to differences in such things as 'parental occupation, income, size of family, degree of overcrowding, and neighbourhood', in other words – class. The Committee noted, indeed, that such factors were related to differences in IQ among whites and accounted for the much better achievement levels of some Asians.[62] Psychologists researching ethnicity and intelligence have demonstrated the pitfalls of using seemingly objective models of evaluation which often only prove the cultural assumptions of the evaluator. Their insights can easily be transposed to class and gender.[63]

In the early 1960s Brian Jackson and Dennis Marsden's in-depth study of 88 working-class children in a northern industrial city who had been selected for grammar school and stayed on into the sixth form, corroborated other research that selection in schools was social as well as academic. They discovered, too, that twice as many middle-class youngsters obtained A levels as working-class and the latter tended to make subject choices which limited their future options at 18. This was exacerbated by the bewilderment of working-class parents and students alike about the educational system. Students often had troubles over the way they spoke and 15 per cent became very anti-school, preferring their local links and culture. Those who conformed often had to learn to live in two different worlds of home and school. Sixteen girls and 38 boys went to university, nine of the latter going to Oxbridge. But nearly a third got very low degrees or failed. On the other hand four of the five who went on to do Ph.D.s had been to the less prestigious grammar schools and the fifth had been in the bottom class of the most prestigious. Interestingly, amongst those who had left grammar school early, the ones who had attended two co-educational primary schools had been happy there but confused and demoralized by the fast pace of the grammar school, its testing and streaming. Placed in B or C streams, most had never recovered from the first setbacks.[64]

This dichotomy between seeming success at 11 and failure to fit into an unresponsive atmosphere meant that entrance to grammar school was not necessarily a golden path for working-class children. But then neither certainly was that to secondary modern school. Kathleen Gibbard, visiting a variety of state primary and secondary modern schools in the early 1960s, ended with an overriding impression of people working against fearful odds. Admittedly somewhat patronizing, nevertheless she deplored so many overcrowded, badly designed schools in bleak areas, with too few teachers or ancillary staff. At the same time she gave many examples of what respect for the pupils, care and imaginative teaching could do to motivate those deprived of many material advantages.[65]

The difficulties of the bright working-class child have been wonderfully expressed by Andrea Ashworth. At her inner-city comprehensive school she had to learn how to escape bullying and racism; the cultured middle-class world seemed an alien one she could not enter nor read its books until she learnt to hide them at home. Eventually, her entrance to Hertford College, Oxford proved that educational mobility was possible for the bright and determined in the 1980s although much might have to be endured to overcome social disadvantage.[66] Gillian Plummer has similarly shown the social isolation working-class pupils could experience in the 1950s to 1970s if they were selected either for a higher school or stream from others in their neighbourhood. At the same time the knowledge and skills they had picked up from their homes were ignored or silenced at school. The women she interviewed were all in grammar streams yet none was encouraged to go to university and only two took A levels. Plummer, in common with others examining various educational reforms and reports throughout the century, believes that education for the working class is about socialization as much as anything else.[67]

On the other hand, the Plowden Report exemplified a commitment to raising standards in education for all, although its proposed educational priority areas were not seriously taken up by government and its emphasis on child-centred, active learning became associated with political struggles in education.[68] There have been some famous attempts at pupil-centred schools such as A.S. Neill's at Summerhill, but largely these have been in small private schools deliberately chosen by supportive parents.[69]

Nevertheless, opportunities for all pupils have grown since 1944. The advent of comprehensive schooling particularly has seen an increasing number of pupils succeeding in national exams at 16, staying on at school until 18 and going on to further or higher education. The vast majority of 16-year-old school leavers who continue in education actually enter further education, although the fight for parity of esteem between vocational and academic qualifications has still to be resolved. Here they are offered a range of technical, vocational and academic subjects which have changed much in the last few decades to suit changing economic, industrial and business demands. Further education now takes as many women as men and increasing numbers of ethnic minorities, thus fulfilling many needs.[70] At the same time, by 1968, a 'considerably higher proportion' of students from manual working-class homes went on to universities from comprehensives than from other types of school. Since then, although it can be argued that true comprehensive education has not yet existed for the most part in England, it can also be acknowledged that educational standards are now no longer just about 'top people' but about all pupils and students in school and college. Most pupils had the chance by 1994 to experience a common curriculum and assessment system with their peers, despite distortions from a system beset by divisions old and new.[71]

That the abolition of selection at 11 could benefit children of all classes was shown in Solihull in the 1980s when it was the middle-class parents who vociferously opposed its reintroduction. At the same time the LEA's attempt to demonstrate that schools in the poorer part of the borough were failing their pupils backfired. Comparisons of expected performance at 16 with National Foundation for Educational Research (NFER) scores at 11 showed that the schools were succeeding against the odds and could, according to one local headteacher, have achieved more with smaller classes and greater resources.[72] In the late 1990s such remarks have been borne out by other case studies in the Midlands.[73]

Such successes have hardly prevented continuing debates about what different pupils need to gain full educational chances both within and without the state sector. For example Nick Davies' searing analysis of life and pupils in three 'failing' secondary schools in Sheffield in 1999, argued that all educational debate must include an analysis of the 'corrosive impact' of soaring child poverty. He was attacked by some for having 'lower expectations on the basis of class', but supported by other reports mapping the effects of social and economic deprivation on education in various regions, not excluding rural or otherwise wealthy areas.[74]

Negative perceptions about standards of education and behaviour in secular state schools have made religious schools increasingly popular with some parents. The general academic success of Anglican and Catholic schools has led the present government to back an expansion of such schools. At the same time there is a small but significant growth of Jewish, Muslim and Sikh schools which allow pupils to study their families' cultural traditions within an ethical atmosphere approved by their parents. Arguments about ghettoization or, conversely, middle-class privilege, have to counter the undoubted popularity of these schools with many.[75] Other initiatives include that of Peter Lampl who provides financial assistance to enable bright children from poor homes and underprivileged backgrounds to attend independent schools.[76]

How far the social privilege of schools such as Eton, Roedean and Winchester accounts for their academic performance, of course is another matter. Interestingly, an examination of A level results and fees in 2000, proved that money does not necessarily buy the highest academic results.[77] Assuredly, however, parents pay for social kudos and other cultural advantages which will matter as much if not more. In the late 1990s, the apparent continuing bias of universities towards students from private schools and away from those from lower social classes stimulated a range of initiatives to raise the educational ambitions of both young children and post-16 students from inner urban boroughs. Those of lower income appear to be welcomed most by the new universities formed from former polytechnics, as are an increasing number of students from ethnic minority groups, although this varies enormously according to locality.[78]

Statistics in 2000 encapsulate the trends of the preceding century. In 1900 only 1.2 per cent of 19-year-olds in Great Britain were in higher education, including teacher training. The slow increase by the late 1930s, followed by the rapid post-war increase and huge expansion after the Robbins Report of 1963 meant there were some one million students in higher education by 1998. Widening participation was helped enormously when the Open University opened in 1971. This has offered a gateway to higher education to many who missed out at school, left early and/or changed direction in later life. Entering university by vocational routes has helped others and since 1978 disadvantaged groups have also benefited by access courses. By 2000, therefore, access to university is no longer denied on account of gender and is far less so than formerly for mature students or most ethnic minorities, although Asian women lag behind Asian males. But class remained a huge factor throughout the century and impinges upon all these groups. In 1997 the Higher Education Funding Council for England (HEFCE) showed the differences with regard to university entrance between the well off, those from suburbia and those on low income, with 75, 35 and 7 per cent entrants respectively. Furthermore, this last group are less likely to enter high status jobs than their better-off peers on graduation.[79]

Such class distinctions might become worse since the gradual abolition of mandatory grants for undergraduates in the 1990s and the prospect for many students of ending their degrees about £10,000 in debt. This is a strong deterrent for those already disadvantaged materially while the government option of bursaries to help the poorest has yet to be proved.[80] At Ruskin College, Oxford, for example the number of students in debt has increased from about 33 per cent in the early 1980s to 92 per cent in 1998. This has had a major impact on women, lone parents, mature, black and lower income students, the backbone of the Ruskin constituency.[81]

Ruskin itself is a prime example of those institutions which have sought to give higher education to those excluded from usual routes. A vigorous yet 'contested place', its students have notably been involved, not only in the general student unrest of 1968, but also in many civil rights movements and the first Women's Liberation Movement conference in 1970. Yet there has been ambivalence over questions of equality while financial problems and uncertainty have continuously beset the college.[82] Its history reflects the paradoxical vibrancy and difficulties of all those fighting on the margins of education.

Conclusion

An examination of the experiences of pupils and students in twentieth-century English education reveals a complex range of difference in which gender, ethnicity and class have played a significant role. The interrelationships of these three factors cause further wide variations of experience within each one. Generally speaking, for example, the gap between females and males has been greatly narrowed over the century despite some prevailing inequities in curriculum and attitudes. Even so, the chances for success of an upper-class white girl are likely to be far higher than those of a black girl from the working class. Variations on this theme could be played for boys, for those from different ethnic communities or social classes or any cross-relationship of these. Further inequalities such as physical disability and refugee status could be added to the list. All these can disable pupils and students from both participating fully in the evolving system of English education or reaching their full potential. There have been changes that have helped dismantle some inequalities and the chance of receiving a positive, lively education or not will always vary according to school and teacher. In the end, too, schooling reflects the society of which it is a part. Nevertheless, gaps remain and have even widened in some cases, particularly for some ethnic groups and the poorest in society. Endless educational initiatives flow from a government ostensibly determined to raise educational standards for all and thereby increase national prosperity,[83] yet a system that rewards some while shaming others can prevent the needs and potential of all students being catered for and thus diminish truly high standards. To avoid accusations of English education still being underpinned by sexist, racist and class prejudices it is crucial that the sensitivities and aspirations of all pupils and students are attended to, especially when they are learning side by side. Historians of education have much to contribute to this cause.

Key reading

Official primary sources include: *15 to 18*, Report of the Central Advisory Committee for Education (Crowther), London, HMSO, 1959; *Half Our Future*, Report of the Central Advisory Committee for Education (England) (Newsom), London, DES, 1963; *Higher Education Report*, Report of the Committee on Higher Education (Robbins), London, HMSO, 1963; *West Indian Children in our Schools*. Interim Report of the Committee of Inquiry into the Education of Children from Ethnic Minority Groups (Rampton), London, HMSO, 1981; *Education for All*, The Report of the Committee of Inquiry into the Education of Children from Ethnic Minority Groups (Swann), London, HMSO, 1985.

More personal accounts can be found in: R. Roberts, *A Ragged Schooling*, Glasgow, Fontana, 1978; G. Greene (ed.) *The Old School Tie*, Oxford, Oxford University Press, 1984, (1st edn, 1934); M. Evans, *A Good School. Life at a Girls' Grammar School in the 1950s*, London, The Women's Press Ltd, 1991; R. Kirkley, *Thursday's Child*, London, Minerva, 1995; A. Ashworth, *Once in a House on Fire*, London, Picador, 1998.

Important studies of gender issues in education include: F. Hunt (ed.)

Lessons for Life: The Schooling of Girls and Women 1850–1950, Oxford, Basil Blackwell, 1987; C. Heward, *Making a Man of Him: Parents and their Sons' Education at an English Public School 1929–50*, London, Routledge, 1988; M. Mac an Ghaill, *The Making of Men: Masculinities, Sexualities and Schooling*, Buckingham, Open University Press, 1994; C. Dyhouse, *No Distinction of Sex? Women in British Universities 1870–1939*, London, University College London Press, 1995; K. Myers (ed.) *Whatever Happened to Equal Opportunities in Schools? Gender Initiatives in Education*, Buckingham, Open University Press, 2000.

Ethnic and other issues are considered in: D. Gillborn, *'Race', Ethnicity and Education*, London, Unwin Hyman, 1990; P. Woods and M. Hammersley (eds) *Gender and Ethnicity in Schools. Ethnographic Accounts*, London, Routledge, 1993; I. Grosvenor, *Assimilating Identities*, London, Lawrence and Wishart, 1997; D. Gillborn and H.S. Mirza, *Educational Inequalities in Mapping Race, Class and Gender*, Ofsted, 2000. Classic studies of the relationships between education and social class include C. Benn and B. Simon, *Half-way There*, Harmondsworth, Penguin, 1972 (1st edn, 1970) and B. Jackson and D. Marsden, *Education and the Working Class*, London, Routledge and Kegan Paul, 1962.

Notes

1 'Ethnicity' is the term used here as preferable to 'race' which, though used widely in popular speech, was deemed as early as 1950 by Unesco to be 'not so much a biological phenomenon as a social myth'. Quoted in I. Grosvenor, *Assimilating Identities*, London, Lawrence and Wishart, 1997, p. 7. 'Ethnicity' itself can be a problematic term as it can also be essentialist and locate people within a fixed, given identity. Ibid., pp. 42–4, 185. Gender is taken to refer to not only sex, that is biological categories of male and female, but also changing social conceptions of femaleness and maleness – see J.A. Scott, 'Gender: a useful category of historical analysis', in J.W. Scott (ed.) *Feminism and History*, Oxford, Oxford University Press, 1996, pp. 152–80.

2 The author accepts Harold Silver's argument about the silence on disability but found there was no room to include it here. On the other hand this is an attempt to think about the experience of education – see H. Silver, 'Knowing and not knowing in the history of education', *History of Education*, 1992, vol. 21, no. 1, pp. 97–108.

3 D. Gillborn and H.S. Mirza, *Educational Inequalities in Mapping Race, Class and Gender*, London, Ofsted, 2000; A. Osler and M. Morrison, *Inspecting Schools for Race Equality: Ofsted's Strengths and Weaknesses*, http://www.cre.gov.uk/publs/dl_ofstd.html; and http://www.cre.gov.uk/media/-nr_arch/nr001026.html.

4 For a definition of class see D. Hill, 'Social class and education', in D. Matheson and I. Grosvenor (eds) *An Introduction to the Study of Education*, London, David Fulton, 1999, pp. 85–6. In census returns, working class has been defined as unskilled to skilled manual workers; lower middle class as routine, low-paid white-collar workers, while various grades of the middle class have been placed above that. 'Working classes' is preferred here rather than 'working class' as a signpost to the variations within the group.

5 See, for example, the series of articles and letters in both *The Guardian* and the *Times Educational Supplement*, May 1999.
6 For example, K. Myers (ed.) *Whatever Happened to Equal Opportunities in Schools? Gender Equality Initiatives in Education*, Buckingham, Open University Press, 2000; G. Plummer, *Failing Working-Class Girls*, Stoke-on-Trent, Trentham Books, 2000; M. Foster, 'A black perspective' in Myers, op. cit., pp. 189–200. 'Black' here is used to denote all those of non-'white' colour. In this chapter I shall follow Ian Grosvenor's use of 'black' as a shorthand for people of South Asian, African and Caribbean origin, although their only uniformity is a common experience of racism and discrimination on account of their colour – see Grosvenor, op. cit., p. 10.
7 See, for example, C. Steedman, *Childhood, Culture and Class in Britain. Margaret McMillan 1860–1931*, London, Virago Press, 1990, passim and especially pp. 173–225; R.J.C. Young, *Colonial Desire. Hybridity in Theory, Culture and Race*, London, Routledge, 1995; I. Brown, 'Who were the Eugenicists? A study of the formation of an early twentieth-century pressure group', *History of Education*, 1988, vol. 17, no. 4, pp. 295–307.
8 V.A. McClelland, ' "Phylacteries of misery" or "Mystic-eyed hierophants"? Some ecclesiastical and educational challenges in England of the Irish diaspora 1850–1902' and M. Hickman, 'Constructing the nation, segregating the Irish: the education of Irish Catholics in nineteenth century Britain', in V. A. McClelland (ed.) *Education and National Identity: the Irish Diaspora, Aspects of Education*, Journal of the Institute of Education, the University of Hull, 1997, no. 54, pp. 20–2, 33–6, 45–8; B. Simon, *Education and the Labour Movement 1870–1920*, London, Lawrence and Wishart, 1974, pp. 121–62, 186–207.
9 R. Watts, 'From lady teacher to professional. A case study of some of the first headteachers of girls' secondary schools in England', *Educational Management and Administration*, 1998, vol. 26, no. 4, pp. 339–51; G.A.N. Lowndes, *The Silent Social Revolution*, London, Oxford University Press, 1937, p. 101.
10 D. Vincent, *Literacy and Popular Culture. England 1750–1914*, Cambridge, Cambridge University Press, 1989, pp. 25–9.
11 R. McWilliams Tullberg, *Women at Cambridge. A Men's University – though of a Mixed Type*, London, Victor Gollancz, 1975; C. Dyhouse, *No Distinction of Sex? Women in British Universities 1870–1939*, London, University College London Press, 1995, pp. 248–9.
12 Dyhouse, op. cit., pp. 18–32; W. Robinson, 'Pupil teachers: the Achilles heel of higher grade girls' schools 1882–1904?', *History of Education*, 1993, vol. 22, no. 3, pp. 241–52.
13 For example, E.W. Vincent and P. Hinton, *The University of Birmingham: Its History and Significance*, Birmingham, Cornish Brothers, 1947, p. 203.
14 Dyhouse, op. cit., pp. 20, 143–5, 189–228, passim.
15 F. Hunt, *Gender and Policy in English Education. Schooling for Girls 1902–44*, London, Harvester Wheatsheaf, 1991, pp. 12–13; 'Divided aims: the educational implications of opposing ideologies in girls' secondary schooling, 1850–1940' in F. Hunt, (ed.) *Lessons for Life. The Schooling of Girls and Women 1850–1950*, Oxford, Basil Blackwell, 1987, pp. 11–16; W. van der Eyken, *Education, the Child and Society. A Documentary History 1900–73*, Harmondsworth, Penguin, 1973, pp. 33–55; S. Kingsley Kent, *Gender and Power in Britain, 1640–1990*, London, Routledge, 1999, pp. 236–53, 260–71, 279, 287–309; J. McDermid, 'Women and education' in J. Purvis (ed.) *Women's History: Britain 1850–1945*, London, University College London Press, 1995, pp. 121–3.

16 Watts, op. cit., pp. 343, 347. J. Burnett (ed.) *Destiny Obscure. Autobiographies of Childhood, Education and the Family from the 1820s to the 1920s*, London, Allen Lane, 1982, p. 292; A. Turnbull, 'Learning her womanly work: the elementary school curriculum, 1870–1914' in Hunt, op. cit., 1987, pp. 83–100.

17 J. Purvis, *A History of Women's Education in England*, Milton Keynes, Open University Press, 1991, pp. 30–1, 54; Hunt, op. cit., 1987, p. 147.

18 P. Summerfield, 'Cultural reproduction in the education of girls: a study of girls' secondary schooling in two Lancashire towns, 1900–50', in Hunt, op. cit., 1987, pp. 149–70.

19 Hunt, op. cit., 1987, pp. 19–20.

20 Burnett, op. cit., pp. 198–211; V. Brittain, *Testament of Youth. An Autobiographical Study of the Years 1900–1925*, London, Victor Gollancz, 1933.

21 R. Watts, 'A medical mind far ahead of her time', *The Birmingham Post, Millenibrum*, 6 Sept. 2000, p. 19; Vincent and Hinton, op. cit.

22 Kent, op. cit., pp. 298–9, 311–23; D. Thom, 'Better a teacher than a hairdresser? "A mad passion for equality" or, keeping Molly and Betty down' in Hunt, op. cit., 1987, pp. 129–30.

23 Ibid., pp. 126–7, 134–45; Van der Eyken, op. cit., pp. 195, 320–1, 369–78; J. Miller, *School for Women*, London, Virago, 1996, p. 130; Anne Madden, 'Challenging inequalities in the classroom: the role and contribution of the Equal Opportunities Commission', in Myers, op. cit., pp. 42–3.

24 R. Kirkley, *Thursday's Child*, London, Minerva, 1995, pp. 30–1.

25 M. Evans, *A Good School. Life at a Girls' Grammar School in the 1950s*, London, Women's Press, 1991, pp. 23, 71, passim.

26 B. Jackson and D. Marsden, *Education and the Working Class*, London, Routledge and Kegan Paul, 1962, pp. 140–6.

27 Thom, op. cit., pp. 128–34; *15 to 18*, Report of the Central Advisory Committee for Education (Crowther), London, HMSO, 1959, pp. 34, passim; *Half our Future*, Report of the Central Advisory Committee for Education (England) (Newsom), London, DES, 1963; Hunt, op. cit., 1991, pp. 3–8.

28 S. Spencer, 'Women's dilemmas in postwar Britain; career stories for adolescent girls in the 1950s', *History of Education*, 2000, vol. 29, no. 4, pp. 329–42.

29 Purvis, op. cit., p. 126.

30 S. Sharpe, *'Just like a Girl'. How Girls Learn to be Women*, Harmondsworth, Penguin, 1976, pp. 121–58.

31 M. Arnot, 'A crisis in patriarchy? British feminist educational politics and state regulation of gender', in M. Arnot and K. Weiler (eds) *Feminism and Social Justice in Education*, London, Falmer, 1993, pp. 192–202.

32 See, for example, T. Grafton, H. Miller, L. Smith, M. Vegoad and R. Whitfield, 'Gender and curriculum choice', K. Clarricoates ' "A dinosaur in the classroom" – the "hidden curriculum" in primary schools' and S. Lees, 'The structure of sexual relations in school', in M. Arnot and G. Weiner (eds) *Gender and the Politics of Schooling*, London, Unwin Hyman in association with the Open University, 1987, pp. 108–21, 155–65, 175–86.

33 See Madden, op. cit., F. Morrell, 'An episode in the thirty years war; race, sex and class in the ILEA 1981–90', V. Millman, 'Was there really a problem? The Schools Council Sex Differentiation Project 1981–3', B. Smail, 'Has the mountain moved. The Girls into Science and Technology project 1979–83', and M. Foster, 'A black perspective', in Myers, op. cit., pp. 27–60, 77–92, 125–42, 143–55, 189–200, passim.

34 Foster, op. cit., pp. 191–2; J. Martin, 'Gender in education', in Matheson and Grosvenor, op. cit., pp. 110–11; A. Wickham, 'Gender divisions, training and the state' in Arnot and Weiner, op. cit., pp. 290–307; L. Raphael Reed, 'Troubling boys and disturbing discourses on masculinity and schooling; a feminist exploration of current debates and interventions concerning boys in school', *Gender and Education*, 1999, vol. 11, no. 1, pp. 97, 100; M. Baker, 'Gender gaps yawn in the silly season', *Times Educational Supplement*, 8 September 2000; C.N. Rackley in *The Guardian*, 23 August 2000.

35 Foster, op. cit., pp. 194–7; *Times Educational Supplement*, 18 and 25 August 2000; *The Guardian*, 24 August 2000; S. Gorard, G. Rees and J. Salisbury, 'Reappraising the apparent underachievement of boys at school', *Gender and Education*, 1999, vol. 11, no. 4, pp. 441–54.

36 *The Guardian*, 23 August 2000.

37 See, for example, D. Mackinnon and J. Statham with M. Hales, *Education in the UK: Facts and Figures*, London, Hodder and Stoughton in association with the Open University, 1995, pp. 177–8.

38 Miller, op. cit., pp. 137–52, 156–7.

39 Myers, op. cit., pp. 217–29.

40 Reed, op. cit., pp. 96–108; 'BERA Conference Report', *Times Educational Supplement*, 8 September 2000; S. Adler, 'When Ms Muffet fought back; a view of work in children's books since the 1970s' in Myers, op. cit., pp. 201–13.

41 A. Phillips, 'Clever lad', *Guardian Education*, 29 August 2000; 'Down with girls', *Guardian Education*, 21 June 2000.

42 C. Heward, *Making a Man of Him. Parents and their Sons' Education at an English Public School, 1929–50*, London, Routledge, 1988, passim.

43 M. Mac an Ghaill, *The Making of Men. Masculinities, Sexualities and Schooling*, Buckingham, Open University Press, 1994.

44 E. Grugeon, 'Gender implications of children's playground culture', J. Stanley, 'Sex and the quiet schoolgirl', J. Draper, 'We're back with Gobbo: the re-establishment of gender relations following a school merger', J. and P. French, 'Gender imbalances in the primary classroom: an interactional account' and M. Hammersley, 'An evaluation of a study in gender imbalance in primary classrooms', in P. Woods and M. Hammersley (eds) *Gender and Ethnicity in Schools. Ethnographic Accounts*, London, Routledge, 1993, pp. 1–5, 11–74, 95–124.

45 Grosvenor, op. cit., pp. 6–10, 49–96; C. Gaine, *Still no Problem Here*, Stoke-on-Trent, Trentham, 1995, pp. 1–58.

46 H. S. Mirza, 'The social construction of black womanhood in British educational research: towards a new understanding' in Arnot and Weiler, op. cit., pp. 32–57.

47 M. Stone, *The Education of the Black Child in Britain. The Myth of Multicultural Education*, Glasgow, Fontana, 1981, pp. 5–10, 26–32, 65–6, 147–67.

48 Grosvenor, op. cit., pp. 154–80, 190–9.

49 I. Grosvenor, ' "Race" and education' in Matheson and Grosvenor, op. cit., pp. 75–80. Many West Indians are Christian but rejection and alienation from the established churches have led them to organize their own. The latter play both a vital cultural and educational role – I. Grosvenor, ' "Faith in the city": religion, racism and education in 1960s Britain', in J. Coolahan, R. Aldrich and F. Simon (eds) *Faiths and Education, Paedagogica Historica* Supplementary Series, vol. V, Gent, C.S.H.P., 1999, pp. 281–97.

50 See, for example, *West Indian Children in our Schools*, Interim Report of the Committee of Inquiry into the Education of Children from Ethnic Minority Groups (Rampton), London, HMSO, 1981; G.K. Verma and Christopher Bagley, 'A critical introduction' in G K. Verma and Christopher Bagley (eds) *Race, Education and Identity*, London, Macmillan, 1979, pp. 5–10; *Education for All*, The Report of the Committee of Inquiry into the Education of Children from Ethnic Minority Groups (Swann), London, HMSO, 1985, pp. 93–100, 105–7.

51 *Times Educational Supplement*, 20 October 2000.

52 A. Osler, *Speaking Out. Black Girls in Britain*, London, Virago Upstarts, 1989, pp. 8–34; L. Ali, 'The case for including black history in the National Curriculum', *Improving Schools*, 2000, vol. 3, no. 1, pp. 50–4; Swann, op. cit,. pp. 98–100; M. Mac an Ghaill, 'Beyond the white norm: the use of qualitative methods in the study of black youths' schooling in England', A. Moore, 'Genre, ethnocentricity and bilingualism in the English classroom', C. Wright, 'Education for some: the educational and vocational experiences of 15–18-year-old members of ethnic minority groups' and P. Foster, 'Case not proven: an evaluation of a study in teacher racism', in Woods and Hammersley, op. cit., pp. 145–222; V. Amos and P. Parmar, 'Resistances and responses: the experience of black girls in Britain', in Arnot and Weiner, op. cit., pp. 211–19; D. Gillborn, *"Race", Ethnicity and Education*, London, Unwin Hyman, 1990, pp. 142–72, 206–7.

53 Gillborn, op. cit., pp. 173–97, 205–6.

54 Stone, op. cit., pp. 65–6.

55 Swann, op. cit., pp. 94, 58–90, 93–8.

56 Swann, op. cit., pp. 58–65, passim; Gillborn, op. cit., pp. 19–44, 72–141; 198–203; Gillborn and Mirza, op. cit., pp. 12–15; *The Guardian*, 27 October 2000.

57 See, for example, G. Greene (ed.) *The Old School Tie*, Oxford, Oxford University Press, 1984 (1st edn, 1934); D. Roker, 'Private education and political socialization', E. Frazer, 'Talk about class in a girls' public school', J. Price, ' "We're here just to make up the numbers really". The experience of girls in boys' public schools', and R. Cresser, 'Take three girls: a comparison of girls' A level achievement in three types of sixth form within the independent sector', in G. Walford (ed.) *The Private Schooling of Girls Past and Present*, London, Woburn Press, 1993, pp. 101–186.

58 Lowndes, op. cit., pp. 109–19; R. Roberts, *A Ragged Schooling*, Glasgow, Fontana, 1978, pp. 156–8; B. Simon, *The Politics of Educational Reform 1920–40*, London, Lawrence and Wishart, 1974, pp. 20–2, 121–2; L. Elvin, *Encounters with Education*, London, Institute of Education, 1987, p. 19.

59 Steedman, op. cit., passim; Lowndes, op. cit, pp. 220–34.

60 Simon, op. cit., pp. 230–50; B. Simon and C. Chitty, *SOS Save Our Schools*, London, Lawrence and Wishart, 1993, passim.

61 Swann, op. cit., pp. 93–4, 77.

62 Swann, op. cit., pp. 70–1, 77, 81–6.

63 E. Stones 'The colour of conceptual learning' and D. Jenkins, S. Kemmis, B. MacDonald and G.K. Verma, 'Racism and educational evaluation', in Verma and Bagley, op. cit., pp. 67–83, 107–32.

64 Jackson and Marsden, op. cit., pp. 104–12, 236–43, passim; Crowther, op. cit., pp. 8–9; J. Floud, A.H. Halsey and F.M. Martin, from *Social Class and Educational Opportunity*, 1957, pp. 139–49 in Van der Eyken, op. cit., pp. 432–9.

65 K. Gibberd, *No Place like School*, London, Michael Joseph, 1962.

66 A. Ashworth, *Once in a House on Fire*, London, Picador, 1998.

67 Plummer, op. cit., pp. 135–200; Stone, op. cit., pp. 20–5, 69; R. Giles, *The West Indian Experience in British Schools*, London, Heinemann, 1977, pp. 1–13.

68 *Children and their Primary Schools*, Report of the Central Advisory Council for Education (England) (Plowden), London, HMSO, 1967; M. Kogan, 'Victim who was cast as the villain', *Times Educational Supplement*, 20 October 2000.

69 A.S. Neill, *Summerhill*, Harmondsworth, Penguin, 1968.

70 Simon, op. cit., pp. 30–1, 101–2, 213, 256–7, 260–1; Mackinnon and Statham, op. cit., pp. 86–7, 189.

71 C. Benn and B. Simon, *Half-way There*, Harmondsworth, Penguin, 1972 (1st edn, 1970), pp. 305–6, 311–12, 315–16, 522; C. Benn and C. Chitty, *Thirty Years On*, London, David Fulton, 1996, pp. 461–91.

72 R.J.L. Watts, 'Comprehensive schooling: a personal perspective', *Forum*, 1997, vol. 39, no. 1, pp. 12–14.

73 Phil Revel, 'Keeping a close eye on the pupils', *Times Educational Supplement*, 3 November 2000.

74 N. Davies, 'Crisis, crisis, crisis: the state of our schools', together with David Blunkett's and readers replies, *The Guardian*, 14–16 September 1999; 'Despair in the classroom', *The Guardian*, 2 November 2000; J. Slater, 'Big cities are not the issues', *Times Educational Supplement*, 10 November 2000.

75 N. Pyke, 'Blunkett backs 100 new church schools', *The Independent on Sunday*, 27 August 2000; S. Rocker, 'Is multi-faith school an impossible dream?', *Times Educational Supplement*, 2 June 2000.

76 D. Ward, 'Merit allows girls to "buy" private education', *The Guardian*, 7 September 2000.

77 R. Smithers, 'Winchester tops public school league', *The Guardian*, 26 August 2000.

78 *The Guardian*, 27 May 2000; P. Lampl, 'Equality before quotas', *Times Educational Supplement*, 24 November 2000; N. Mitchell, 'Get more kids to go to college', *Times Higher Educational Supplement*, 21 July 2000; J. Beckett, H. Carter and M. Wainwright, 'University, eh?', *Guardian Education*, 25 July 2000; L.M. Elliot, 'Upstairs or down?', *Guardian Education*, 18 July 2000.

79 *Higher Education Report*, Report of the Committee on Higher Education (Robbins), London, HMSO, 1963, pp. 16, 50–3, passim; C. Matheson, 'Access to Higher Education', in Matheson and Grosvenor, op. cit., pp. 143–56; D. Matheson, 'The university', in Matheson and Grosvenor, op. cit., p. 163; A. Taher, 'Stuff of dreams', *Guardian Education*, 7 November 2000.

80 P. McGill and D. Macleod, 'Goodbye to all that', *Education Guardian*, 21 November 2000.

81 R. Bryant, 'Counting the cost', in G. Andrews, H. Kean and J. Thompson (eds) *Ruskin College: Contesting Knowledge, Dissenting Politics*, London, Lawrence and Wishart, 1999, pp. 102–18.

82 B. Purdie, ' "Long-haired intellectuals and busybodies": Ruskin, student radicalism and civil rights in Northern Ireland', in Andrews, Kean and Thompson, op. cit., pp. 58–79; H. Kean, 'The place of Ruskin in its own history', in Andrews, Kean and Thompson, op. cit., pp. 167–83.

83 See, for example, *The Guardian*, 13 February 2001.

Chapter 8

Special educational needs

Ian Copeland

The situation in 2000

The report of the Warnock Committee[1] and the ensuing 1981 Education Act provide the backdrop to the current situation in schools regarding special educational needs (SEN). The Committee recommended that the term 'children with learning difficulties' should replace the term 'educationally sub-normal' which had been introduced in the 1944 Education Act. The prevalence of such pupils in special school classes alone had increased from 0.27 per cent of the school population representing 15,173 pupils in 1950 to 1.05 per cent representing 79,239 pupils in 1983.[2] Furthermore a large-scale study of junior-age, Key Stage 2, classes and SEN in 1981 was replicated in 1998. The authors observe that:

> The substantial sample size, the involvement of the same schools and, in particular, the very high response rate from both schools and teachers, provides (sic) a secure base both for a picture of the prevalence of different sorts of SEN and for the change in such prevalence over time.[3]

While there had been an increase between 1981 and 1998 in the proportion of pupils adjudged by their teachers to have SEN from 18.8 per cent to 26.1 per cent, an increase of 38.8 per cent, the proportion of pupils with learning difficulties had risen from 15.4 per cent to 23.1 per cent, an increment of 50 per cent. Over the same period pupils with health, sensory and physical difficulties had declined by 4 per cent from 4.5 to 4.3 per cent.[4]

The main strands of Warnock's deliberations may be summarized as an attempt to change the defining of pupil disability, an enlargement of the pupil target group, a safeguarding of the position of an identified minority of pupils, an endorsement of the policy of the integration of pupils with disability into ordinary schools and the recognition of parents as partners in educational decisions concerning their children.

Warnock's starting point was a rejection of the thinking that had underpinned the 11 categories of handicapped pupils which had been a consequence of the 1944 Education Act; the categories were regarded as unsatisfactory because they concentrated upon the pupils' handicap rather than their educational needs. Warnock concluded that: 'The purpose of education for all children is the same; the goals are the same. But the help that individual children need in progressing toward them will be different.'[5]

The concept of SEN was adopted to re-orientate educational thinking along this line. SEN, it was argued, did not spring from deficiencies within the child but from the dialectical relationship between the strengths and weaknesses of the child and the environment's resources and deficiencies.[6] In addition, because of variations in the degrees of severity and/or permanence in disabling conditions, it made sense to think in terms of a continuum of SEN rather than simply presence or absence. The previous medical categories covered roughly two per cent of the school population which received education largely in special schools or units. Drawing upon a range of published research, Warnock proposed that a further 18 per cent of pupils might have some form of SEN at some point in their educational careers.[7]

The committee acknowledged that the most powerful argument in favour of the medical categories of handicap was that they 'provided a valuable safeguard of the right of a child who fits into one of the categories to an education suited to his needs'.[8] In accord with this principle, Warnock proposed that schools and LEAs should jointly undertake the 'discovery, assessment and recording' of SEN but that 'the LEA should be given the specific duty to record those children whose needs cannot be satisfactorily met within the resources generally available to ... schools and to provide special education'.[9]

The committee endorsed the principle that 'handicapped pupils ... are to be educated in ordinary schools in preference to special schools'.[10] Indeed, it regarded the debate as so exhausted that it was better to consider the practicalities entailed in the three different forms of integration – locational, social and functional.

'Parents as Partners' is the title of one chapter in the report and 'the support of parents' features in sections of four others. The importance of parents is summarized thus: 'The appearance of such recommendations in so many chapters is evidence of the central place of parents in our view of special education.'[11]

Warnock's introduction of the concept of SEN has been characterized as 'rhetoric' because it essentially substituted one set of categories for another.[12] This criticism is misconceived and misguided. Categories are a feature of abstract thought which facilitate generalizations.[13] Hence attention should be directed not to the fact that categories have changed, which is predictable, but rather to the form and impact of change. The impact of the concept of SEN and particularly of continuum was immediately to enlarge the pupil target group to one in five in the school population. The overwhelming majority of the group, some 18 per cent, were already pupils in ordinary schools. Hence the main impact could be described as making the SEN pupil normal. This, in turn, was bound to affect the process of integration. The figure was also close to that identified by the Wood Committee for backward pupils in 1929.

The 1981 Education Act endorsed these principles: indeed, so much so that it is claimed that members of the Government referred to the Act as 'the Warnock legislation'.[14] Thus the concept of continuum of SEN was accepted with an enlarged cohort of pupils. A small minority would have their rights safeguarded through a process of assessment and the issue of a statement of need as appropriate. LEAs were to be responsible: first for assessments, statements and annual reviews and any additional resources implied for this minority, and second for ensuring that schools through their governing bodies and policies identified the pupils who constituted the much larger group, roughly one in six. Parents were given the right to participate in the assessment process, to comment upon any provision which the LEA might propose, to appeal to the LEA to reconsider if dissatisfied and ultimately to appeal to the Secretary of State for Education.

The concept of SEN was central to the legislation and was accordingly defined in the first section of the Act. However, the definition is relative and contingent upon two other statements, both of which are imprecise. Clarification of the meaning of SEN is attempted through its relationship with the ideas of 'learning difficulty' and 'special educational provision'. The Act's first section states that 'a child has SEN if he has a learning difficulty which calls for special educational provision to be made for him'. In this way, SEN, learning difficulty and special provision stand in a circular interrelationship. The section then proceeds to state that:

> a child has a learning difficulty if:
>
> (a) he has significantly greater difficulty in learning than the majority of children of his age;
>
> (b) he has a disability which either prevents or hinders him from making use of educational facilities of a kind generally provided in schools within the area of the LEA for children of his age.

There is a third clause for children under the school age of five. In this way learning difficulty is not defined by reference to objective criteria, but normatively by locating the child in terms of the performance of the peer majority. While 'significant' carries specific connotations in mathematics and statistics,[15] no specific measure is offered for 'significantly greater difficulty'.

'Special educational provision' is defined in the section as 'educational provision which is either additional to, or otherwise different from, the educational provision made generally for children of his age in schools maintained by the LEA concerned'. Again, special provision is defined relatively in terms of what is by custom generally available. Without an inventory of general provision, that statement too is imprecise.

The 1981 Act required LEAs to produce and maintain a statement for some children with SEN. The importance of the issue of a statement was the guarantee of additional resources for the subject. In the general context of governmental cutbacks in expenditure in the 1980s, since no financial memorandum accompanied the 1981 Act, pressure was exerted upon LEA expenditure. The DES published guidelines on statementing in 1983,[16] and subsequently funded research into a sample of LEAs in different regions of the country.[17] The findings revealed that in spite of the guidelines,

LEA statement procedures varied widely;

LEAs varied in the extent to which procedures were adopted;

LEA procedures were often time consuming;

Insufficient collaboration between LEAs, health and social services;

Partnership between professionals and parents was elusive;

Statements often lacked specificity regarding provision.[18]

The obvious inference from this list is that the statementing process raised issues for those enmeshed in it: pupils, teachers, LEA officers, psychologists, health workers and parents. The many issues have been explored at length elsewhere.[19]

As a precursor to subsequent legislation, the Audit Commission and Her Majesty's Inspectorate (ACHMI) jointly undertook research on provision for pupils with SEN.[20] The report chose to present the results of its research into LEAs and schools as a list of issues. One of the most important was the wide variation between LEAs in the percentages (from 3.3 to 0.8 per cent) of pupils issued with statements.

Part III of the 1993 Education Act was devoted to 'children with SEN' and gave notice of introduction in the following year of a 'Code of Practice on the Identification and Assessment of SEN'.[21] A Department for Education (DfE) briefing paper noted that the Code was triggered by 'the publication of the ACHMI Report "Getting in on the Act" which illustrates inconsistencies in LEA practice to a worrying extent'.[22] The original research had involved 12 out of more than 100 LEAs and 77 out of thousands of schools.[23] Variations were now regarded as attaining a 'worrying' level and had been generalized to all LEAs. The ACHMI reported 'serious deficiencies in the way in which children with special needs are identified and provided for. The deficiencies are caused by three key problems: (the first is) lack of clarity about what constitutes SEN.'[24]

The prime aim of the Code 'is to provide national criteria to help LEAs identify the type and level of any SEN of individual children ... The code will require Authorities to use the same national criteria.'[25] Moreover, when the Bill was under discussion in the Commons:

> It became clear from (the Minister's) replies that the Code of Practice would be critical to the new legislative framework ... (and as the Minister remarked) "I am aware that I have raised expectations about the Code to an almost hysterical level."[26]

How does the Code tackle the problem of the 'lack of clarity about what constitutes SEN'?[27] This lack of clarity was considered to arise from 'the definition of SEN'.[28] The Code's definition of SEN, however, is precisely the definition embedded in the 1981 Act with the addition of the female gender.[29] But, as has already been argued, in that context SEN is defined contingently upon the ideas of 'learning difficulty' and 'special educational provision'.

Part IV of the Education Act of 1996 covered the ground of Part III of the 1993 Act. As a publication by the Centre for Studies in Inclusive Education (CSIE) observed, however: 'The 1996 Education Act replaced the 1993 Act in name alone. It is the same law but with a different title and section numbers. There are no changes in the substance of the law.'[30] The Code of Practice has also been revised with the intention that the new edition should be in place in September 2001 after consultation with interested parties.[31] The definition of SEN, however, remains the same as in the 1994 version which stems directly from the 1981 Act. Was the situation in the past clearer when circumstances might have been less complicated?

The situation in 1900

The earliest official attempts to make provision for children with learning difficulties were contained in the deliberations of the Royal Commission on the Blind, the Deaf and Dumb, etc. of the United Kingdom (RCBDD) which reported in 1889. This report contained the discourse which provided the first basis for objectifying the pupil with learning difficulties and the blueprint for segregated special schools and classes.

The general background to the establishment of the commission was, first, Forster's 1870 Education Act which permitted school boards to found schools to supplement the existing places provided by church schools, and second, Mundella's 1880 Education Act which compelled children to attend school. In this way elementary education became comprehensive, and schools for the first time contained children who had previously received no formal teaching and who came from families whose members had not attended school. As a consequence 'the lower classes (in schools) were thronged ... by unwilling and ignorant victims'.[32] The number of pupils in elementary schools expanded rapidly, from 1.7 million in 1870 to 4.8 million in 1891.[33] The size of classes was also very large. Even if pupil teachers who had recently completed their own school lessons and were subsequently apprenticed to teaching, are included in the calculations, then there was a pupil:teacher ratio of 60:1 in 1870 and 48:1 in 1891.[34] In addition, the teaching regime in elementary schools was dominated by Robert Lowe's Revised Code of 1862 with its central principle of payment by results. In accordance with this principle, the amount of grant which schools were paid was determined in small part by each pupil's general attendance and merit rate, but in larger part by pupils' performance in examinations of the three Rs. In sum, classes were large, teaching methods were mechanical and primarily directed towards preparing pupils for the examination.[35]

The conditions in elementary education did not elude the attention of politicians. Early in January 1886 the membership of a Royal Commission under the chairmanship of Lord Cross to examine the working of the elementary education acts was announced.[36] Within a few days the membership of another Royal Commission to examine the education of the blind, the deaf and dumb, and others was reported.[37] The establishment of this latter had been convoluted and incremental; a Royal Commission to enquire into the education of the blind having been set up in 1885. Some few months later, however, following Lord Egerton's lobby on behalf of the deaf and dumb, its terms of reference 'were extended by the inclusion of the deaf and dumb and of such other cases as from special circumstances would seem to require exceptional methods of education'.[38]

The co-existence of the two Royal Commissions was to be a profound historical conjuncture. The chief consequence was the division of the school population in terms of theory and planning into two unequal groups. The Cross Commission determined at an early stage that 'exceptional children', 'the dull and deficient' in the words of a Senior Inspector of Schools,[39] should be the concern of the other Commission chaired by Lord Egerton. This proposal was accepted and Egerton observed that 'there are a great many backward children in our Elementary schools who require a different treatment to that of the ordinary children'.[40] The *Oxford Dictionary* defines 'exception' as 'thing which does not follow the rule' and 'exceptional' as 'unusual'. Thus, in terms of the fracture of thinking about the groups in the elementary school population, there was considered to be a group which consisted of the unusual as opposed to all the rest. The division was made between the ordinary and normal, and the abnormal or subnormal.

Egerton's terms of reference had conjoined the physical and mental categories, the blind, the deaf and dumb, with those children with other learning difficulties. That decision had two profound consequences for pupils with learning difficulties: first, the physical and mental categories together became a part of the domain supervised by the medical profession; and second, such supervision tended to close off the quest for an educationally based solution.

The Egerton Commission received evidence from 143 witnesses concerning the education of the blind and the deaf and dumb. In contrast, only seven presented evidence on the children in the exceptional section. However, in this section of the report very nearly half of the references draw upon the evidence presented by Dr George Shuttleworth, then Medical Superintendent of the Royal Albert Asylum for Idiots and Imbeciles at Lancaster. In Shuttleworth's evidence the 'exceptional' children were conceived as being idiots or imbeciles, and this definition was subsequently reiterated in the report. In Shuttleworth's view no real distinction between idiots and imbeciles could be made simply because it was a distinction of degree and not of kind. Hence, he averred that 'idiocy means a lower degradation of intellect, a greater deficiency of intellect, and imbecility means a lesser degree of such deficiency'.[41] Shuttleworth offered no explanation of what was meant by intellect nor did any member of the Commission ask him to do so. Nevertheless it is evident that intellect is the norm which first distinguishes this group of exceptional children from their peers and then organizes the group hierarchically in terms of degrees of deficiency. The definition is both decontextualized and relativistic. In Foucauldian terms, the discourse of intellect creates its object which becomes the exceptional, abnormal child. Shuttleworth averred that the efficacy of the definition was confirmed by his case notes which, in his own words, 'contained accurate histories' of several thousand patients treated at the Royal Albert Asylum.[42] In this way the condition is confirmed by the diagnosis and the diagnosis by the condition. The science and discourse is securely circular.

Another witness, indeed, openly acknowledged the efficacy of the definition as an organizing principle and declared:

> In other words, idiocy is a deeper mental defect than imbecility. This view meets all requirements whether for scientific purposes or for purposes of medical treatment, or for practical purposes connected with care, management and education.[43]

In contrast, however, the Commission also received evidence which disagreed with Shuttleworth's, at least in terms of aetiology. Francis Warner was a paediatrician in a London hospital and a professor of physiology. From the basis of case notes collected over a period of 12 years he submitted evidence regarding physically and mentally defective children. Warner calculated that some one in 20 or five per cent of children in large urban areas were unable to cope with elementary education in its then current state. To back up the calculation he had surveys of child outpatients in hospital and pupils in school. Among the reasons he put forward were irregular development in eyesight and hearing; diseases of the lungs and the heart; being orphaned; large classes in schools with their mechanical teaching and examinations; and the sometimes brutal and cruel methods of correction in schools.[44] While the detail of differences between Warner's and Shuttleworth's positions has been set out elsewhere,[45] it is manifest that there was available to the Commission an alternative rationale to recommend the provision of education for the exceptional group of children.

The 1893 Elementary Education (Blind and Deaf Children) Act obliged school authorities to assume responsibility for the education of blind and deaf pupils. Such education was from the age of 5 to 16 years for the blind and from the age of 7 to 16 years for the deaf. School authorities could either establish their own school or contribute towards an existing one but both types were to be certified by the Education Department. By the year 1898 there were 23 residential schools for the blind pupil of which all but three were supported by independent bodies. Seventeen day schools were wholly provided by school boards. In the same year, 1,089 boys and girls were educated in residential schools and 275 in day schools. In the former the proportion of boys to girls was three to two but in the latter was almost precisely equal.[46]

Statistics for the deaf were not presented in a similar fashion so that direct comparison is not possible. In 1898 there were 17 boarding institutions, of which all but three were provided by independent bodies, and 44 day schools, only one of which was independent. There were 1,788 pupils in the boarding schools and 1,742 in day schools.[47]

While arrangements were made for the blind and for the deaf and dumb, the Commission's recommendations left the issues surrounding provision for the exceptional children unresolved. Some ten years later the question was taken up in a special committee of the Education Department, the Departmental Committee on Defective and Epileptic Children (DCDEC). The seven members of the committee included Shuttleworth who was called upon to present the very first piece of evidence upon 'the definition of terms'.[48] He repeated the definition of imbeciles and idiots, the hierarchy of deficiency, which he had presented to the previous Commission,[49] and also linked a prior medical examination with educational provision. Although this definition was decontextualized, relativistic and judgmental, nevertheless it featured alongside the medical examination in the ensuing permissive legislation, the 1899 Elementary Education (Defective and Epileptic Children) Act. This definition subsequently appeared in legislation which required local authorities to make assessments of exceptional children. These were the 1913 Mental Deficiency Act and the 1914 Elementary Education (Defective and Epileptic Children) Act. The first Section of this latter Act 'defines and classifies mentally defective persons ... into the following four groups which graduate from a low to a high type: Idiots ... Imbeciles ... Feeble-minded ... Moral Imbeciles'.[50] 'Feeble-minded' was the term the Egerton Commission had used to identify the imbecile judged educable. The Education Department employed the term, 'moral imbecile', to explain the seemingly inexplicable; for example a girl who could read and write well but was a habitual thief. The original definition proved an enduring cornerstone in the educational provision for these exceptional children.

Francis Warner, who had offered evidence to the Royal Commission which suggested an alternative explanation to that of Shuttleworth, presented similar evidence to the Departmental Committee, which contained three senior members of the Education Department. The Department had also commissioned evidence from two groups of inspectors, the one inspectors of urban areas and the other of rural districts. The former group was opposed to medical practitioners acting as the gatekeepers of special education on the grounds that they lacked details of schools and such children in school. They argued that the schoolteachers' judgements were more reliable because they were often continually with these pupils in school.[51] The rural inspectors also argued that teachers were experienced in the teaching of these pupils in small schools. They were also strongly opposed to residential special schools whose need would arise almost automatically because of the small size of scattered rural communities. Additionally, they argued that there was a stigma attached to a special school and it was inappropriate to uproot a child from a family and village context to be taught a skill which might have no relevance on return to village life.[52] For whatever reason, the Committee chose to ignore these arguments.

In the period 1901 to 1914 the number of certified schools for epileptic children increased from one to six and the numbers on roll from ten to 474.[53] The schools for mentally defective children rose in the same period from 79 to 179 and the numbers on roll increased from 2,965 to 13,651.[54] To judge by the statistics alone this was an issue of considerably greater magnitude than the education of the blind and the deaf. Moreover, it was only the tip of the iceberg since the numbers of LEAs which had taken up the 1899 permissive legislation had only risen from an initial 14 to 56 per cent in 1913.[55] In addition the proportion of mentally defective pupils discovered at routine medical inspections varied from 0.07 per cent in the county of Dorset to 0.5 per cent in Surrey and Cambridgeshire alike. The range for towns was even wider: 0.02 per cent in Tynemouth and 4.3 per cent in Sunderland.[56]

The Leicester School Board established the first special class for pupils with learning difficulties but considered educable in April 1892. The class was located within an existing elementary school and the admission criteria were educational – reading, arithmetical computation and science. It was also agreed that a pupil's attainment in each might vary.[57] There were 12 members of the class. By the turn of the century Leicester had opened another similar class.

The London School Board (LSB) established two 'special schools ... for those children who by reason of ... mental defect, could not be taught "in ordinary standards or by ordinary methods"'.[58] Those two schools with five teachers and 208 pupils on roll in 1892 expanded to 2,154 pupils, 199 teachers and 53 schools in 1900.[59]

The London board consciously pursued a policy of separate, segregated special schools based upon the German auxiliary schools scheme. In 1880 the German Minister of Education had instructed all towns with more than 20,000 inhabitants to provide auxiliary schools for 'children who, after two years at a State elementary school had proved themselves incapable of doing the work'.[60] The LSB's special schools subcommittee readily adopted the medical science formulation of the exceptional child set out in the Egerton Commission's deliberations and, indeed, within a few years Shuttleworth was appointed as the board's examiner for admission to the special classes. The principle of classification lay at the centre of the subcommittee's thinking, planning and establishment of these schools. 'My idea ... was to classify as much as we could', declared the chairman of the subcommittee who was also the vice-chairman of the board itself.[61] To achieve classification efficiently, the policy was adopted that there should be normally at least three classes on any one site with a minimum of two and a maximum of five.[62] The deep irony was that classification was embedded in the concept of the hierarchy of mental deficiency where it was conceded that there were no differences of kind within the hierarchy. Finally, London inaugurated a further degree of separation of special schools from the rest of the education system by requiring the headteachers of the special schools to report to the superintendent of special schools who in turn reported to the board's special schools subcommittee.

There is a sense in which the concept of the hierarchy of mental deficiency in harness with the principle of classification made an apparent reality of these abstract ideas in the concrete existence of segregated special schools. The abstract ideas legitimated the school buildings and their organization; obversely, the buildings legitimated the ideas. The London model served as the blueprint for this part of the system since other authorities embarking upon the establishment of special classes for mentally defective pupils routinely dispatched intending teachers to become familiar with the London procedures. Quoting from an Education Department report, the

London board observed that 'the example is being followed in other large centres of population'.[63]

Changes and continuities

The London board's personnel were influential in another respect. In October 1903, the National Special Schools Union (NSSU) held its inaugural conference. London's superintendent of special schools was vice-president while Shuttleworth was a committee member. The Union's declared aims were 'to promote the interests of Special School Teachers', 'methods of training teachers for Special Schools' and the encouragement of the formation of local branches.[64] A 'physician for nervous diseases' who had also presented evidence to the Egerton Commission and the Departmental Committee was the first speaker to address the national conference. He produced a taxonomy of 13 'types of mental deficiency' which were based upon the 1899 Act's definition.[65] In this way the science of mental deficiency was further elaborated in harness with the growth of a network of special schools serviced by specially trained teachers.

In 1913 Cyril Burt was appointed by the London County Council (LCC) to refine the tests designed by Simon and Binet to separate those children considered capable of deriving benefit from education from those who could not. This is not the place to present a critique of Burt's psychometry, especially since there is already available a lengthy and incisive exegesis on Burt's work.[66] One example taken from Burt's work illustrates its impact concisely. In 1920 'in London special schools there is accommodation for 1.51 per cent of the population during the ages at which (mental) defectives are admitted ... the lowest 1.5 per cent ... is equivalent to ... a mental ratio of 69.4 ... The borderline is taken as 70 per cent of the chronological age.'[67] In this way the purely pragmatic consideration of the number of places available in special schools determined the cut off point in a test of mental ability. Thus 'in time, the 70 per cent cut off became "frozen" in people's minds as a convenient criterion for selection (for special classes)'.[68]

Burt's appointment was symbolic of the increasing standing of psychometric tests in the identification of the mentally defective pupil. From that time on the Chief Medical Officer of the Board of Education in his annual reports encouraged medical officers undertaking examinations of pupils to make themselves familiar with the tests.

The 1921 Education Act consolidated no fewer than 27 previous acts. Part V brought together into one section the measures contained in the 1893 Elementary Education (Blind and Deaf Children) Act, the provisions of the permissive 1899 Elementary Education (Defective and Epileptic Children) Act and the compulsory measures in the 1914 Act of the same title. It recognized five categories of disabled children: blind, deaf, mentally defective, physically defective and epileptic. For the previous year the Chief Medical Officer of the Board of Education had reported the numbers of pupils in special schools as being: 2,934 blind, 4,048 deaf, 15,077 mentally defective, 6,467 physically defective and 458 epileptic.[69] An appendix offered further details for all the categories. Regarding the mentally defective, in addition to the figure in special schools it was reported that 9,389 feeble-minded pupils attended elementary schools, 1,196 had been notified to the local authority and 3,103 were not at school. Also 467 pupils classified as idiot, the next lower ranking, were in elementary schools.[70] It is evident that the adjudged mentally defective pupils were substantial in number and formed by far the largest subgroup in special education. The 1921 Act laid down that following assessment and medical certification, provision for these five categories of children could only be in special schools and certified classes.

Commentators are agreed that financial restraints consequent upon the onset of the First World War severely restricted the necessary assessment and provision for the backward pupil.[71] On top of this factor, however, the 'Geddes axe' in 1922 recommended a total of £75 million savings across the whole range of government activities but concentrated a sharp attack upon the education service. In these circumstances expansion of provision from the 1921 Act was unlikely. Indeed, the Board of Education ruled that expenditure on special schools in 1922–3 should not exceed that of 1921–2.

In a section of his report for 1923 the Chief Medical Officer of the Board of Education concentrated upon the difficulties attendant upon the assessment of the mentally defective pupil. These difficulties, in his opinion, stemmed from two sources: first, the reluctance on the part of LEAs to accept that effective provision was possible for such pupils once ascertained. Hence it was thought that medical officers could spend their time more profitably on other tasks; and second, the ambiguities in the definition in Section 55(I) of the 1921 Act. This, briefly, defined mentally defective pupils as those 'incapable of receiving proper benefit from the instruction in the ordinary Public Elementary Schools but not incapable ... of receiving benefit from instruction in ... Special Classes or Schools'. The difficulties hinged upon the interpretations of the words 'proper' and 'beneficial' and here LEAs differed widely in their practices. The Chief Officer's solution was to issue a revised, more detailed schedule of ascertainment and to emphasize that the task was the responsibility of a 'medical man' and must not be undertaken 'by teachers and other non-medical persons'.[72]

The Chief Officer also declared that special provision should be located in mainstream schools: 'The ideal arrangement for every child is *that he should go to the ordinary school* which is attended by his usual companions and playmates.'[73] The cynic might argue that this was not a statement of policy but rather, given the previous figures, an acceptance of reality. This reality was subsequently confirmed by extensive research undertaken by the Wood Committee which was established in 1924 and reported in 1929.[74] The ambiguities in ascertainment and provision rumbled on through the 1930s, producing a large pamphlet from the Ministry of Education in 1937.[75]

The 1944 Education Act can be characterized as a tripartite system of classification based upon a belief in the accuracy of psychometry and in a more or less fixed innate intelligence. A profound irony suffused the Act. Its expressed aim was to provide education for all children according to age, ability and aptitude. However, the subsequent Handicapped Pupils and School Health Service Regulations[76] defined 11 categories of pupils whose education was to be the responsibility of the health authorities. These categories were based upon those in the 1921 Act but also contained subdivisions such as partially sighted and partially deaf, together with new categories such as maladjusted. The enlarged list of categories created the potential for expansion of special education, particularly in the area defined as educational subnormality (ESN) which was based upon ability and maladjustment, based upon behaviour. It is argued that the engine for expansion was the pressure from personnel, teachers and others within the special school system and the desire that mainstream schools should function efficiently.[77] The Ministry subsequently acknowledged that 'the period under review (1945–55) witnessed a rapid expansion of the special school system'.[78]

The Regulations defined 'Educationally sub-normal pupils' (ESN) as 'pupils who, by reason of limited ability or other conditions resulting in educational retardation, require some specialised form of education wholly or partly in substitution for the education normally given in ordinary schools'.[79] It was estimated that ESN pupils might constitute ten per cent of registered pupils. ESN arose from 'limited intelligence' which 'cannot be substantially improved by any methods known'.[80] The retarded were pupils whose standard of work was below that of average children who were 20 per cent younger; for example a ten-year-old whose work was below that of an eight-year-old. Children with an intelligence quotient (IQ) 'below about 55' were judged ineducable in school. An IQ 'of about 55 to 70 or 75' characterized the ESN pupil. Eight or nine per cent of such pupils over the age of seven were to be found in ordinary junior schools and more in secondary moderns, which was the most efficient setting 'if he were a steady, stable child who received full support in his efforts from his parents and sympathy from his classmates'.[81] Boarding schools were to be the destiny of 'public assistance children, those from unsuitable homes and those unmanageable in day special schools'.[82] The social and judgmental dimensions are evident.

Between 1951 and 1973 numbers of special schools for ESN pupils expanded from 126 to 758 day schools and from 68 to 147 boarding schools – a massive sixfold increase for the former and more than twofold for the latter.[83] In that same period the number of pupils ascertained as being ESN rose from 15,173 to 79,556. This represented a rise from 0.27 to 0.93 as a percentage of the school population, although the ratio of boys to girls remained roughly constant at 3:2.[84]

The 1970 Education (Handicapped Children) Act transferred responsibility for the care and training of ineducable or severely ESN pupils from the health to the education authorities. On this basis between 1974 and 1983 the number of ESN schools increased from 784 to 786 day schools and declined from 143 to 133 boarding schools. In that same period the number of ascertained ESN pupils rose from 77,005 to 79,239 which constituted a rise in prevalence in the school population from 0.87 to 1.05 per cent.[85]

Following the changes in nomenclature in the 1981 Education Act, data concerning the previously classified ESN pupils were published in terms of curriculum need between 1984 and 1988 when they ceased. The figures reveal a decline in absolute numbers from 114,746 to 102,142, which also represents a decline in the prevalence in the school population from 1.56 to 1.52 per cent. That latter, however, was a very large increase, almost a half, from the 1.05 per cent of 1983.[86]

Conclusion

In a persisting context where the backward pupil, the feeble-minded, the mentally defective or the ESN pupil has consistently proved to be the largest group numerically and increasing, one puzzling thread runs through all the legislation from its inception: the inadequacy of the definition of the phenomenon. In the most recent instance, that of the revised Code of Practice to be launched in the year 2001, this arises despite the fact that an official critique of the deficiency was published almost a decade ago.[87] One consequence has been the wide variations in the rates of ascertainment or statementing both between and within authorities.[88] One possible explanation is that this form of definition permits flexibility in the oversight of the application of policy. There is certainly an awareness of the relative cost of special education,[89] and the unit cost per pupil/student in special schools is calculated as being nearly six times greater than primary school costs and four times that of secondary school.[90] Hence there may be an official desire to minimize costs through variations in the application of policy.

The 1981 Act introduced the concept of the statement, which was, in effect, a guarantee of additional resources for the pupil. From inception the prevalence of statemented pupils within the school population has increased remorselessly from two per cent in 1991 to three per cent in 1999.[91] A study commissioned by the Society of Education Officers in 1996 estimated that five per cent of pupils would be statemented in the year 2000 and demonstrated that expenditure on special educational needs already cost 12.5 per cent of LEAs' schools' budget.[92] A more recent study reveals that such expenditure in one London borough amounts to 16.75 per cent of the schools' budget.[93]

Addressing a conference in the mid-1990s, Baroness Warnock stated that the idea of a 'Code of Practice lies very uneasily within the 1988 Education Reform Act and competition between schools'.[94] Ironically, that same Act encouraged the idea of parents as consumers and parental rights. One way for parents to pursue their perceived rights was to appeal to the Secretary of State against decisions made by LEAs. Parents also began to seek judicial review of LEA decisions in the courts and through the local government ombudsmen.[95] The 1993 Education Act established eight regional Special Educational Needs Tribunals which were intended to be independent of both local and national government. In the first year of operation, 1994–5, 242 appeals were heard. Since that date both the number of appeals has increased steadily to 1,220 in 1998–9 and the parental success rate to three-quarters of all appeals.[96] This trend is most likely to continue.

If the definition of special educational needs is ambiguous, the one way to try to establish clarity is through the legal process. Initially in the 1980s legal challenges centred upon issues such as school placement or responsibility for the provision of speech therapy. A decision of the House of Lords in July 2000 'in the case of Pamela Phelps, who was awarded £45,650 damages against Hillingdon council because her former school failed to identify her dyslexia ... fundamentally alters the landscape'.[97] The Lords ruled that just like any other members of professions, teachers and particularly headteachers, had a duty of responsibility. A group of 30 families in the Midlands was awaiting the outcome eagerly. The group has initiated a class action to sue a county council for three-quarters of a million pounds 'claiming their dyslexic children did not get enough support at school ... leaving with few or no qualifications'.[98] It is reported that a London law firm has more than 40 similar cases which it intends to bring to the courts,[99] and a Manchester law firm has brought a group action for ten people.[100] Given the circumstances, this trend too is likely to persist in the case of pupils with learning difficulties.

Baroness Warnock has expressed her disappointment over these tendencies. The committee's intention had been to redirect attention away from the hard core of pupils with serious handicap toward a larger group which might require additional help at some point in their educational careers. This, however, had not proved to be the case:

> The 'statement' has been a disastrous mistake. As money for education lessened so it became clear that little would be done to meet the needs of a child unless he or she had a statement and so parents increasingly demanded that their child be 'statemented' ... local authorities began to list the child's needs to match what they could afford.[101]

In this way the ambiguous definition drives the policy and the application of policy the litigation. In a context of spiralling costs this situation is likely to persist.

Key reading

The reports of Royal Commissions provide a rich source of primary historical data in the form of witness evidence. That of the Royal Commission on the Blind, the Deaf and Dumb, etc. of the UK, London, HMSO, 4 vols, 1889, is an excellent example. The Education Department's, Departmental Committee on Defective and Epileptic Children, London, HMSO, 2 vols, 1898, is another. The annual reports of the Chief Medical Officer of the Board of Education, London, HMSO, 1908–38 often contain original contributions on a variety of topics submitted by school medical officers in the field. Frequently, there are accounts of experiments and/or research. The Department of Education and Science, *Special Educational Needs* (The Warnock Report), London, HMSO, 1978 contains details of the research and arguments which informed the Committee's thinking.

A. Morton, *Education and the State from 1833*, Kew, PRO Publications, 1997, is a guide to educational documents in the Public Record Office and contains a section on 'Special Educational Treatment' (8.2). I. Mortimer (ed.) *Record Repositories in Great Britain*, Kew, PRO, 1999, lists national, university and special repositories in the UK and local repositories in GB. Through the examination of committee minutes and school log books information can be derived about local responses to policy and decisions.

D.G. Pritchard, *Education and the Handicapped, 1760–1960*, London, Routledge and Kegan Paul, 1963, draws upon countless primary and secondary sources in his narrative of the development of special education in Britain up to just beyond the middle of the last century. T. Cole, *Apart or A Part? Integration and the Growth of British Special Education*, Milton Keynes, Open University Press, 1989 reveals how arguments in favour of integration and segregation have moved one way and then another in changing circumstances. I.C. Copeland, *The Making of the Backward Pupil in Education in England 1870–1914*, London, Woburn, Press, 1999, draws upon primary and secondary sources to give an account of the early stages of learning difficulties in state education. M. Thomson, *The Problem of Mental Deficiency*, Oxford, Clarendon Press,

1998, draws heavily upon primary sources and shows how conceptions of mental deficiency and eugenics were interwoven in the period 1870–1960. Although the focus is upon adults, there is much salient information on pupils and school policy. J. Corbett, *Special Educational Needs in the Twentieth Century: a cultural analysis*, London, Cassell, 1998, presents a radical reappraisal of policies and practices in special education as they unfolded over the past century and suggests what could develop in the twenty-first century.

Notes

1 Department of Education and Science (DES), *Special Educational Needs*, London, HMSO, 1978.
2 Ministry of Education (MoE), *Statistics of Education: Schools*, London, HMSO, 1951; DES, *Statistics of Education: Schools*, London, HMSO, 1984.
3 P. Croll and D. Moses, *Special Needs in the Primary School. One in Five?*, London, Cassell, 1999, p. 22.
4 Ibid., p. 23.
5 DES, op. cit., p. 5.
6 Ibid., pp. 36–7.
7 Ibid., pp. 37–41.
8 Ibid., p. 44.
9 Ibid., p. 48.
10 Ibid., p. 100.
11 Ibid., p. 150.
12 B. Norwich, *Reappraising Special Needs Education*, London, Cassell, 1990, pp. 6–17.
13 P.B. Medawar, *The Art of the Soluble: Creativity and Originality in Science*, London, Methuen, 1967, pp. 113–16.
14 National Union of Teachers (NUT), *The Education Act 1981: A Union Guide*, London, NUT, 1982, p. 6.
15 T.G. Connolly and W. Slukin, *An Introduction to Statistics for the Social Sciences*, London, Macmillan, 1971, pp. 137–59.
16 DES, *Assessments and Statements of SEN, Circular 1/83*, Stanmore, DES, 1983.
17 B. Goacher, J. Evans, J. Welton and K. Wedell, *Policy and Provision for Special Educational Needs*, London, Cassell, 1988.
18 Ibid., pp. 50–96.
19 I.C. Copeland *et al.*, 'Statements and issues in special educational needs', *Curriculum*, 1993, vol. 14, no. 2, pp. 104–12.
20 Audit Commission and Her Majesty's Inspectorate (ACHMI), *Getting in on the Act: Provision for Pupils with Special Needs*, London, HMSO, 1992.
21 Department for Education (DfE), *Code of Practice on the Identification and Assessment of Special Educational Needs*, London, DfE, 1994.
22 B. Norbury, *Education Bill: SEN*, London, DfE, 1993, p. 1.
23 ACHMI, op. cit., p. 5.
24 Ibid., p. 1.
25 Norbury, op. cit., p. 3.
26 R. Morris, E. Reid and J. Fowler, *Education Act 93: A Critical Guide*, London, Association of Metropolitan Authorities, p. 54.
27 ACHMI, op, cit., p. 51.

28 Ibid., p. 13.
29 DfE, op. cit., p. 5.
30 Centre for Studies in Inclusive Education (CSIE), *Meeting SEN: CSIE Summary of Part IV of the Education Act 1996*, Bristol, CSIE, 1997, p. 2.
31 Department for Education and Employment (DfEE), *SEN Code of Practice on the Identification and Assessment of Pupils with SEN*, London, DfEE, 2000.
32 F. Smith, *A History of English Elementary Education, 1760–1902*, London, University of London Press, 1931, p. 307.
33 Board of Education (BoE), *Report of the BoE 1899–1900*, London, HMSO, 1901, vol. iii, p. 104.
34 Ibid., p. 105.
35 Smith, op. cit., pp. 254–61; D. Wardle, *English Popular Education, 1780–1975*, Cambridge, Cambridge University Press, pp. 68–89.
36 Report of the Royal Commission on the Elementary Education Acts (RCEEA), 1886, pp. 3–4.
37 Report of the Royal Commission on the Blind, the Deaf and Dumb &c., (RCBDD), 1889, vol. i, p. 2.
38 Ibid., p. v.
39 RCEEA, op. cit., p. 131.
40 RCBDD, op. cit., vol. i, p. 104.
41 Ibid., vol. iii, p. 705; see also vol. i, p. 95.
42 Ibid., vol. iii, p. 706; see also J. Alston, *The Royal Albert: Chronicles of an Era*, Centre for North West Regional Studies, University of Lancaster, 1992, pp. 30–2.
43 RCBDD, op. cit., vol. iii, p. 670.
44 Ibid., pp. 698–9.
45 I.C. Copeland, 'The establishment of models of education for disabled children', *British Journal of Educational Studies*, 1995, vol. 43, no. 2, pp. 179–200.
46 BoE, op. cit., p.153.
47 Ibid., p. 154.
48 Report of the Departmental Committee on Defective and Epileptic Children (DCDEC), London, HMSO, 1898, vol. ii, p. 1.
49 Ibid., p. 2.
50 J. Wormald and S. Wormald, *A Guide to the Mental Deficiency Act 1913*, London, P.S. King, 1915, p. 8.
51 DCDEC, op. cit., p. 225.
52 Ibid., p. 202.
53 BoE, *Report of BoE, 1902*; *Report of BoE, 1916*.
54 Ibid.
55 Chief Medical Officer of the BoE, *Annual Report 1913*, London, HMSO, 1914, p. 213.
56 Ibid., p. 210.
57 DCDEC, op. cit., pp. 134–7.
58 School Board for London, *Final Report of the London School Board 1870–1904*, London, P.S. King and Son, 1904, p. 162.
59 Ibid., p. 163; see also E.M. Burgwin, 'The physically and mentally defective', in T.A. Spalding (ed.) *The Work of the London School Board*, London, P.S. King and Son, 1900, p. 256.
60 DCDEC, op. cit., p. 249.
61 Ibid., p.101; Burgwin, op. cit., p. 255.
62 Burgwin, op. cit., p. 256.
63 School Board for London, op. cit., p. 184.

64 National Special Schools Union, *Report of the First National Conference of the NSSU*, Liverpool, C. Tinling, 1904, pp. 9–10.

65 Ibid., pp. 13–27.

66 S.J. Gould, *The Mismeasure of Man*, Harmondsworth, Penguin, 1984, pp. 234–320; N. Rose, *The Psychological Complex: Psychology, Politics and Society in England 1869–1939*, London, Routledge and Kegan Paul, 1985, pp. 90–145.

67 C. Burt, *Mental and Scholastic Tests*, London, P.S. King and Son, 1921, p. 168.

68 W. Swann, *Psychology and Special Education*, Milton Keynes, Open University Press, 1982, p. 14.

69 Chief Medical Officer of BoE, *Annual Report 1920*, London, HMSO, 1921, p. 117.

70 Ibid., p. 211.

71 D.G. Pritchard, *Education and the Handicapped, 1760–1960*, London, Routledge and Kegan Paul, 1963, p. 188; G. Sutherland and S. Sharp, *Ability, Merit and Measurement: Mental Testing and English Education 1880–1940*, Oxford, Clarendon Press, 1984, p. 18; T. Cole, *Apart or A Part? Integration and the Growth of British Special Education*, Milton Keynes, Open University Press, 1989, p. 71.

72 Chief Medical Officer of the BoE, *Annual Report 1923*, London, HMSO, 1924, p. 61.

73 Ibid., p. 66, original emphasis.

74 Board of Education and Board of Control, *Report of the Joint Departmental Committee on Mental Deficiency*, 3 vols, London, HMSO, 1929.

75 MoE, *The Education of Backward Children*, Educational Pamphlet No. 112, London, HMSO, 1937.

76 MoE, *Handicapped Pupils and School Health Service Regulations*, London, HMSO, 1945.

77 S. Tomlinson, *A Sociology of Special Education*, London, Routledge and Kegan Paul, 1982, p. 51.

78 MoE, *Education of the Handicapped Pupil 1945–1955*, Pamphlet No. 30, London, HMSO, 1956, p. 5.

79 MoE, *Special Educational Treatment*, Pamphlet No. 5, London, HMSO, 1946, p. 7.

80 Ibid., p. 18.

81 Ibid., p. 22.

82 Ibid., p. 25.

83 MoE, *Statistics of Education : Schools*, London, HMSO, 1951; DES, *Statistics of Education: Schools*, London, HMSO, 1975.

84 Ibid.

85 DES, *Statistics of Education: Schools*, London, HMSO, 1975; DES, *Statistics of Education: Schools*, London, HMSO, 1984.

86 DES, *Statistics of Education: Schools*, London, HMSO, 1985; DES, *Statistics of Education: Schools*, London, HMSO, 1988.

87 ACHMI, *Getting in on the Act: Provision for Pupils with Special Needs*, London, HMSO, 1992, pp. 1, 51.

88 Chief Medical Officer of the BoE, *Annual Report 1910*, London, HMSO, 1911, pp. 206–7; B. Norwich, *A Trend Towards Inclusion: Statistics on Special School Placements and Pupils with Statements in Ordinary Schools, England, 1992–96*, Bristol, Centre for Studies in Inclusive Education, 1997, pp. 6–18.

89 Chief Medical Officer of the BoE, *Annual Report 1923*, London, HMSO, 1924, p. 27.

90 DfEE, *Education and Training Statistics for the UK 1999*, London, TSO, 1999, p. 10.
91 DfEE, *Statistics of Education, Special Needs in England: January 1999, Issue No. 12/99*, London, TSO, 1999, p. 5.
92 N. Pyke, 'Warnock fears for special needs code', *Times Educational Supplement*, 12 May 1996.
93 T. Bowers and T. Parrish, 'Funding of special education in the US and England and Wales', in M.J. McLaughlin and M. Rouse (eds) *Special Education and School Reform in the US and Britain*, London, Routledge, 2000, p. 173.
94 Pyke, op. cit.
95 I.C. Copeland, 'The special needs code of practice: antecedents and outcomes', *Cambridge Journal of Education*, 1997, vol. 27, no. 1, pp. 709–22.
96 J. Slater, 'Special educational needs', *Times Educational Supplement*, 14 July 2000.
97 J. Rabinowicz, 'A risk any professional may run?', *Times Educational Supplement*, 24 August 2000.
98 R. Bushby, 'Dyslexics sue council', *Times Educational Supplement*, 15 September 2000.
99 R. Verkaik, 'Dyslexic sues for £60,000 over her "Lost Education"', *The Independent*, 10 October 2000.
100 I. Herbert, 'Dyslexia sufferers sue councils for neglect', *The Independent*, 17 October 2000.
101 H.M. Warnock, 'If only we had known then', *Times Educational Supplement*, 31 December 1999.

Chapter 9

Curriculum

Peter Gordon

The situation in 2000

In a survey of the curriculum in English schools over the last century, it may seem appropriate that a major review of this area came into effect in the year 2000. As we shall see later, the first National Curriculum, introduced between 1988 and 1992, was heavily criticized as being overloaded and too prescriptive. A review of the curriculum carried out by Sir Ron (now Lord) Dearing in 1993–4 attempted to tackle some of the more immediate problems: many teachers found that they had to reinvent the wheel by preparing personal teaching plans based on the curriculum, and that the National Curriculum was failing to engage a significant minority of 14-year-olds who were as a consequence becoming disaffected with learning. Another serious aspect was that over a third of pupils were leaving primary schools without reaching the expected level of achievement in English and a similar proportion were not meeting adequate standards in mathematics.[1]

In order to try and meet these shortcomings, the Secretary of State for Education and Employment, David Blunkett, ordered the Qualifications and Curriculum Authority (QCA) to undertake a further review in order to advise him of necessary changes in current curriculum subjects. In 1999 the QCA reported and drew up a list of key themes for the future.[2]

The Secretary of State accepted particularly the recommendations for some relaxation in aspects of the National Curriculum, though as there are statutory tests in the core subjects of English and mathematics at seven, 11 and 14 and in science which is assessed at seven but tested at 11 and 14, and given that there are national targets for 11-year-olds in English and mathematics set for the year 2002, proposed changes in these subject should be kept to a minimum. The more important changes recommended included: a more explicit rationale for the school curriculum; a more inclusive curriculum framework, with individual subject statements in all subjects; a less prescriptive and more flexible National Curriculum, with revised programmes of study for the core subjects. Two new areas, personal, social and health education and citizenship, would be introduced in order to prepare pupils for life and also a wider range of vocational qualifications to support work-related learning.[3]

The situation in 1900

Similar dramatic changes in the curriculum were occurring at the beginning of the twentieth century. At the elementary level, a system of 'payment by results' had been in operation since the Revised Code had been introduced by Robert Lowe, the Vice-President of the Committee of the Privy Council on Education, in 1862. In future, grants were paid to managers of schools largely based on an annual examination of all children in the three Rs – reading, writing and arithmetic, together with plain needlework for girls. From the age of six, children were examined in six stages or standards. The narrowness of the curriculum and the nature of the examination which led to mechanical teaching resulted in protests from the profession and a gradual softening of the regulations took place over the next 40 years. For example, extra grants were made in 1867 for schools if they included at least one 'specific' subject such as history, geography and grammar, and eight years later a third category, 'class' subjects, were introduced. The last category was based not on the proficiency of individual pupils but on the attainment of the class as a whole. By the 1882 Code, a new Standard seven – a recognition that children were now staying longer at school – was introduced and new subjects, including chemistry, electricity and agriculture, were allowed.[4]

The 1890s saw a remarkable loosening up in the control of the elementary curriculum. In 1888 an official report on elementary education by the Cross Commission had advised that many changes were needed not only in the subjects taught but also in the teaching methods then employed. Alternative schemes of work were subsequently allowed in small schools in English, geography, elementary science and history; manual instruction was recognized and drawing was made compulsory; and commercial subjects, particularly bookkeeping and shorthand, became immediately popular. Similarly, the 1893 Circular on *The Instruction of Infants* contained a list of varied occupations embodying Froebelian principles which marked the acceptance of modern teaching methods. Finally, in 1895 the Code for that year took the logical step of abolishing the annual examination for older scholars, thus signalling the ending of payment by results. Teachers were now free to pursue a broader curriculum and were encouraged to experiment with their pedagogical approaches.

The Elementary Code of 1900 introduced a new and simple method of block grants to schools for the first time, and contained the first official statement of what the elementary curriculum should comprise: English, arithmetic, geography, history, singing, physical education, drawing for boys and needlework for girls with, where practicable, a science, French and algebra for the older pupils. No specific syllabuses were prescribed. By the beginning of the twentieth century, almost all elementary schools were subject to general inspection only.

There was also much less uniformity of curriculum in the secondary sector. There were several providers, outstanding of which were the public schools. For the most part they offered a curriculum heavily biased towards the Classics. Because of mounting criticism of the public schools in the mid-nineteenth century, a Royal Commission, chaired by Lord Clarendon, enquired into the curriculum and teaching methods as well as the endowments and administration of nine leading public schools, including Eton and Harrow. The exclusivity of Classics was condemned and 'modern sides', with emphases on modern languages, mathematics and natural science, were recommended. That at Harrow, created in 1869, is a typical example. Boys unable to learn Latin were set Milton and Coleridge and a state of the art laboratory was established.[5]

Some 800 endowed or grammar schools, like their public school counterparts, were also examined by a Commission headed by Baron Taunton, 1864–8. Unlike elementary schools, they did not come within the jurisdiction of the Committee of the Privy Council on Education and the curriculum ranged from copies of a public school to one no different from that of an average elementary school. An important outcome of the Commission was that endowed schools were reformed into one of three categories, first, second and third grade, each with its own curriculum corresponding to the perceived class of pupil attending each school. The first grade, mainly preparing pupils for university, were predominantly classical schools; the second grade for boys preparing for business, the armed forces or the professions, with a more modern type of curriculum, and the third grade, for future artisans, leaving at the age of 14 with a more utilitarian and practical curriculum. It is interesting to compare this tripartite division of secondary schools with a similar typology promoted by the Norwood Committee some 75 years later, and which is discussed below.

The lack of science and technical education in schools was a constant worry towards the end of the century. Evidence from Continental countries such as France and Germany gathered by the Samuelson Commission on Technical Instruction in 1882–4 showed that foreign industrial competition had been helped by the establishment of technical education institutions in many countries. To stem the decline, a Technical Instruction Act of 1889 encouraged county councils and county boroughs to levy a penny rate for technical instruction and abolished the restriction that limited the work of the Science and Art Department to the 'industrial classes'. One local authority which took the matter seriously, London, provided a good secondary education which was not confined only to a few subjects. As Sidney Webb, chairman of the London Technical Education Board, claimed, 'We can now lawfully teach anything under the sun, except ancient Greek and theology.'[6]

By the last decade of the century, the lack of a central authority for a well-organized system of education was obvious. The Bryce Commission on Secondary Education in 1895 called for a central authority which would include the educational aspects of the Charity Commission, the Science and Art Department and the Education Department under the direction of a single minister. This became an accomplished fact when the Board of Education came into existence in 1900. It is, however, worth noting that the Bryce Commission considered that it was not 'desirable to lay down definite model curricula for schools of various types'. Whilst this could be interpreted as an assertion of the continuing independence of secondary schools from state supervision and interference, it could also be construed as an attempt to avoid the tightly controlled elementary curriculum which in itself was then coming to an end.

Another factor was the fear of higher grade schools, then operated by school boards, which offered a curriculum which straddled the elementary/secondary divide and was often superior to the latter in breadth. In an attempt to curb the activities of these schools, a Higher Elementary Minute was promulgated, curbing the scope by limiting the curriculum to future manual workers and with a leaving age of 15. The matter was contested in the High Court which decided that the London School Board had spent money illegally and not in accordance with the Code. The so-called Cockerton Judgment of 1901 henceforward sharpened the curriculum distinction between secondary and elementary education.

Changes and continuities

If we look at the development of the school curriculum during the past century we can discern five fairly distinct phases.

Beginnings of central policy, 1900–11

The establishment of the Board of Education was followed by the 1902 Education Act which created local education authorities (LEAs). These LEAs took over responsibility from the School Boards including the supervision of the secular curriculum and they were also permitted but not compelled to be responsible for building secondary schools, popularly known as grammar schools. However, the Board of Education came to exercise detailed control over the curriculum at both elementary and secondary levels. Much of the influence on the shape of the curriculum was due to Robert Morant, the first Permanent Secretary of the Board of Education, 1903–11. He put forward the view that there was 'a necessity for having a really expert Central Authority for the whole of our National Education, a localised "guidance of brains", which will watch, consider and advise upon all our national educational arrangements of all grades, of every type, as one whole'.[7]

Morant now set about putting those aims into practice. In the Introduction to the Code for Elementary Schools, 1904 which he drew up, he stated:

> The purpose of Public Elementary Schools is to form and strengthen the character, to develop the intelligence of the children entrusted to it, and to make the best use of the school years available, in assisting both girls and boys, according to their different needs, to fit themselves, practically as well as intellectually, for the work of life.

Whilst some historians have interpreted the Code as a recipe for 'training in followership',[8] others have seen it as a more enlightened document. For the first time in a Code, the Board endeavoured to state the proper aims of elementary schooling and also outlined a more co-ordinated curriculum in place of the relatively haphazard list of possible branches of knowledge which were formerly presented. To effect this change, a companion volume to the Code was issued in the following year, *Suggestions for the Consideration of Teachers and others concerned with the work of Public Elementary Schools*, renamed from 1927 *Handbook of Suggestions for Teachers*. The first publication stated in the Preface that its aim was to offer guidance to teachers 'and even more to encourage careful reflection on the practice of their profession'. One memorable passage in the *Suggestions* reads:

> The only uniformity of practice that the Board of Education desire to see in the teaching of Public Elementary Schools is that each teacher shall think for himself, and work out for himself such methods of teaching as may use his powers to the best advantage and be best suited to the particular needs and conditions of the school.[9]

A separate chapter is devoted each to English, arithmetic, observation lessons and nature study, geography, history, drawing, singing, physical training, needlework, housecraft, handicraft and gardening. The *Handbook* was a collaborative venture between Board officials and leading members of His Majesty's Inspectorate (HMI), with the addition of a few distinguished outside experts.[10] This initiative was widely welcomed.

If the elementary curriculum was seen as a liberalization from its former fetters, a much more rigid approach was applied to the secondary stage. Morant who himself had been educated at Winchester College and Oxford, saw the task of secondary schools as being to provide an education for leadership, and favoured a curriculum based on the majority of public schools with little emphasis on the practical and scientific. The 1904 Regulations for Secondary Schools recommended that instruction should be 'general' and that specialization in science or literature should only begin after a good deal of general ground had been covered. The precise allocation of time to be devoted to each part of the curriculum left little space for teachers to innovate. Morant's achievement here though was that for the first time a coherent pattern of secondary schooling with recognizable boundaries was established.[11] This rigidly academic view of the curriculum was relaxed to some extent by the Board's 1907 Regulations. The minimum time prescribed for English language and literature, geography, history, science and one foreign language was withdrawn and more practical subjects, particularly physical education and manual work, were allowed.

One interesting by-product of the 1907 Regulations was the introduction of a scholarship ladder whereby 25 per cent of the annual entry to secondary schools was reserved for pupils passing the approved tests. But as only a small minority of elementary pupils was admitted, this tended to widen the curriculum gap between the elementary and secondary schools.

Effects of official reports and new philosophies, 1911–25

As long ago as 1868, Matthew Arnold in his *Reports on European Systems* had recommended an unpaid central council to supervise examinations, school books and questions of the curriculum. Apart from the establishment in 1880 of a Code Committee consisting of HMI, civil servants and the political head of the Department to scrutinize the operation of the school codes, little action was taken. The 1899 Board of Education Act included provision for a Consultative Committee to advise the Board on any matters referred to it. At least two-thirds of its 18 members represented universities and other bodies concerned with education. It was acknowledged that Royal Commissions were cumbersome and slow in their deliberations and that the new body could take more decisive action. Not all politicians welcomed the new move. Hicks Beach, a leading Conservative, wrote to the Lord President, the Duke of Devonshire, in 1899, 'I hope the Committee will not be given a permanent character. I look with horror on the projects which would be started directly or indirectly by a Committee of educational faddists.'[12] In practice the Consultative Committee proved to be of great value in investigating a range of curriculum issues until almost the end of the Second World War.

One important topic was the place of examinations in secondary schools, as their growth was increasingly affecting the curriculum. One result of the expansion of secondary education since the 1902 Act was the increase in the number of pupils taking a wide variety of examinations at

14 or 15. Clearly, some national guidelines were required and the Consultative Committee was asked to consider 'in what circumstances examinations are desirable for boys and girls'. The Committee considered the question at three levels: on entrance to school, during school life and at leaving school. It decided that external public examinations should be conducted in order to emphasize the principle that every secondary school should provide a sound liberal education for school leavers at the age of 16, and that examinations should be a means of planning and directing the content of the school's curriculum.

The Board of Education saw examinations as merely a means of testing rather than influencing the curriculum. A number of circulars stated that 'the cardinal principle is that examinations should follow the curriculum and not determine it', an admirable principle but one not easy to operate. This can be seen when in 1917 the Board set up the Secondary School Examinations Council to supervise the newly created School Certificate Examination for pupils who had experienced five years of secondary education, and the Higher School Certificate, taken after a further two years in the sixth form. Prolonged negotiations with university examination boards and other interested parties led to a five-subject examination in which one had to be chosen from each of the three groups, English, mathematics, science, together with a foreign language. Candidates sitting the Higher School Certificate Examination specialized in one of three groups: Classics, modern studies or science and mathematics. This selection of subjects was criticized as representing only those of high prestige. It was not until 1923, for instance, that a further group was allowed for the School Certificate Examination which included art, drawing, handicraft and housecraft.[13]

Wars have generally stimulated countries to apply their minds to reappraising their educational systems. As we have seen, examination reform was carried out in Britain during the First World War. A year before the Secondary School Examinations Council was formed, a memorial signed by leading industrialists and educationists was presented to the Prime Minister, H.H. Asquith, calling for a reappraisal of the whole education system. Instead, the Board of Education set up four subcommittees to investigate specific subject areas: natural science, modern languages, Classics and English. Although the Prime Minister's Committees were slow to publish – that on English did not appear until 1921 – nevertheless they were, on the whole, enlightened documents.

The Committee which enquired into the position of modern languages, for instance, took evidence from Civil Service departments, the Army and Navy, the world of business and foreign administration. It showed that in Europe the Dutch, Germans, Russians, Scandinavians and Swiss were better equipped in foreign languages than Britons, thus placing British business at a disadvantage.[14] The Teaching of English Committee, chaired by Sir Henry Newbolt, emphasized the importance of 'language across the curriculum' and coined the phrase that 'every teacher is a teacher of English'.[15] One outcome of the Prime Minister's Reports was Circular 1296, *Curricula of Secondary Schools in England*. It summarized the findings of the four Committees and concluded that the curriculum was congested and the timetable overcrowded. The Circular argued that it was impossible for the secondary curriculum to be general and supported the idea of an increase in specialization. Once again the Board specified carefully the allocation of time to be spent on the teaching of each subject.[16]

After the war one outstanding issue received official attention for the first time, girls' curriculum. Since the Revised Code of 1862 when girls were examined in plain needlework, curriculum differentiation was practised in schools. The 1904 Secondary Regulations pointed out that 'at many Girls' Schools it is not practicable to have the regular after-school meetings which are a matter of course in a Boys' School' – and encouraged more flexible arrangements. In 1913, Circular 826 on the curriculum of secondary schools warned of over-pressure caused by a shorter school day combined with too many subjects, especially in mixed schools. In the latter, therefore, the Board of Education recommended that girls might with advantage postpone the taking of public examinations to 'an age rather later than that which is usual for boys'.

One of the matters taken up by the 1923 Consultative Committee on the Differentiation of the Curriculum for Boys and Girls in Secondary Schools was that the curriculum for girls was modelled too much on that for boys,[17] a legacy of Frances Buss and Emily Davies in the nineteenth century. The Report made some interesting recommendations in order to alleviate the situation. It proposed the elevation of art and music to equal standing with other subjects at School Certificate level and that girls sharing a special aptitude for manual instruction should be allowed to pursue a suitable course; similarly boys with a predilection for cookery should be accommodated. It was recommended that girls be allowed to develop their own interests and encouraged to take initiatives, such as organizing games for themselves rather than being led by a mistress.

More importantly the Committee advised a greater assimilation of teaching methods for boys and girls. New ways of teaching mathematics had been introduced into boys' schools: the Committee suggested that such teaching should also be made available for girls and that they might be taught elementary physics in closer association with mathematics. Other practical steps recommended were the gathering of data by teachers and psychologists on the intellectual and emotional differences between the sexes and their bearing on academic achievement, as well as noting which combination of curriculum subjects seemed most appropriate for girls. However, timidity was shown in implementing these innovations. The Committee mentioned that as secondary education for girls was only about 60 years old, it could still be regarded as experimental. 'It would', the Committee solemnly stated, 'be too easy to make mistakes' at that stage. As a result no larger scale attempt at reform was made for the next half century.

Another important element in the educational climate of the time was the philosophy of the progressives, especially in the elementary sector. The 'New Education' as it came to be called had its antecedents in the writings and practice of Herbart and Froebel in the nineteenth century. Its renaissance in England was largely due to the writings of an ex-school inspector, Edmond Holmes, who published his creed, *What Is and What Might Be*, in 1911. The book was an attack on the existing practices of elementary education: Holmes believed the child should be set free from these through his or her schooling and put on 'the path of self-realisation'. Holmes' writings, which had a strong Montessorian basis, proved an inspiration to many other educationists. Pioneering progressives included Homer Lane, director of the Little Commonwealth community in Dorset, A.S. Neill at Summerhill and the Russells at Beacon Hill. In the more conventional school setting teaching methods came to be used which were in the spirit of the new philosophy. Caldwell Cook at the Perse School, Cambridge, introduced the Play Way method. Helen Parkhurst, who had experimented successfully with liberal teaching methods at the Dalton High School, Massachusetts in the United States, wrote of her experiences in *Education on the Dalton Plan*, published in 1922. Her ideas were eagerly adopted in Britain: by 1926 some 2,000 schools were using the Dalton Plan.[18]

Not all innovations in curriculum and teaching methods were due to the followers of the New Education. Geography teachers for instance had been influenced by H.J. Herbertson's paper on 'The Major Natural Regions: an Essay in Systematic Geography', the beginnings of the new geography, published in 1904. In music, Cecil Sharp was a potent force in enlarging the subject, introducing folk songs and dancing in schools and colleges during the first quarter of the twentieth century. Franz Cizek, an Austrian painter and art teacher, was a leading figure in the Child Art movement. His theories aimed at encouraging the creative rather than the imitative nature of previous teaching.[19] These changes in educational philosophy and methods had an impact on curriculum which were echoed in the important official inquiries which took place in the inter-war period.

War, reorganization and the curriculum, 1926–45

In January 1924 the first Labour government briefly came into office. Two years before, a Labour party policy document, *Secondary Education for All*, edited by R.H. Tawney, had set out the blueprint under which 'primary education and secondary education are organised under two stages in a single continuous process; secondary education being the education of the adolescent, and primary education being preparatory thereto'. All children at the age of eleven plus would be transferred to 'one type or another of secondary school' and remain there until 16 years of age. Within ten days of taking office the Labour government had set up a Consultative Committee on the Education of the Adolescent chaired by Sir W.H. Hadow. Its terms of reference were 'to consider and report upon the organisation, objective and curriculum of courses of study suitable for children who will remain in full-time attendance at schools other than Secondary Schools, up to the age of 15'.

One of the lesser-highlighted recommendations of the Report was its support for a tripartite system of secondary education. It assumed a high-flying secondary grammar school, a modern school determined by local conditions and a technical school for 13 plus pupils, the latter consisting mainly of the junior technical schools created in 1913. The Commission declared strongly against admission of pupils aged 11 to a school with a vocational curriculum, thus losing a golden opportunity.[20]

Hadow's best-known recommendation was that primary and secondary education should be separated at about the age of 11: 'There is a tide which begins to rise in the veins of youth at the age of eleven and twelve', an obvious acknowledgement of the findings of educational psychologists. The secondary grammar school was left out of the Commission's considerations. As the majority of pupils would leave the modern school at 15, as distinct from those at grammar school who left school at 16 or 17, 'the course must be shorter and the subjects handled in a simpler way'. Unlike the grammar school, the modern school would not be influenced to the same extent by the requirements of an external examination. A more instrumental education was recommended:

> The teachers will accordingly be free to frame courses in the several subjects of the curriculum (with some bent in many cases towards, agriculture, commerce or the local industry or group of industries) which should, so far as they go, constitute a coherent body of knowledge in each several branch and in the curriculum as a whole.[21]

By the time the Report had been published, a Conservative government was once more in office. Even before the Committee's deliberations had been completed, a Board of Education Circular 1350, *The Organisation of Public Elementary Schools*, stated that in future, schemes of school planning would not be approved unless provision were made for the advanced instruction of children over 11.[22]

A remarkable fact was that the 1926 Code removed all parliamentary control over the elementary school curriculum, possibly in order to play down the differences between the curriculum of secondary modern schools and grammar schools.[23] But two benefits at least had arisen from the

Report: first, it recognized the need for a distinctive primary school rather than an elementary school, necessitating a massive reorganization of educational provision; second, it recognized the need to rethink the curriculum. In 1928, a Board of Education pamphlet, *The New Prospect in Education*, acknowledged, 'if we cannot adjust our curricula so that they meet these varying needs, the compulsory attendance of the child at school becomes a mere constraint, which may well prejudice him for all time against educational influences'.[24]

The Report of the Consultative Committee on the Primary School, 1931 was the logical sequence to the 1926 Report and marks an important advance in the development of primary education. So far, the elementary tradition had assumed that pupils would be drawn from what may be termed 'the labouring poor'. Now, in a more progressive spirit, it could be seen as a type of schooling appropriate for all children up to the age of 11. Whilst adopting a mildly conservative approach to curriculum, advising some 'drill' in the three Rs and expressing doubts on the relevance of project methods, the Report nevertheless coined the memorable phrase that 'the curriculum was to be thought of in terms of activity and experience rather than of knowledge to be acquired and facts to be stored'.[25] The Report of the Consultative Committee on Infant and Nursery Schools in 1933 was more adventurous, putting forward a new synthesis in the development tradition whilst paying due attention to the importance of basic skills at the infant stage.[26]

Shortly before the outbreak of the Second World War, a very important Report on the curriculum appeared. So far, the secondary school had not come under official scrutiny for many decades. The Consultative Committee on Secondary Education with special reference to Grammar Schools and Technical High Schools, 1938, under the chairmanship of Sir Will Spens looked particularly at the framework and content of the 11 to 16 age group in those schools. It was to have important consequences for the future curriculum of secondary schools.

The Report concluded that a 'single liberal or general education for all is impracticable'.[27] Different forms of general and quasi-vocational education were needed to meet the widely differing intellectual and emotional capacities of pupils and a broader curriculum was required. Spens stressed the strain and overwork of the less academic pupils in secondary schools and therefore recommended that there should be three kinds of secondary schools, grammar, modern and technical, each with its own curriculum. There was to be parity of esteem between all three kinds of school with transfer possible between them. Much of this had been foreshadowed in the 1926 Hadow Report.

With the coming of the Second World War, no action was taken on the Report, but within two years, in 1941, a second Committee, chaired by Cyril Norwood, began work 'to consider changes in the secondary school curriculum and the question of School Examinations in relation thereto'. The investigation, carried out by the Secondary School Examinations Council, was in response to those concerned, including Board of Education officials, that the Spens Report had expressed the need for existing grammar schools to be reformed.[28]

Norwood, a former headmaster of Harrow School and President of St John's College, Oxford, had in 1936 written a book called *The Curriculum in Secondary Schools*, which displayed his thinking on the topic. Much of the Report bore his imprint. It stated on 'Types of Curriculum' that pupils 'of a particular type of mind' would receive the training best suited for them 'and would lead to an occupation where their capacities would be suitably used'. Three types of mind would correspond to three main types of curriculum. One would consist of fields of higher knowledge for the grammar school pupil and would not be geared to occupation. The second would be directed to the skills of an occupation related to industry, trade and commerce, and the third type would study humanities, science and the arts which would make 'a direct appeal to interest which would awaken by practical touch with affairs'. The Report equated the first group with future university students, the second to advanced studies or branches of industry; the future of the third group was not spelled out.[29] It also rejected the multilateral school which could accommodate grammar, technical and modern schools on one site.

The Norwood Report, as commentators have observed, was not concerned with evidence but with assertion.[30] The Committee's philosophy was accepted by R.A. Butler in the 1944 Education Act, which was widely interpreted along Norwood tripartite lines. Two aspects of the Report raised public discussion. One was on the nature of the mix of curriculum subjects at secondary level, and problems of framing a curriculum. The second was a call for the reorganization of public examinations, stating that the existing system was inappropriate and outdated.[31]

Developments in post-war curriculum, 1945–64

It is a surprising fact that the 1944 Education Act made no mention of the word curriculum, except to state that religious education was a requirement in all schools. Nevertheless, important changes in curriculum planning were taking place. In 1945, the Secondary Regulations were discontinued and secondary school curricula were henceforth not subject to central control, the situation achieved by the elementary sector some 20 years earlier.

But the spirit of Norwood was still alive. The Education Act merely stated that public education should be organized in three progressive stages – primary, secondary and further – whilst in practice most local authorities adopted the tripartite system. Of these the technical school was the weakest link and faded away in many areas, as it lacked a distinctive curriculum. With the advent of the Labour government in 1945 it might have been expected that a return to the spirit of *Secondary Education for All* would have been attempted. Instead, in 1945 the Labour Minister of Education, Ellen Wilkinson, commended the publication of a Ministry pamphlet, *The Nation's Schools*, which endorsed the tripartite system. Two years later, under a different Minister, George Tomlinson, a publication, *The New Secondary Education*, used language reminiscent of the Hadow Report about the curriculum of the modern school: it should not focus primarily on the traditional subjects but develop out of children's interests.

A group of academics including J.W. Tibble, Eva Hubback, J.A. Lauwerys, and Herbert Read, calling themselves the Council for Curriculum Reform, pointed out that when the functional relationship between a society and its schools is not considered, and when further the functional relationship between the purpose and the content of education is overlooked, 'discussions on the curriculum become anaemic and sterile. If a society wants unity, it will provide for common experience in pre-adult life; if it wants division in society it will provide different types of curricula for different schools.'[32]

Much of the energy of educational administrators after the Second World War was, however, necessarily devoted to other issues: the consequences of the population explosion, the catching up of the building programme which had lapsed during the war and the raising of the school leaving age to 15 in 1947. One reform was the replacement in 1951 of the School Certificate Examination by a subject examination, the General Certificate of Education Ordinary (GCE O) Level. Thus the examination no longer necessarily reflected the testing of a full secondary school course.

During the war the Consultative Committee had fallen into abeyance, and with the replacement of the Board of Education by the Ministry of Education in 1945 it was felt that a new body was required which could report back more quickly to the Minister. R.A. Butler convened a body with a wider term of reference and wider representation. 'My idea', wrote Butler, 'was to attach to the administrative machine which runs the general education within the state system, a body which could concern itself with the content of education itself, thus inspiring and helping the central machine.'[33] So was born the Central Advisory Council for Education (CAC).

One of the more important investigations carried out by the CAC was that of the education of boys and girls between 15 and 18 in relation to the changing social and industrial needs of society. The Crowther Report, entitled *15 to 18* and published in 1959, dealt with the problems of the curriculum at sixth form level. It decided that there was too much over-specialization and that those taking science subjects should be exposed to the humanities.[34] Crowther called also for the raising of the school leaving age to 16 and the establishment of county colleges, a successor to the day continuation schools, offering a relevant curriculum to those who had left school for work.[35] No action was taken on this enlightened proposal because of lack of funds.

The Crowther Report had shown the inadequacies of the education given to pupils attending modern schools. The CAC was subsequently requested in 1961:

> to consider the education between the ages of 13 and 16 of pupils of average or less than average ability who are or will be following full-time courses, either at school or in establishments for further education. The term education shall be understood to include extra-curricular activities.

Curiously, the foreword by the Minister, Sir Edward Boyle, to what became known as the Newsom Report contained the statement that 'all children should have an equal opportunity of acquiring intelligence and of developing their talents and abilities to the full'. The Report steered a middle course between promoting a traditional modern school with concentration on the basics to a more progressive notion of the curriculum.

> Very high in this list we should place improvement in powers of speech: not simply improvement in the quality and clearness in pronunciation, although that is needed, but a general extension of vocabulary, and with it a surer command over the structures of spoken English and the expression of ideas. That means seizing the opportunity of every lesson, in engineering or housecraft, or science, as well as in English, to provide material for discussion – genuine discussion, not merely testing by teacher's question and pupil's answer.[36]

Stress was laid on the importance of the humanities as a means of advancing the capacity of thought and judgement. Once again it was urged that the school-leaving age should be raised to 16, and links established between school and industry. One important recommendation was that the school day should be extended so that the differences between what were considered curricular and extra-curricular activities would be lessened.

The impact of the Report on schools was impressive. So-called 'Newsom' courses became popular in modern schools and the spotlight was turned on the need to provide a suitable and relevant curriculum for the less able child. 'Nevertheless', it concluded, 'a universal fixed curriculum ought to be ruled out if only because of the wide range both of capacity and of tastes among the pupils with whom we are concerned.'[37]

Politicization of the curriculum, 1964–2000

Between 1945 and 1964 the differences expressed between the two major political parties on educational policy and the curriculum were comparatively small. At the secondary school level, especially, there was ambivalence within the Labour party about the effect that possible comprehensivization might have on the future of grammar schools. This led to the compromise notion put forward by the Labour leader, Hugh Gaitskell, of 'grammar school education for all'. After 1959 the issue of comprehensive education seemed to become less prominent politically.[38]

However there was soon an early signal that government intended to play a greater part in determining educational policy. In March 1960 the Conservative Minister of Education, Sir David Eccles, announced in the Commons that he intended to 'try to make the Ministry's voice heard rather more often and positively, and no doubt more controversially'. This opportunity arose with the publication of the Beloe Report that year which recommended a new examination, the Certificate of Secondary Education (CSE) for pupils not entering for the GCE. Eccles added, 'The section in the Report on the Sixth Form is an irresistible invitation for a sally into the secret garden of the curriculum.'[39]

A Curriculum Study Group (CSG) was formed within the Ministry consisting of civil servants, HMI and a university professor. Its remit was to advise the Minister and carry out research on the new examinations. The CSG was headed by Derek Morrell, a vigorous Assistant Secretary. He told a conference of researchers the following year:

> In the area of curriculum and examinations a new approach is needed that will reduce to a minimum the waste and frustration resulting from excessive reliance on *ex post facto* criticism as a means of furthering society's interests ... the work of curriculum development now requires the active participation in some form or other of agencies other than the teachers including central and local government.[40]

Such statements raised worries in the teaching profession of a future centrally directed curriculum. Some of these fears were allayed when Eccles was replaced by Sir Edward Boyle: a working party under Sir John Lockwood was set up to consider the need for co-operative machinery on school curricula and examinations. The Lockwood Report of March 1964 recommended the establishment of a Schools Council for the Curriculum and Examinations. It would take over the work of the Secondary School Examinations Council (SSEC), and whilst the Council would not determine school curricula it would make available a wide range of materials and suggestions. The Council itself was to be made up of Ministry officials, local authorities and teachers, the latter having a majority on the Governing Council.

The Council quickly set to work. In regard to the primary curriculum, the Plowden Report of 1967 had recommended a new structure of first and middle schools. Some of the Schools Council projects which had an impact on curriculum development included Science 5–13 and Social Studies 8–13. The secondary school curriculum projects placed emphasis on catering for the average pupil. The coming of the raising of the leaving age in 1972 added urgency to such work; besides producing materials, the Council produced influential curriculum documents, such as the Working Paper No. 11, *Society and the Young School Leaver* in 1967. Provision was also made for a broader new sixth form curriculum. The Council, however, was less successful in relating curriculum to examinations. Much work was done towards devising a common system of examinations which would have helped schools operating a common curriculum up to 16, but the Council's proposals were not accepted by the government.

A new element in the curriculum debate was the Conservative counter attack against comprehensive schools and their curricula and the progressive 'methods' advocated by the Plowden Report. A decline in standards was alleged, especially in the three Rs. In 1969 and 1970 three so-called Black Papers consisting of a series of essays, were sent to every MP, and received widespread public support as well as within the teaching profession. These allegations received dramatic confirmation with the William Tyndale School scandal where some teachers appeared to be preaching politics whilst neglecting their traditional duties of teaching basic skills. The incident also revealed the difficulty of a local education authority taking action on an inadequate curriculum unless much stronger guidelines were laid down nationally.

More direct intervention was forthcoming. In 1974 the Assessment and Performance Unit was set up by the Department of Education and Science which had superseded the Ministry of Education in 1964, to monitor and assess school children in English and mathematics, science and modern languages on a national basis. An Organization for Economic Co-operation and Development (OECD) Report on the DES, published in 1976, pointed out that 'it is true to say that it has both enlarged its authority and it has great powers'.

In retrospect, it is now clear that from the 1970s there were at least two different official views of the most appropriate national curriculum model: the HMI view of a common curriculum and the DES view of a core curriculum.[41] A Curriculum Publications Group of HMI had been set up to develop a secondary school curriculum and in 1978 it produced a so called Red Book, *Curriculum 11–16*, setting out the basis for a common curriculum. This consisted of eight areas of experience, including the aesthetic, physical, social and spiritual. A third Red Book in 1983 looked to an entitlement curriculum for all pupils, irrespective of type of school or level of ability.

The DES took a stronger and different line from the beginning. In 1975 the Labour Prime Minister, James Callaghan, concerned about education standards, ordered a report known as the 'Yellow Book', to be drawn up by the Department. Two of the four areas considered were the teaching of the three Rs in primary schools and the curriculum of comprehensive schools.[42] One of the key statements in the Yellow Book was that 'the time has probably come to try and establish generally accepted principles for the composition of the secondary curriculum for all pupils, that is to say a "core curriculum"'.[43] In his speech at Ruskin College in 1976, Callaghan opened the debate, mentioning the core curriculum as necessary in an overcrowded timetable and in order to establish parity in curriculum content between schools.

There was a strong contrast between the HMI response and the DES outlook. In 1980 the latter issued a brief document, *A Framework for the School Curriculum*, setting out a compulsory curriculum in terms of percentage of the total time which each subject should be allocated; the HMI response, *A View of the Curriculum*, 1981, restated the need for a more liberal outlook. The House of Commons Committee on Education, Science and the Arts attacked a further DES publication, *The School Curriculum*, 1981, as being 'a confused document, lacking in intellectual distinction and practicality alike. Many have doubted the DES's competence in this area of the curriculum and this document will do nothing to dispel these doubts.'[44]

Another path-clearing exercise towards curriculum control was carried out in the 1980s. In April 1982, the Secretary of State for Education, Sir Keith Joseph, announced in the Commons that he intended to disband the Schools Council and replace it with two centrally appointed bodies, the School Curriculum and Development Committee and the Secondary Examinations Council. No official reason was given for the decision.[45] There were also government initiatives directed towards a larger vocational element in the curriculum such as the Technical and Vocational Education Initiative (TVEI) from 1983. This marked a change in tactics as the project, under the Manpower Services Commission, was financed by the Department of Employment thus by-passing the DES.

At the 1987 general election, the Conservative party announced in its manifesto that there would be a national core curriculum if a Conservative government came into office. Following their election victory there were published in rapid succession a consultation document, *The National Curriculum 5–16*, in July and an Education Bill in November of that year. Kenneth Baker, the Secretary of State, was in charge of the Bill, steering it through Parliament despite criticism that the National Curriculum consisted mainly as a subject listing without consideration of underlying aims. There were three core subjects, mathematics, science and English, together with seven compulsory foundation subjects – history, geography, technology, music, art, physical education and a foreign language.

Religious education was to be taught in all schools. For each foundation subject there was to be specification of general skills and understandings called Attainment Targets (ATs) which would be tested at the end of each Key Stage (KS) at ages seven, 11, 14 and 16. The National Curriculum applied only to maintained and not to independent schools.

Many other changes were subsequently made in government machinery which had a strong bearing on curriculum policy. For instance the 1988 Education Reform Act set up two curriculum councils, the National Curriculum Council (NCC) and the School Examinations and Assessment Council (SEAC). These in turn were both replaced in 1993 by the School Curriculum and Assessment Authority (SCAA) and subsequently, in 1997, the Qualifications and Curriculum Authority (QCA). As a sign of the government's intention to link more closely education and industry, the DES changed its title in 1991 to the Department for Education and in 1995, to the Department for Education and Employment.

Conclusion

In surveying the curriculum in England over the past hundred years, six important features can be seen. Perhaps the most remarkable one is the conservative nature of curriculum change. This is borne out by the 1988 National Curriculum, which consists of a list of subjects very similar to that contained in the Secondary School Regulations of 1904. A second feature has been the several attempts made during the period to link school examinations with the curriculum rather than direct it, a problem which still remains to be settled. Third, changes in curriculum theory and practice have been influenced by the deliberations of advisory bodies such as the Consultative Committees and the Central Advisory Council, replacing the more ponderous Royal Commissions. A fourth feature has been the growing realization throughout the century that the child is at the centre of the curriculum, as can be seen, for instance, in the recommendations of the Hadow Reports on Nursery, Infant and Primary Schools and the Newsom Report. Similarly, increasing attention has been paid to the inequalities between boys' and girls' curricula and ways of alleviating this situation. A fifth feature has been the failure to bring about a consensus on the curriculum by all the interested parties, though briefly attempted by the Schools Council. The sixth feature has been the increasing politicization of the curriculum and government intervention, both features of the second half of the century. At the beginning of the twenty-first century, 12 years after the introduction of a National Curriculum, many questions and criticisms still remain unanswered. The extent to which curriculum activities best fulfil overall aims and how far they should be compulsory, as well as the untangling of the lines between the political and professional spheres in delivering the curriculum, are two of the important issues which have yet to be confronted.[46]

Key reading

Many of the official reports on education contain background chapters giving information on the history of the curriculum. *The Report of the Board of Education 1910–11*, 1912, pp. 2–41, gives an account of the history of the elementary school curriculum, as does R.D. Bramwell, *Elementary School Work 1900–1925*, Durham, University of Durham Institute of Education, 1961. This may be supplemented by reference to successive editions of the Board of Education's *Suggestions for the Consideration of Teachers and Others*, later the *Handbook of Suggestions*, from 1905 to 1944. Post-war official reports devote more space to the curriculum, for example, Central Advisory Council for Education, *Children and their Primary Schools* (Plowden), London, HMSO, 1968, chapter 17 'Aspects of the Curriculum', pp. 203–61. Histories of individual subjects abound, for example, E.W. Jenkins and B.J. Swinnerton, *Junior School Science Education in England and Wales since 1900*, London, Woburn Press, 1998.

Stuart Maclure, *Educational Documents. England and Wales 1816 to the present day*, London, Methuen, 1965 and following editions, gives an excellent summary of the main commissions on education. R.J. Montgomery, *Examinations*, London, Longman, 1965 covers the history of the links between examinations and the curriculum in detail. Two publications by the History of Education Society are devoted to curriculum issues, *The Changing Curriculum*, 1971, and *Post-War Curriculum. An Historical Approach*, 1978. An overall picture of the background to curriculum development is contained in P. Gordon, R. Aldrich and D. Dean, *Education and Policy in England in the Twentieth Century*, London, Woburn Press, 1991.

The increasing politicization of the curriculum is discussed in B. Simon, *The Politics of Educational Reform, 1920–1940*, London, Lawrence and Wishart, 1974 and D. Lawton, *The Politics of the School Curriculum*, London, Routledge and Kegan Paul, 1980. There are numerous publications, official and otherwise, on issues raised by the introduction of the National Curriculum, such as B. Moon (ed.) *New Curriculum – National Curriculum*, London, Hodder and Stoughton, 1991, M. Barber (ed.) *The National Curriculum. A Study in Policy*, Keele, Keele University Press, 1996 and R. Aldrich and J. White, *The National Curriculum beyond 2000: the QCA and the aims of education*, London, Institute of Education, University of London, 1999.

Notes

1 School Curriculum and Assessment Authority, *The Review of the National Curriculum. A Report on the 1994 Consultation* (Dearing), London, SCAA, 1994.
2 QCA/DfEE, *The Review of the National Curriculum in England. The Consultation Materials*, London, QCA, 1999, pp. 3–11.

3 QCA/DfEE, *The Review of the National Curriculum in England. The Secretary of State's Proposals*, London, QCA, 1999, pp. 1–16.

4 P. Gordon and D. Lawton, *Curriculum Change in the Nineteenth and Twentieth Centuries*, London, Hodder and Stoughton, 1978, pp. 11–16.

5 C. Tyerman, *A History of Harrow School*, Oxford, Oxford University Press, 2000, p. 331.

6 For Webb's work, see E.J.T. Brennan, 'Sidney Webb and the London Technical Education Board', *Vocational Aspects of Secondary and Further Education*, 1959, vol. 11, pp. 85–95.

7 B.M. Allen, *Sir Robert Morant*, London, Macmillan, 1934, pp. 125–6.

8 E.J.R. Eaglesham, *The Foundations of Twentieth Century Education in England*, London, Routledge and Kegan Paul, 1967, p. 53.

9 Board of Education, *Suggestions for the Consideration of Teachers and Others Concerned with the Work of Public Elementary Schools*, London, HMSO, 1905, p. 6.

10 P. Gordon, 'The Handbook of Suggestions for Teachers: its origins and evolution', *Journal of Educational Administration and History*, 1985, vol. 17, pp. 43–4.

11 P. Gordon and J. White, *Philosophers as Educational Reformers. The Influence of Idealism on British Educational Thought and Practice*, London, Routledge and Kegan Paul, 1979, p. 149.

12 Sir Michael Hicks Beach to 8th Duke of Devonshire, 28 February 1899, Chatsworth Mss 1340.2792.

13 P. Gordon, R. Aldrich and D. Dean, *Education and Policy in England in the Twentieth Century*, London, Woburn Press, 1991, p. 300.

14 *Report of the Committee Appointed by the Prime Minister to Enquire into the Position of Modern Languages in the Education System of Great Britain*, London, HMSO, 1918, p. 9.

15 *Report on the Teaching of English in England* (Newbolt), London, HMSO, 1921, section 64.

16 Board of Education, Circular 1296 *Curricula of Secondary Schools in England*, London, HMSO, 1922, p. 2.

17 *Report of the Consultative Committee on the Differentiation of the Curriculum for Boys and Girls Respectively in Secondary Schools*, London, HMSO, 1923, pp. 63–4.

18 R.J.W. Selleck, *English Primary Education and the Progressives, 1914–1939*, London, Routledge and Kegan Paul, 1972, p. 4.

19 W. Viola, *Child Art and Franz Cizek*, Vienna, Austrian Junior Red Cross, 1936, pp. 13–14.

20 H. Loukes, 'The pedigree of the secondary modern school', *British Journal of Educational Studies*, 1959, vol. 7, p. 138.

21 *Report of the Consultative Committee on the Education of the Adolescent* (Hadow), London, HMSO, 1926, p. 87.

22 B. Doherty, 'The Hadow Report, 1926', *Durham Research Review*, 1964, vol. 4, p. 119.

23 J.P. White, 'The end of the compulsory curriculum', in *The Curriculum*, The Doris Lee Lectures, London, University of London Institute of Education, 1975, p. 28.

24 Board of Education, *The New Prospects in Education*, London, HMSO, 1928, p. 9.

25 *Report of the Consultative Committee on the Primary School*, London, HMSO, 1931, p. 93.

26 N. Whitbread, *The Evolution of the Nursery-Infant School. A History of Infant and Nursery Education in Britain, 1800–1970*, London, Routledge and Kegan Paul, 1972, p. 98.

27 *Report of the Consultative Committee on Secondary Education with special reference to Grammar Schools and Technical High Schools* (Spens), London, HMSO, 1938, p. 2.

28 G. McCulloch, *Educational Reconstruction. The 1944 Education Act and the Twenty-First Century*, London, Woburn Press, 1994, pp. 74–5.

29 *Report of the Secondary School Examinations Council, Curriculum and Examinations in Secondary Schools* (Norwood), London, HMSO, 1943, p. 4.

30 J. Lawson and H. Silver, *A Social History of Education in England*, London, Methuen, 1973, p. 122.

31 Norwood, op. cit., pp. 45–6.

32 Council for Curriculum Reform, *The Content of Education*, London, University of London Press, 1945, pp. 13–14.

33 M. Kogan and T. Packwood, *Advisory Councils and Committees in Education*, London, Routledge and Kegan Paul, 1974, p. 16.

34 *Report of the Central Advisory Council for Education (England), 15–18* (Crowther), London, HMSO, 1959, para. 77.

35 Ibid., para. 274.

36 *Report of the Central Advisory Council for Education (England), Half our Future* (Newsom), London, HMSO 1963, p. 29.

37 Ibid., p. 124.

38 M. Parkinson, *The Labour Party and the Organisation of Secondary Education, 1918–65*, London, Routledge and Kegan Paul, 1970, pp. 86–7.

39 *Hansard*, House of Commons, 5, 620, 21 March 1960, col. 52.

40 D.H. Morrell, 'The freedom of the teacher in relation to research and development work in the area of curriculum and examinations', *Educational Research*, 1963, vol. 5, pp. 88–9.

41 C. Chitty, 'Two models of the National Curriculum: origins and interpretation', in D. Lawton and C. Chitty (eds) *The National Curriculum*, Bedford Way Papers, No. 33, London, Institute of Education University of London, 1988, p. 35.

42 D. Lawton, *The Politics of the School Curriculum*, London, Routledge and Kegan Paul, 1980, p. 37.

43 Department of Education and Science, *School Education in England. Problems and Initiatives*, London, DES, 1976, p. 11.

44 House of Commons Committee on Education, Science and the Arts, Report, 1982, i, p. xxv.

45 P. Gordon, 'The Schools Council and curriculum developments in secondary education', in R. Lowe (ed.) *The Changing Secondary School*, Lewes, Falmer, 1989, p. 65.

46 S. Bramall, and J. White, *Will the New National Curriculum Live up to its Aims?*, London, Philosophy of Education Society of Great Britain, 2000, pp. 46–7.

Chapter 10

Qualifications and assessment

Alison Wolf

The situation in 2000

Britain in the year 2000 possesses an education system dominated by the pursuit of formal qualifications. Teaching and learning are shaped largely by public examinations and state-mandated testing; schools and teachers are judged by pupils' examination performance; further education colleges are funded on the basis of the qualifications they offer (and the number that students obtain). Universities are less affected but here, too, the prevalence of modular degrees and multiple subject combinations means that course and unit assessments and examinations dominate both staff and student time.

Public examinations, leading to nationally recognized academic qualifications, involve virtually every teenager in the land. In the school year 1999–2000, 94 per cent of all 15–16-year-olds achieved at least one pass in the General Certificate of Secondary Education (or its Scottish equivalent, Standard Grade), the examination taken, in a variety of different subjects, at the end of compulsory schooling. No fewer than 5,480,000 GCSEs were sat by English candidates, and 5,367,000 awards made: some to older or younger entrants but the vast majority to teenagers at the end of 'Year 11' schooling.[1]

At the same time, 603,000 A levels (Advanced level of the General Certificate of Education) were taken by students who made up 40 per cent of the country's 18 year olds – more than double the participation rate just 20 years before. Another 118,000 A levels were taken by older candidates. In Scotland, similar proportions sat for 'Standard Grade' examinations at 15 as for GCSE in England, but take-up of 'Highers' (mostly taken one year after Standard Grade) is half as high again as for A Levels. In both countries current reforms are adding yet more examinations to the total, with 'Higher Still' in Scotland introducing Intermediate, Higher and Advanced Higher levels and 'Curriculum 2000' in England and Wales swelling Advanced Supplementary (AS) level take-up between GCSE and A level.

Post-compulsory vocational education, adult training, and adult ('lifelong') learning are also heavily structured around and by qualifications.

Well over three-quarters of young people stay in education or government-funded training after they reach the compulsory school-leaving age. Rather over half of these follow academic tracks, and a variety of other qualifications structure alternative programmes – notably General National Vocational Qualifications (GNVQs) (in the process of being replaced by vocational A levels and vocational GCSEs), National Diplomas and National Vocational Qualifications (NVQs). Modern Apprenticeships, introduced in 1996, offer government subsidies to apprenticeship programmes in which employers commit themselves to certain conditions, including apprentices working towards NVQs – the first time there has been a formal link between apprenticeship in the UK and national qualifications.[2]

Large numbers of adults also work towards and obtain formal qualifications – partly for their perceived labour market value, but also because government funding mechanisms mean that virtually all publicly funded courses (including those for part-time evening students) must now offer formal qualifications. Some 528,000 full-time students and 1,617,000 part-time students were enrolled in further education (FE) colleges. Adults take academic courses but also register for a very wide range of vocational qualifications. Among the latter, NVQs are the single largest group, but their total number is equalled by what are termed, by policy makers, 'traditional' qualifications. In 1998[3] 458,000 NVQs and NVQ equivalents were awarded, along with at least as many other vocational awards. Four per cent of the population as a whole report they are working for non-academic qualifications, compared to 12 per cent for academic ones, but among those over 20, the ratio shifts to four and nine per cent; and for those over 30 (which excludes most university students), the figures are three and four per cent respectively.[4]

Every qualification at pre-university level – and it is a vast array – is formally regulated by the Qualifications and Curriculum Authority (QCA), the powerful central quango established in 1997. However, the actual examining/assessing process and awarding of certificates is the task of a large number of 'awarding bodies'. These include, notably, three large competing unitary awarding bodies which offer both academic and vocational awards, including all the GCSEs and A levels in England. Equivalent bodies for Wales, Scotland and Northern Ireland respectively are effective monopolists in their countries.[5]

QCA also has direct responsibility for the other major assessment activity which structures education in the year 2000 – the 'Key Stage' tests which monitor the progress of all children enrolled in publicly funded compulsory schooling. These tests, instituted in 1991[6] alongside the National Curriculum are taken by all state school pupils at age 7, 11 and 14 (end of Key Stage 1, end of Key Stage 2, end of Key Stage 3 respectively). The QCA has direct responsibility for the setting, analysis and reporting of results from these tests which cover English, mathematics and science (the last at Key Stages 2 and 3 only): much of this work is subcontracted, but in the case of mathematics the test items are actually written in-house. QCA also makes available voluntary tests for use with students in any of the other compulsory curriculum years: in 1999 take-up of these tests rocketed as teachers sought evidence that their students had improved, in order to gain performance-related pay increases offered by government.

The role of tests and qualifications is entwined with the growing importance and visibility of targets and performance indicators.[7] These are especially visible in England and Wales – in Scotland national testing has been far less centralized and visible, while in Northern Ireland steps are being taken to make it less so. In England and Wales, however, the results feed into published and widely reported 'league tables'. These rank schools by the performance of their pupils on examination results (and especially the proportions gaining five or more GCSEs at grades A*–C), and on their pupils' Key Stage 1, 2, and 3 test results. English children, in particular, take numbers of publicly set and regulated tests and examinations which are among the highest, if not the highest in the world. The system is also, internationally, highly distinctive. In 1900, as we shall see, it was also distinctive, if in rather different ways – but enormously less concerned with either formal testing or formal qualifications.

The situation in 1900

The situation at the start of the twentieth century was dramatically different. In 1900, education was compulsory – but the vast majority of students were found in elementary schools, which they left as early as 12 without having taken any formally recognized examination. Even in the grammar and public schools which offered secondary education to a tiny minority, most students were unconcerned with obtaining formal qualifications, leaving without any externally awarded certificates or apparent need for them.

The precursors of today's vast GCSE and A level industry were nonetheless present. In its examinations the UK followed a very different pattern from that of most other developed countries. Instead of creating a national and nationalized system *ab initio*, systems grew organically in response to public demand. This was similar to elementary schooling as a whole, where systems of church schools developed which were then incorporated, half-digested, into a national system. In this case, the key organizations were the examination boards, established by individual universities partly on government urging, and partly as a useful way of establishing that students were ready to matriculate. Nineteenth-century charters for the new 'red-brick' universities and university colleges such as Leeds, Liverpool, Manchester and Sheffield explicitly included powers for such institutions to 'examine into the efficiency of schools', and award certificates to individual students who had demonstrated their academic achievement. Thus by the start of the twentieth century, universities – alone, or in consortia – were setting, administering and marking examinations through boards whose names would be familiar to schools for most of the next hundred years. They included, for example, the joint Oxford and Cambridge Board; the Joint Matriculation Board (JMB), the Cambridge Locals Syndicate, and the London University Board.[8] However, as already noted, the numbers taking their examinations were tiny. Their clientele was also almost entirely drawn from the independent sector: the public schools and the fee-paying grammar schools, for which only very few state scholarships were available. The government's own involvement in secondary level examinations was confined to sponsoring examinations in science and in art. The schools of art were the precursors of the later, tertiary institutions, but there were also 183 schools of science in the country. Of their 25,000 students, only 4,000 were on advanced courses and eligible to take the examinations. Other schools also offered science classes, but largely for part-timers and evening students. The schools of science were still eligible for payment by results (see below), and in this year had a total of 1,459 advanced successes which brought payments. Students outside the schools registered 30,000 elementary passes, and a further 5,362 advanced. This in a population of 37 million people!

Formal examinations of a vocational or professional nature were also well established by 1900 – but again on a far smaller scale than a century later. Written examinations were used increasingly from the late nineteenth century by professional and would-be professional groups as a way of defining and certifying their expertise (and/or creating barriers to entry or a closed shop). Lawyers, doctors,[9] chartered accountants, municipal engineers, architects, electrical engineers and veterinary surgeons were all setting their own examinations by 1900. Here the major differences between 1900 and 2000 lie less in the structure of examinations as an entry into the professions than in the far smaller role played by the universities in 1900 for these examinations and the smaller absolute number of candidates, and professionals in the occupational structure.[10]

Qualifications for non-professional callings also grew organically during the late nineteenth and much of the twentieth century. The Royal Society of Arts offered some 'technological' examinations in the 1870s, but the single most important development was the creation of the City and Guilds of London Institute, established by the City of London Corporation in conjunction with the City Livery Companies in 1878.[11] The purpose of 'City and Guilds' was to set technological examinations and thereby encourage technical instruction and technical expertise throughout British industry. Growth was extremely steady, but the numbers involved were, again, very small – 14,500 entries and 8,000 passes in total in 1900.

Unlike the professions, there was no move to link technical or craft occupations to compulsory registration and licensing procedures. Very large numbers of young school leavers (almost all of them male) entered apprenticeships on leaving school – as was, indeed, the case throughout Europe. However, apprenticeships were not regulated by the State in any way, and there was no compulsory system of examination. The largest single component of post-school training in the Britain of 1900 was thus effectively examination-free.

Elementary schools, which provided most children with all the formal education they ever received, were also far less examination driven than in 2000. Indeed, the hand of the State was actually lighter than a couple of decades before, when the 1862 'Revised Code' still dominated the elementary school curriculum, tying school payments to pupils' results on tests of the three Rs administered by Inspectors. This system of 'payment by results' ended for the bulk of schools in 1897, replaced by payments tied to hours of instruction. Thus for most older elementary school pupils, school was largely a question of sitting things out until they were free to leave for a job and real life.

Changes and continuities

During the twentieth century the State took not merely responsibility for, but also control over, examinations and assessment. It thus offers a parallel to the nineteenth, when the State effectively nationalized schooling and semi-nationalized the universities. In 1900 the government took very little account of public examinations and qualifications. By 2000 as described briefly above, academic and vocational qualifications at pre-university levels were tightly regulated and controlled and public tests created for almost every year a child spends in compulsory schooling.

This section traces the expansion of government activity. It deals first with public academic examinations; second, with technical and vocational awards; and third, with testing against national curriculum targets. In each case, government activity has gone hand in hand with major expansions in the scale of schools, colleges and universities, and a commensurate increase in the importance of formal qualifications for people's future careers.

The growth of academic examinations

The examination boards responsible for the examining of secondary school pupils have been in existence, in more or less continuous form, throughout the twentieth century. Nonetheless, in absolute terms, the boards of 1900 were minnows to today's whales. At the beginning of the century, their clientele was concentrated in the public and grammar schools. Board of Education statistics for the period immediately before the First World War show that pupils in state (grant-aided) secondary schools amounted to less than ten per cent of the relevant age-group: and of these, more than four-fifths left without sitting for any public examinations. The proportion in the grammar and public schools was almost certainly higher: nonetheless, many of their pupils likewise left without ever taking any formal external examinations.

The scale of growth over the century that followed can be illustrated from one of the Boards for which unusually good statistics are available: the Joint Matriculation Board.[12] The JMB was one of the largest boards, typically registering around 20 per cent of all English candidates. Table 10.1, for entries on the eve of central government's first major intervention, shows how tiny the boards still were. Fewer than 2,000 candidates took Matriculation or the Senior certificate; in 1976 and 1998 comparable figures for that board were 52,000 and 105,000 A level entries respectively.

Table 10.1 JMB entries for matriculation and certificate examinations 1917 [13]

Matriculation examination	1223
Senior school certificate (old regs)	442
Housecraft certificate	28
Junior school certificate (old regs)	96
School certificate (new regs)	847

Although numbers in 1917 were tiny, they were nonetheless growing steadily. The more important secondary education became, the more important the examinations which offered certification as well as possible entry to university. Those pupils who did sit examinations sat more and more – partly because of the overlapping requirements of different universities, partly because of the proliferation of examinations set by professional bodies,[14] and partly because schools liked to demonstrate and boast of their examination successes.

In 1911, the Board of Education commissioned a report on Examinations in Secondary Schools (the 'Dyke Ackland' Report) which duly recommended a major centralization and rationalization of secondary school examining. The Report's concerns were to find direct echoes in the 1980s and 1990s – for example, 'the absence of any sound criterion by which schools may be judged by the public', or the 'difficulty of finding, under present conditions, an accepted standard for external examinations … the difficulty is not that the existing standards are too high or too low but rather that those different bodies vary'.

The Report considered three options – a system of external examinations controlled by provincial authorities; a system organized by the Board of Education itself; and a system held under a new examinations council with executive powers – the Report's preferred option. The system which developed during the inter-war years left rather more freedom and autonomy to the examination boards than the Dyke Acland Report envisaged. It nonetheless followed its broad outline, with a Secondary School Examinations Council which was the arbiter of which examinations could be taken in state funded secondary schools, and the establishment of the School Certificate examination, which influenced and structured the whole of inter-war secondary education.

In historical perspective the most striking feature of the School Certificate was that it was a grouped award.[15] To obtain School Certificate or, later, Higher School Certificate, a candidate had to pass a number of different subjects, selected according to quite complex rules, rather than taking subject-specific examinations and gaining separate certificates for each. In this, the Certificate was far more in the European and indeed global mainstream than the examinations which succeeded it. The school-leaving certificates of almost every contemporary European country – for example the German *Abitur*, the French *Baccalaureate* – require the student to complete, successfully, a range of subjects. The same is true for high school graduation in the USA. Until 1950, England and Wales were firmly within this tradition.

Conversely, the School Certificate did establish the other distinctive characteristic of early twenty-first century UK examinations – namely the existence of *two* high-stakes hurdles. The two levels (School and Higher School Certificate) continued the system of providing for both university matriculation *and* certificates for secondary school leavers: and led, in their turn, first to the two levels of GCE (Ordinary and Advanced) and then to the current system of GCSE and A levels (or in Scotland, Standard or Intermediate Grade and Highers). Other countries, especially in Europe, had comparable double demands on their systems,[16] and also developed certificates for those completing elementary or early secondary schooling. But perhaps because these lower level certificates tended to be pass/fail certificates, and therefore not very useful as a discriminator, they never achieved the labour market importance of England's School Certificate, 'O' levels or GCSE.

Figure 10.1 shows the rapid growth of School Certificate and Higher School Certificate entries in the inter-war period: though these were still, pending the arrival of universal secondary education, very much a minority concern. Higher Certificate was not even a general attribute of university students: a significant proportion of Oxbridge students entered without it, from the public schools, via the colleges' own entry test.[17] Post-war, however, free secondary education for all was – after years of debate and delay – enacted through the 1944 Education Act. The post-war reforms involved the creation of quite distinct schools, for which children

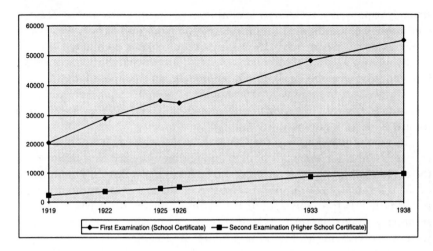

Figure 10.1 Public examinations in the inter-war years: England and Wales[18]

were selected by the eleven-plus examination and immediately made examinations at 11 (involving English, arithmetic and an IQ test) a major
concern to large proportions of primary age children and their families. It
also had both an immediate, and a longer-term, impact on examination
policy at secondary level.

The new Ministry of Education created under the 1944 Act developed
quite definite views on the type of examination scheme appropriate for the
new school system and on the role of the Ministry in establishing it. These
in turn reflect two quite different impulses in the educational and
Whitehall politics of the time, both found in the Norwood Report of 1943
which laid the foundations for the 1944 Act itself.

The Norwood Report is best known for its tripartite legacy, based on
the supposed way in which children can be grouped into those 'interested
in learning for its own sake', those whose 'abilities lie markedly in the field
of applied science or applied art', and those who deal 'more easily with
concrete things than with ideas'.[19] The last group, destined for the
'modern' schools, were, according to a pamphlet of 1945 intended for
'employment (which) will not demand any measure of technical skill and
knowledge', and therefore did not need to take formal examinations either.
On the contrary, 'Free from the pressure of any external examination,
these schools can work out the best and liveliest form of education for
their pupils'.[20]

This statement was later withdrawn following attacks at the Labour
Party conference. But it did not just reflect disdain for the non-grammar-
school child. There was also, at this period, a strong reforming element in
both the Labour Party and the educational world generally, which was

strongly opposed to external examining as harmful to the process of education. The Committee that produced the Norwood Report was critical of the extent to which School Certificate requirements dominated teaching in the grammar and secondary schools. They wanted to encourage a broader, teacher-and-pupil-centred approach; and proposed that, in the near future, examinations at 16 should be entirely replaced by teacher assessment. Only at 18, prior to university admission, did they see the need for any external examinations.

The result, post-war, was the General Certificate of Education, designed entirely by the Secondary School Examinations Council and delivered to the examination boards (and universities) as a *fait accompli*. The influence of the reformers' vision is evident in its initial format. No candidate was to be admitted before the age of 16 – thus freeing the earlier years of secondary schooling from examination pressure, but also ensuring that, with school-leaving at 15, no secondary modern schools would prepare students for the examinations. Second, there were to be two levels – Ordinary and Advanced – but no grades at either level, merely Pass or Fail. Finally the new examinations would be tests of separate subjects, not grouped awards like the old School Certificates.

Of all this, only the last survived. Most of the other changes vanished within the first two years in the face of a storm of protest from the schools. The creation of the General Certificate of Education (GCE) marked a huge increase in central control over examining; but it could not abolish the latter's underlying functions in a modern society. Universities, parents, employers and students were alike in using, and wanting to use, formal certificates for university and labour market selection and entry. Grades for Advanced level GCEs accordingly were allowed within two years, and for O levels soon thereafter. The age limit on entrants also vanished. Reformers would have liked A level candidates to skip O level altogether; the public felt otherwise, much as they do today.

From the advent of the GCE, examination statistics become subject specific, with huge increases in numbers as single candidates started to take seven, eight, nine, ten or more subjects. New subjects were introduced, notably by the Associated Examining Board, established in 1953 as a new board with a special remit to develop GCE courses for technical, further and other non-traditional, non-grammar school entrants.[21] It also became feasible for schools to spread entries between boards: and while wholesale mixing was rare at first, it grew steadily throughout the next half-century.

What could not be done was to provide a viable GCE examination for the majority of the age cohort found in the secondary modern schools. GCEs were intended to be difficult – and they were. Demand for the prestigious, formal certificate meant that by 1959 around a third of O level candidates were from institutions other than grammar and public schools;

but there was effectively no examination suitable for the majority of secondary modern pupils. The vast bulk left school at 15 with no formal qualifications, and only a very few transferred to grammar schools to continue full-time education.

The labour market of the 1950s was characterized by more and more white-collar jobs, and the decline of old settled working-class communities where school leavers were channelled into jobs through informal networks. In this context, lack of formal certificates became less and less acceptable but, unlike the nineteenth century, any change had to come from government. Throughout the 1950s the Ministry deprecated the idea of a new formal examination. However, in 1960, the Beloe Report, commissioned by the Secondary School Examinations Council,[22] reflected public (and parental) opinion with its firm recommendation of just that – albeit with the pious determination that it 'must not shape the curriculum as the School Certificate examination did'. The Minister (and the Ministry) hesitated and delayed, but in 1962 the creation of the Certificate of Secondary Education (CSE) was announced.

The CSE was born of public demand for formal qualifications for young people. In key respects, however, it differed markedly from the GCE. Though graded from the start, it was placed in the hands of a completely new set of 14 regional examining boards (raising the overall total to 22). These were not only allowed but also encouraged to develop a multiplicity of new syllabuses, including 'Mode 3' syllabuses: assessed internally by teachers, but leading to a full blown CSE award certificated by whichever Board had approved it.[23]

The CSE was thus partly the child of that recurrent strain in UK assessment policy which abhors the straitjacket that public examinations place on the curriculum, the way they label candidates and their exclusion of informed teacher judgement. The second half of the twentieth century saw repeated reforms based on these ideals, and their repeated defeat. The root cause of failure was, and is, a socially mobile society with a continually changing industrial and occupational structure, in which formal qualifications are more and more important to the young. These created CSEs – and also doomed them.

By the late 1970s the same pressures that had produced universal secondary education were apparent in post-compulsory education. More and more young people were staying in school beyond the minimum age, and more and more wanted higher education in some form. A CSE certificate which was visibly and avowedly inferior in status to the GCE was nonetheless decreasingly viable.[24] If selection at 11 had continued (as it has, for example, in Germany or the Netherlands), changing aspirations might have been met by changes in the CSE. But by now most British children were in comprehensive secondary schools, where the division of 13 and 14 year olds between the GCE and CSE streams was highly visible and contested. Educational opinion was increasingly in favour of a unified examination. Keith Joseph, then Education Minister in the first Thatcher cabinet, was convinced by the arguments and, in 1986, O levels and CSEs were superseded by a joint exam: the General Certificate of Secondary Education (GCSE), administered by five 'groups' of boards from both pre-existing stables.[25]

The GCSE is now taken by the overwhelming majority of the nation's young, for whom it also provides a set of signals that structure and decide much in their future lives. Research into young people's choices at this period indicates that the GCSE itself boosted staying-on rates, presumably by giving young people a clear indication that they possessed the necessary credentials for further progress. At the same time it provides a sorting device for post-compulsory education options. Courses for 16–19 year olds form a clear hierarchy according to the average GCSE results of entrants: top scorers into A levels, next best into Advanced GNVQs ('vocational A levels'), and so on.[26]

The launching of the GCSE also immediately predated an unprecedented centralization of education policy and administration in England and Wales, including the creation of a national curriculum, national testing, the emasculation of LEAs, and the development of league tables as an instrument of accountability as well as an aid to parental choice. In rapid succession, England and Wales saw the creation and disbanding of the Secondary Examinations Council, the School Curriculum Development Committee, the National Curriculum Council, the School Curriculum and Assessment Authority and, in 1997, the arrival of the Qualifications and Curriculum Authority (QCA). QCA is in many ways a classic late-twentieth-century quango – officially independent of its parent department, but in practice highly dependent on the ministry that created and pays for it. Under its aegis, there has been an ever-increasing regulation and oversight of the whole examining process. QCA's remit also runs well beyond GCSEs and A levels to encompass all qualifications offered in publicly-funded, non-university provision.

The nationalization of vocational qualifications

The extension of tight central control that took almost a century in the case of academic school-based examinations has been paralleled in the vocational arena, but at four times the speed. There is also a contrast between vocational and academic fields in the qualification structures themselves. The organizational history of academic examination boards is neat enough: university-linked boards, gradually losing autonomy; an expansion in board numbers with the creation of the CSE; then shrinkage again, to just three bodies in England, and one each in Scotland, Northern Ireland and Wales. For vocational qualifications there is no such neatness, strive for it as the government has in recent years. Instead, we find a multiplicity of examining organizations and qualifications, some tiny and some large, some gatekeepers to powerful professions, others existing entirely by virtue of short-lived government initiatives.

The contrast derives from the fact that in this area, unlike secondary schooling, there is no single, largely nationalized sector, where the vast bulk of funding comes from government, and where qualifications are a major output in themselves. In contrast, vocational qualifications gain their meaning and currency from a highly complex labour market, in which companies and employers are often highly aware of (and trusting of) their own sector's training history but marginally, or not at all, concerned with government education policy.

As noted above, written examinations have been widely used since the late nineteenth century by professional and would-be professional groups as a way of defining and certifying their expertise (and/or creating barriers to entry or a closed shop). Today, such examinations remain extremely important in the middle- and upper-middle-class job market: accountancy, banking, and law. Control of them is fiercely guarded by the professional associations who rightly see this as central to the principle of self-regulation, and who seek chartered status as a safeguard of such professional independence and a sign of status.[27]

Qualifications for non-professional callings also grew organically during the late nineteenth and twentieth century, and for much of that time also remained largely outside state control.[28] The number of candidates and awards grew hugely during the twentieth century, indeed for much of this period apprentices comprised a good third of male school leavers. Although British apprenticeships were not state regulated until the 1990s,[29] and did not have any formal requirements for examinations, apprentices increasingly often studied for City and Guilds qualifications while on day release, or in the evenings. Adults also enrolled in large numbers at evening classes, and in addition City and Guilds developed a large number of specific certificates for particular companies and industries' training programmes. Alongside them, the Royal Society of Arts developed a raft of clerical and secretarial qualifications, whose predominantly female entry mirrored male domination of the older crafts and technical occupations.

Alongside these large, multi-occupation examining bodies, there also developed a large number of others, often tiny, with specific occupational remits and high visibility in their own occupational sector. These included areas as specific as diamond cutting or horse dressage, or as large as banking. Since they developed organically, in response to demand from a particular sector, they also covered only a portion of the labour market. In many areas, such as retail, there were no qualifications since the sector had not felt any major need to develop its own 'awarding body'.

The vocational qualifications system obtaining by the 1970s was, at one level, highly complex, in that it involved a very large number of qualifications with different names, and a large number of different bodies setting examinations and awarding qualifications. It is not so obvious that it was *overly* complex, and therefore deficient, from the point of view of employers. Most employers were (and are) only interested in one particular part of the qualifications spectrum and they tended to know that part very well. To a catering manager, the nature and content of 'C & G 706' were very clear indeed, and the existence of myriad awards in non-catering sectors was neither here nor there. If we take the analogy of a supermarket, we don't, on the whole, find ourselves bemused by the number of goods on sale. On the contrary, if we are looking for a box of teabags or a fresh aubergine we tend to find them fairly quickly, because we can follow a number of simple choices and directions to get to where we want to be. Employers were in a similar situation in the case of pre-1990s qualifications. What government spokesmen labelled the 'jungle of qualifications' was actually criss-crossed by very well marked paths.

However, reform it was, primarily because governments and the policy community of the 1980s became convinced that the UK's economy was being harmed by a shortage of vocational qualifications in its workforce.[30] A determination to increase take-up of vocational qualifications both by the young and by the adult workforce led to a major 'National Review of Vocational Qualifications' which duly concluded that a major barrier to take-up was the aforementioned qualifications 'jungle'. It recommended, again as predicted, that a new body be set up to create and oversee a completely new qualification system based on employer-defined 'occupational standards'; and the National Council for Vocational Qualifications (NCVQ) was duly established with this remit.

In order to develop 'National Vocational Qualifications', the government provided funding for large numbers of sector-specific standards-setting bodies ('lead industry bodies'), for NCVQ itself, and for companies and training schemes which offered the new awards. Enormous pressure was also placed on the big vocational awarding bodies – notably City and Guilds and RSA – to convert their traditional awards into NVQs. The latter had a large number of demanding and defining characteristics laid down by the National Council as preconditions for approval. They were, for example, all based on a large number of exhaustively defined 'outcomes', every single one of which had to be demonstrated and recorded before someone could obtain the NVQ, and thus supposedly ensuring that awards were indeed 'transparent'. They also had to mirror, as closely as possible, workplace activities. If they could not be assessed in the course of normal work, then close simulations were required.

The problems that beset the NVQ reforms have been amply documented – not least the fact that, of the 800 or so NVQs developed and made available, almost half proved to have no market whatsoever, and were never taken by anyone, while many of the rest registered only single-figure candidatures.[31] Meanwhile many of the older awards which NVQs were expected to displace remained popular with employers and refused to fade away. However, rather than withdraw from the vocational sector which it had so recently entered, the government determined to replace the troublesome NCVQ and to strengthen rather than reduce central government involvement.

As already noted, the Qualifications and Curriculum Authority (QCA), was formed in 1997. It merged NCVQ with the schools body, the Schools Curriculum and Assessment Authority. One motive for the change was unquestionably to defuse the growing controversy surrounding NVQs – and in this the move succeeded, as NVQ development and administration became a low-profile component of the QCA's activities. However, far from reversing the move towards nationalization of vocational qualifications, the creation of the QCA signalled the wholesale, statutory regulation of all qualifications authorized for provision in publicly-funded institutions. Any qualification, however small, however specialized, however well-established, must meet a stringent set of 'quality' requirements in order to join the list. The only exceptions are university-based, university-level diplomas.

The underlying rationale for this is that students are entitled to expect that the government has secured quality; while for those studying at the public expense the taxpayer is entitled to value for money. Official QCA documentation explains that 'Statutory regulation is used to safeguard the public interest where other mechanisms – including awarding bodies' own quality assurance arrangements – would not be sufficient'. These are, in principle, legitimate concerns; although there have not been, in fact, any major failures in non-governmental organizations that would support the argument in practice. In fact, at the time of writing, the only major failure in quality control which had occurred in recent years was that of the Scottish Qualifications Authority, in 2000: and this is not a regulated awarding body, but rather a governmental monopoly, which for Scotland combines QCA's regulatory functions with the actual design, delivery and marking of both academic and vocational qualifications. Politicians' determination to reform vocational qualifications was fuelled by the belief that other countries' economic performance was being strengthened by their possession of a fully structured and regulated system. In fact, this latter belief was something of a misconception. Further vocational training for adults (whether certificated or not) is a complex, fluid affair in every country, and most countries also have rather few formal qualifications for adults outside higher education/tertiary institutions.[32] What many other countries do possess, however, are well-structured qualifications for young people who complete their initial education in a vocational or vocationally related context. The absence of such qualifications in the UK remains evident today after a quarter century of 'reform'.

The UK came late to mass upper secondary education – in part because the public examinations at 16 (O level, CSE, GCSE) provided a credible and differentiated (graded) labour market entry qualification. Nonetheless, from the 1970s on more and more 16 year olds started to remain in school for whom traditional A levels (or Highers) were not really suitable. The older vocational awarding bodies, City and Guilds and RSA, developed full-time courses and certificates for this market, but the really successful 'products' were those offered by a newer organization, the Business and Technician Education Council (BTEC), originally set up by the government as two bodies – BEC and TEC[33] during a panic about the supply of technicians. However, it quickly built up, as its main market, a quite different group: full time students in FE colleges who were looking for a post-GCSE level course, with a strong general vocational flavour but also the opportunity to obtain a certificate leading on to higher education. This the BTEC diplomas, in subjects such as business, engineering or tourism, were able to provide.

While numbers were small compared to the higher status A levels, growth was steady and by the late 1980s ten per cent of the cohort were registering for BTEC diplomas. The governments of the 1980s nonetheless expected that these awards would be converted into practical, specific, vocational NVQs. BTEC resisted angrily and young people continued to register for BTEC awards in preference to NVQs. Consequently in 1992 there was a sudden change of government policy. The Department of Education and Science (DES) recognized that the strong demand for a full-time alternative to A levels, essentially for those with weaker GCSEs,[34] was not going to vanish. A new set of governmentally conceived and designed qualifications was therefore launched, which BTEC could award but on which it was not to have a monopoly. These were named General National Vocational Qualifications (GNVQs)

The policy of establishing a nationally recognized qualification alongside the GCSE and A level should finally have brought England and Wales into line with the prevalent form of upper secondary education in the developed world. The new GNVQs offered the additional attraction of a progression route – a one-year Intermediate GNVQ could be taken by the weakest post-GCSE candidates as a prelude to the two-year Advanced GNVQ. The government's target was 25 per cent of the age cohort taking GNVQs by 1996; early uptake suggested that this was a realistic target.

Unfortunately, the complex and hugely demanding design of the GNVQs set them on a course for self-destruction. Like NVQs, but unlike any of the other public examinations in the UK, the GNVQ was designed from scratch entirely by government agencies, in this case NCVQ, who were inspired by a particular assessment philosophy. This involved very detailed specifications of multiple outcomes, each of which must be assessed and, in the strong UK reformist tradition, a resistance to formal examinations. The government insisted on some formal examining, which took the form of short module-based multiple-choice tests, playing only a small part of the award. The result was an administrative nightmare, with teachers spending up to 20 hours a week on assessment of the award, lack of consistent standards between different schools and colleges and very low completion and success rates.[35]

At the beginning of the GNVQ experiment, BTEC started to convert their old diplomas to GNVQs. As the problems with GNVQ implementation became clear, this stopped. Unconverted diplomas were retained and even new ones were developed. Meanwhile, a new set of government ministers with a strong commitment to maintaining standards via formal examinations had taken office and GNVQs' creators, the NCVQ, had been merged into the QCA. In 2000 it was announced that GNVQs were to disappear, to be replaced by 'vocational GCSEs' and 'vocational A levels'. In a major policy speech by David Blunkett, the Secretary of State for Education and Employment, GNVQs were simply airbrushed from history as though they had never been.[36]

Integration of vocational awards with academic ones is administratively easier than at any time in the past because, under direct government pressure, further amalgamations of the examining and awarding bodies have taken place. As mentioned above, there are now three monster 'awarding bodies' combining the old examination boards with, in each case, one of the large vocational ones. Thus BTEC, for example, is now part of the Edexcel awarding body, along with the former University of London Examination Board. In other ways, however, major problems remain. There is still no clear, simple structure of awards post-16, other than for academic students. In a context of high upper secondary participation, and a government target of 50 per cent participation in higher education, this is likely to cause major stresses very soon. However, what the history of GNVQs does demonstrate, once again, is the progressive nationalization of assessment and examination policy, and the direct day by day involvement of ministers in decisions.

The introduction of national testing

The third major development of the twentieth century is rather different: a coming full circle rather than a story of gradual but consistent assertion of government control. In 1900 schools had very recently been freed from the payment-by-results approach whereby they were not simply judged but also recompensed on the basis of children's performance in the three Rs together with needlework for girls. In 2000, schools were once again being examined annually on the basis of children's performance, not just in public examinations but on 'Key Stage' tests. Payment was again attached, albeit rather less directly; for there were both direct discretionary rewards for good performers and indirect rewards, as parents favoured 'successful' schools and funding followed numbers on the rolls.

The national testing programme was developed in full during the 1990s, following the introduction of a national curriculum for the first time in British history. Scottish developments, however, have been quite distinct and a full testing programme has never been applied there. An attempt to carry out such a programme, in advance of the first English tests, was boycotted by parents.

The testing programme – even more than the National Curriculum itself – was the result of growing concerns among politicians and the media about the standards of achievement in UK schools. The belief grew that primary schooling, in particular, had been taken over by a 'progressive' philosophy which emphasized free choice and self expression to the exclusion of effective teaching of basic skills. The reforms were instituted under Margaret Thatcher, whose vision was always of a sort of eleven-plus without the selection consequences. However, the early testing programme had a much more ambitious and wide-ranging remit. Based on the proposals of the government-established Task Group on Assessment and Testing (TGAT), the intention was to test the whole curriculum, through a mixture of centrally designed and teacher assessments, and to do so using 'authentic' means of assessment, which would not distort teaching by centring it around a few, paper-and-pencil-based objectives.

This proved to be a hugely over-ambitious task – not least because of the complexity of the curriculum itself. The first pilot tests in 1991 were carried out with seven year olds at the end of 'Key Stage 1', the age at which English children generally move from infant to junior schools. The test programme proved completely unmanageable, taking a minimum of 40 hours for an average class (and often more), and completely disrupting normal teaching, since many of the tasks involved the teacher working with a group of just four pupils while the others were – somehow, somewhere – otherwise engaged. The 1992 tests took rather less time, as the Prime Minister exerted her influence to move them towards a more limited and conventional form of testing. Nevertheless, the looming prospect of Key Stage 2 and 3 tests sparked a national revolt by teachers, backed not only by their heads but also by school governors.[37]

The Secretary of State for Education was sacked, an enquiry into the testing programme set up under Ron (now Lord) Dearing, and a much simpler testing programme of a highly conventional type was introduced. Although teachers record their judgements on a number of additional areas and subjects, the tests that matter are the centrally set ones of English and maths at age seven, and of English, maths and science at ages 11 and 14. These are the tests which are used to compile league tables of schools, examined by Ofsted inspectors, and which, under a Labour Minister, have become the subject of increasingly ambitious and high-profile 'targets' for children's achievement. In their current form, they signal another victory for centralized, public testing and examining and another defeat for the idealistic but recurring opposition to exams and to the assessment-driven curriculum.

Conclusion

Overall, the events of the twentieth century seem to signify total victory for formal tests and qualifications and a commensurate and apparently unstoppable increase in the domination of the classroom by their requirements. To a degree, this development probably was inevitable. Modern labour markets demand 'objective' criteria for selection. The government's drive for 'accountability' is imposing extensive measurement and reporting requirements (and formal league tables) on all public services, not just education. The competitive scramble for desirable university courses also generates the need for quantitative sorting mechanisms such as certificates and marks supply.

It thus seems unlikely that the number of qualifications will fall much in the near future, or, indeed, that key stage testing will disappear entirely from the schools. Nonetheless, it is already apparent that the pendulum of opinion is beginning to swing. Not only teachers, but parents and (most importantly) journalists and politicians, are becoming aware of how much schools are being forced to 'teach to the test', and of the effects on education of so tightly examination-driven an approach. The financial cost of all this testing, and the difficulty of maintaining high standards of accuracy and efficiency and increasing volume, are also increasingly apparent. It is extremely unlikely (I would venture inconceivable) that the recurring reform ideal of an education unshackled and undistorted by formal, competitive examinations, will prevail in the new century. We may, nonetheless, see some recurring interest in the broader aspects of curriculum, and in the benefits of greater curriculum freedom, in the years immediately ahead.

Key reading

Readers with a direct interest in the history of the examination boards or more recent (post-1980) vocational qualification reforms will find the key texts in the chapter footnotes – see for example the entries for Petch. A. Wolf. *Competence-Based Assessment*, Buckingham, Open University Press, 1995 gives an especially full account of the history and approach of NVQs. R. Murphy and P. Broadfoot, *Effective Assessment and the Improvement of Education – A Tribute to Desmond Nuttall*, London,

Falmer, 1995 is highly recommended, as it pulls together key publications by the leading UK writer on assessment policy of his generation and provides a full flavour of assessment issues and controversies in the hyper-active decades between 1970 and 2000. D. Koretz, P. Broadfoot and A. Wolf (eds) *Assessment in Education. Special Issue: Portfolios and Records of Achievement*, 1998, vol. 5, no. 3 and H. Torrance (ed.) *Evaluating Authentic Assessment*, Buckingham, Open University Press, 1995 provide in-depth discussions of the more idealistic and learning-orientated approaches to assessment which have figured large in policy and academic circles, but increasingly have been obscured by the relentless rise of centrally prescribed testing. C. Gipps, *Assessment in Primary Schools: Past Present and Future*, Milton Keynes, The British Curriculum Foundation, 1997 and C. Gipps, B. McCallum and E. Hargreaves, *What Makes a Good Primary School Teacher? Expert Classroom Strategies*, London, Falmer, 2000 provide interesting insights into how key stage testing has actually affected primary classrooms. G. Stanton and W. Richardson (eds) *Qualifications For The Future: a Study of Tripartite and other Divisions in Post-16 Education and Training*, London, Further Education Development Agency, 1997 provides a broad perspective on post-16 developments, and D. Lambert and D. Lines, *Understanding Assessment: Purposes, Perceptions, Practice*, London, RoutledgeFalmer, 2000 a good factual overview of the current (2001) arrangements at school level. For a more theoretical perspective, including some international context, the best single publication is H. Goldstein and T. Lewis (eds) *Assessment: Problems, Developments and Statistical Issues*, Chichester, John Wiley and Sons, 1996, while H. Goldstein, and A. Heath (eds) *Educational Standards*, Oxford, Oxford University Press, 1999 provides a comprehensive overview of the debate over standards which is so important in UK politics. A. Little (ed.) *Assessment in Education. Special Issue: The Diploma Disease Twenty Years On*, 1997, vol. 4, no. 1 demonstrates how far the UK's recent experiences are echoed elsewhere. In general the journal *Assessment in Education* provides an ongoing overview of developments in assessment, both in the UK and internationally.

Notes

1 Awards at grades A*–C (generally regarded as a creditable pass) totalled 3,102,770, or 56.6% of the total.
2 In 1999, 136,000 young people were enrolled on Modern Apprenticeship programmes.
3 The last year for which these data have been published at the time of writing.
4 Labour Force Survey. It is impossible to give precise figures for vocational awards. NVQ totals include 'notional' NVQs added to the total while the total for non-NVQ or 'other' vocational awards applies only to those awarded by the three big all-purpose awarding bodies in England and the Scottish Qualifications Authority.

5 This is not a statutory monopoly: Scottish schools can enter pupils for English exams and vice versa. In practice, however, such cross-country entries are tiny in number.

6 There was a pilot in 1990; the first full implementation of Key Stage 1 tests was in 1991. Key Stage 3 was piloted in 1991 and 1992 and implemented in 1993. Key Stage 2 was implemented in 1994.

7 A. Wolf, 'The evaluation of non-advanced adult and continuing education in England and Wales: the triumph of formal audit?', in K. Künzel (ed.) *Internationales Jahrbuch der Erwachsenenbildung. International Yearbook of Adult Education*, Köln, Böhlau Verlag GmbH & Cie, 1999, pp. 131–44.

8 The origins of the different boards were apparent well into the late twentieth century, with each having a quite distinct clientele. For example, the JMB and its successor bodies was established by predominantly northern universities, and maintained schools in the north of England who continued to use its exams almost exclusively until quite recently. The Oxford and Cambridge Board, by contrast, had been established in response to public schools' desire to gain exemption for their pupils from Oxbridge college entrance tests and first university examinations at those universities: it continued until very recently to be the preferred board for boys' public/independent schools.

9 The medical profession was prepared to allow universities to offer pre-clinical training but retained tight control over clinical training.

10 For a full discussion of the role of examinations in the UK professions, see G. Sutherland, 'Examinations and the construction of professional identity: a case study of England 1800–1950', *Assessment in Education*, 2001, vol. 8, no. 1, pp. 51–64.

11 See especially S.E. Cotgrove, *Technical Education and Social Change*, London, George Allen and Unwin, 1958; City and Guilds of London Institute, *A Short History: 1878–1992*, London, City and Guilds of London Institute, 1993.

12 The excellent historical statistics for the JMB are the work of its long-time Secretary, James Petch. See especially J.A. Petch, *Fifty Years of Examining*, London, Harrap, 1953; J.A. Petch, *The Joint Matriculation Board: What it is and what it does*, Manchester, JMB, 1963. For assistance with these and more recent statistics I am extremely grateful to Ms H.T. Nicholls, the librarian of the JMB's successor, the Assessment and Qualifications Alliance,

13 Petch, op. cit., 1953.

14 Many of these were taken by school students prior to articles.

15 For a full account of the structure and evolution of the examination requirements, including the gradual relaxation of subject requirements, see Petch, op. cit., 1953.

16 By contrast, from a very early date in the USA and Canada the defining certificate was that of high school graduation.

17 See Petch, op. cit., 1953.

18 Board of Education reports.

19 Committee of the Secondary Schools Examination Council, *Curriculum and Examinations in Secondary Schools* (Norwood Report), London, HMSO, 1943, pp. 2–3.

20 Ministry of Education, *The Nation's Schools*, London, HMSO, 1945. For a discussion of this controversial pamphlet see B. Simon, *Education and the Social Order 1940–1990*, London, Lawrence and Wishart, 1991, pp. 104–9.

21 See H.G. Earnshaw, *The Associated Examining Board for the General Certificate of Education: Origin and History*, Aldershot, AEB, 1976.

22 The sub-committee of the SSEC which published the report was itself only authorized after repeated blocking of any such enquiry by the Ministry.

23 Strictly speaking, O level grades remained unofficial until 1974, though few candidates were aware that, in public policy terms, it remained a pass/fail ungraded exam. CSE grades were five in number to reflect the (unofficial!) GCE O level grades, with grade 1 equivalent to an O level pass/an O level grade C.

24 This inferiority was not only something of which everyone was aware but was actually institutionalized, in that only the top grade of a CSE was counted as the equivalent of an O level. This formal equivalence was created in response to teacher and public demand and effectively recognized the prevailing view that CSEs as a whole were of lower status.

25 In its announcement of the new award, the government emphasized that, under the old dual system, there were 'too many awarding bodies and too many syllabuses', DES, *Examinations at 16-plus: a statement of policy*, London, HMSO, 1982. In future there should be four groups in England – the Northern Group, Midland Group, London and East Anglian Group, and Southern Group – and one in Wales. The former CSE boards were fully incorporated into the older and larger GCE ones at speed, but the latter retained distinct identities and syllabuses within their groups for most of the period until the late 1990s when further 'rationalization' was imposed.

26 Further Education Development Agency, Institute of Education and The Nuffield Foundation, *GNVQs 1993–1997. A National Survey Report. The final Report of a joint project: the evolution of GNVQs: enrolment and delivery patterns and their policy implications*, Bristol, FEDA, 1997.

27 By the end of the twentieth century, most professions had developed a graduate entry policy, tied to exemption from some examinations for entrants who had obtained a particular type of degree. This link is itself under strain as universities expand. The chartered engineering institutes are now willing to recognize only certain universities' degrees: the Royal Institute of Chartered Surveyors is (2001) in the process of adopting a similar policy.

28 The tight control over qualifications (effectively a state monopoly) which characterizes many other European countries means that they tend to have far fewer formal qualifications than the UK, especially at post-initial levels.

29 Strictly speaking, they are still not, but if firms opt to provide a 'Modern Apprenticeship' they are subject to state regulation but also qualify for state funding.

30 See National Economic Development Office, *Competence and Competition: Training and Education in the Federal Republic of Germany, the United States and Japan*, London, National Economic Development Office and Manpower Services Commission, 1984; A. Wolf, 'Politicians and economic panic', *History of Education*, 1998, vol. 27, no. 3, pp. 219–34.

31 See especially P. Robinson, *Rhetoric and Reality: Britain's New Vocational Qualifications*, London, Centre for Economic Performance, London School of Economics, 1996; and M. Eraut, S. Steadman, J. Trill and J. Porkes, *The Assessment of NVQs*, Research Report No. 4, University of Sussex Institute of Education, 1996.

32 A. Green, A. Wolf and T. Leney, *Convergence and Divergence in European Education and Training Systems*, London, Institute of Education, 2000.

33 Business Education Council and Technician Education Council. BEC and TEC were originally housed within City and Guilds but broke away to form an independent organization.

34 See FEDA, op. cit., for a comparison of the GCSE grades of A level and GNVQ students.

35 A. Wolf, R. Burgess, H. Stott and J. Veasey, *GNVQ Assessment Review Project: Final Report*, Technical Report No. 23, R&D Series, Sheffield, Employment Department Learning Methods Branch, 1994; Centre for Curriculum and Assessment Studies and International Centre for Research and Assessment, *Evaluation of the Use of Set Assignments in GNVQ. Final Report*, University of Bristol and University of London, Institute of Education, 1995.

36 D. Blunkett, *Education into Employability: The Role of the DfEE in the Economy*, London, Department for Education and Employment, 2001.

37 The tests have always been quite popular with English parents, since they provide a fairly objective verdict of a child's progress, against national norms, at important points in their school career. Prior to their introduction – and with the disappearance of the eleven-plus – parents had no such measure. In Scotland, their unpopularity was bound up with growing opposition to Margaret Thatcher and the perception that, yet again, an English policy was being foisted on Scottish schools.

Conclusion

Richard Aldrich

This conclusion draws together the detailed conclusions supplied in the several chapters of this book. It begins by providing an explanatory framework and then briefly summarizes the features of this century of education within four, overlapping categories: continuities, cyclical changes, unprecedented changes, continuing areas of concern.

The twentieth century was a century of education. As the preceding chapters clearly demonstrate, the expansion of education extended across a whole spectrum – more pupils in schools, more students in higher education, more teachers, more examinations. The 1997 election, indeed, was fought by the Labour Party on the slogan, 'Education, education, education', an indication both of education's importance in the political arena and of its prominence in popular consciousness. Such importance and prominence may be seen in countries around the world. Efficient education is now widely regarded as being essential to both economic success and social harmony. Indeed, as the artist, architect and conservationist, César Manrique, has written, 'A country's biggest business is its education'.[1]

Nevertheless, during the twentieth century educational expansion was not continuous on all fronts. Its development was subject to those economic, social and political events, such as wars and slumps, outlined in the 'Introduction'. For example, the mid-1970s, characterized by economic and demographic downturn and the Ruskin Speech, signalled a reduction in the proportion of gross domestic product (GDP) spent on education, and fuelled major debates and divisions about its nature and purposes.[2] Writing in 1970, Harold Dent subtitled his study of the 100 years from 1870 to 1970, *Century of Growth in Education*.[3] This was an appropriate appellation, but given the events of the last three decades of the twentieth century the celebratory tone of Dent's work, written explicitly to 'emphasize our triumphs rather than our tragedies',[4] now seems improbably optimistic and naive. For this century of education must be interpreted not simply in terms of quantity but also with reference to quality, including quality of opportunities and outcomes. As Roy Lowe and Ruth Watts argue in their contributions to this volume, while access to education broadened overall, old hierarchies in terms of institutions and social class proved remarkably resistant to change. Indeed, as George Smith has recently concluded,

> despite the massive expansion in all aspects of education, and the quite dramatic increases in staying-on rates and qualifications in the last two decades of the century, the relative chances of children from different social backgrounds were still apparently as unequal as they had been at the start of the century.[5]

Such paradoxes mean that the educational continuities and changes of the twentieth century can be interpreted in different ways and an explanatory framework of contests between traditionalists and progressives, both with reference to the making and writing of history, provides a useful starting point. Whilst such a framework is open to criticism and caricature it does reflect deep-seated divisions about the purposes and achievements of education in modern and post-modern societies. Richard Peters has defined education as 'initiation into worthwhile activities'.[6] Debates over which activities, knowledge and values are of most worth, however, have a long history.[7] Priorities have differed and will no doubt continue to do so. Traditionalists emphasize the role of education in the preservation and transmission of the best of the nation's culture, for example in terms of institutions, curricula, religion and morality. For progressives,[8] on the other hand, the major purpose of education is to promote greater freedom, equality and access to new knowledge and ideals, both in education and in society more broadly. For the first group, Oxford and Cambridge, Eton and Winchester, represent all that is best in English education – exemplars indeed. For the second, the ancient universities and boys' public schools may be seen as part of the problem rather than the solution.

Continuities in English education are based upon a general tendency to amend and supplement rather than to remove and replace. In education this tendency has been strengthened by the hierarchical nature of English society and by the reluctance of central government to assume full responsibility for education – for example by direct ownership of schools or employment of teachers. In the twentieth century the English failed to develop a significantly new and more inclusive concept of 'national education'. Instead, official attitudes often still reflected the concept of national education expressed in the name of the largest single provider of schools in the nineteenth century – the National Society for Promoting the Education of the Poor in the Principles of the Established Church, founded in 1811. The major Education Acts of 1918 and 1944 have properly been attributed in part to the wartime wish to better the lot and life chances of all citizens. In both cases, however, post-war economic problems and a sense that national institutions and qualities had been confirmed by ultimate victory led to retrenchment. Even the deficiencies of technical education, so evident during both World Wars, were soon forgotten, as demonstrated by the fate of continuation schools and county colleges.

At the beginning of the century traditional attitudes predominated. Given the nation's position of world leadership the prime purpose of education was intellectual, social, economic and political stability and reproduction. Moderate reform was permitted, encouraged indeed, but the integrity of institutions and the stability of society were paramount. In education, as in other spheres of life, continuity was more important than change. Thus in boys' public schools an elite group of young men were equipped with symbols of authority – in terms of speech, manner, dress and Classical knowledge – to assume positions of leadership in a nation which God had manifestly called to rule over much of the world. The model was selectively exported: in the shape of 'plain and basic straw-roofed "Winchesters" in Africa or ornate and elegant domed "Etons" in India, of sun-baked scholastic playing fields on the South African veld or in the Australian suburbs'.[9] Most children, however, boys and girls, attended elementary schools. There they were taught to be grateful for being English, to recognize their social superiors and to defer to them, and to accept that poverty was a virtue and, coupled with humility, a sure passport to a better life in the next world.

Thus the Education Act of 1902 was based upon the principle of filling up the gaps in secondary school provision, just as that of 1870 had filled up the gaps in the map of elementary schools. In both cases schools maintained by local authorities with financial assistance from the State were initially seen as adjuncts to existing educational institutions whose longevity was taken as clear proof of their worth and of their superiority over the new 'Board' or 'Council' schools. Such hierarchies continued to exist and at the end of the twentieth century were frequently confirmed by league tables of schools and universities based upon examination successes and other criteria. The children of the wealthy and powerful still attended fee-paying schools where expenditure per pupil might be twice as high, or more, as in maintained secondary schools. Even at the end of the twentieth century some half of undergraduate students at Oxford and Cambridge were recruited from independent schools which catered for a mere seven per cent of the population.

Philip Gardner's chapter on teachers provides some of the strongest evidence for continuities across the century. Changes did occur, with more teachers, better qualifications and a greater sense of professional unity; yet continuities remained in terms of low status and salary levels, and cultural and classroom constraints. In the year 2000, as in 1900, the majority of schoolteachers were women. In spite of technological advances, the organization, timetables and pedagogy of many schools and classrooms still bore a significant resemblance to those of a century before; indeed in some cases teaching and learning were still taking place in the same premises. Some continuities, however, were welcome, for many of the essential features of good teaching and a worthwhile education were the same at the end of the twentieth century as at the beginning. Good teachers may be defined as those with a sound knowledge of their subject matter and of pedagogy, steady application of principles of management and organization, genuine care and concern for those whom they teach and the ability to inspire and enthuse. Worthwhile education is about the promotion of knowledge over ignorance, truth over falsehood, concern for others over selfishness, effort over sloth, mental and physical well-being over despair and debility.

Cyclical changes in education may be allied with continuities and attributed to a variety of factors. For example, war and other national emergencies were catalysts for educational change; peace and success for continuity. In some situations the options were limited. Thus the control of the formal education system was shared between central and local government, school managers and governors, voluntary bodies, teachers, parents – with one or other group in the ascendancy in a particular time or situation. As Paul Sharp demonstrates, in the early years of the twentieth century increases in Local Education Authority (LEA) powers produced a decline in those of central government and of governors and managers. From the 1980s this situation was reversed as central government curtailed the remit and responsibilities of LEAs and increased those of governing bodies. Indeed, the situation at the end of the twentieth century was reminiscent of that prior to the establishment of school boards in 1870, when the central authority for education, established in 1839, dealt directly with the managers of individual schools. Teacher powers also waxed and waned throughout the century. So, too, did teacher supply. Full employment led to shortages of teachers and minor improvements in their pay and conditions. In contrast, rises in general unemployment produced an oversupply of teachers and a decline in rewards and status.

Similarly, the school curriculum may be seen as an amalgam of child-centred, vocational, subject-based and social disciplinary approaches, with recurring cycles of emphasis. Thus the last 30 years have seen the child-centred dimensions of Plowden, the vocational initiatives of the MSC, the subject-based National Curriculum of 1988, the addition of citizenship as a subject at the start of the twenty-first century. Increasing central government direction of the curriculum from the 1980s harked back to previous eras. Indeed, the 3Rs of the Revised Code, abandoned in the last decade of the nineteenth century, seemed to be replicated in the national testing and literacy and numeracy strategies of the last decade of the twentieth. In addition, the list of subjects prescribed under the National Curriculum of 1988 bore an uncanny resemblance to those of the Secondary School Regulations of 1904.[10]

Many of the educational changes of the twentieth century, however, were novel. The sheer expansion of the system – for example in terms of pupils and students – was unprecedented. Secondary schooling, once the province of a small section of the community, became compulsory for all until age 16. In 1900 less than one per cent of the age group entered university; a century later this had risen to more than 30 per cent. Another major change occurred in the qualifications of teachers. Whereas at the start of the century many schools were staffed by untrained teachers and pupil-teacher apprentices, in the year 2000 children were taught by trained graduates, although in primary schools increasing use was being made of classroom assistants.

Educational expansion reflected and promoted substantial structural and social changes. Structural change was exemplified by the transformation of the all-embracing, social-class based elementary school into a primary school which supplied only the first stage in a child's education. At the start of the twentieth century, the majority of children from the working classes would have attended but one school, leaving at the age of 12 or 13 to proceed directly into employment. In contrast, in the year 2000 all children attended at least two different schools, with the great majority of school leavers proceeding to further or higher education. Perhaps the most significant social changes, as Ruth Watts suggests in her chapter, were the expansion and successes of female education. In 1900 secondary and higher education were construed predominantly in male terms. A century later, girls would outperform boys in GCSE and GCE A level examinations and constitute the majority of undergraduate students in higher education. The decline of the former male dominion was evident in many ways. Relationships between teachers and pupils became less formal and corporal punishment, once the accepted means of dealing with recalcitrant or underachieving pupils, was abolished.

The growth in qualifications and assessment reflected not only the general expansion of education, but also the growth of accountability in a credentialled society. As Alison Wolf shows, by the end of the twentieth century children in English schools were amongst the most frequently examined in the whole world. In the 1890s concerns about over-examination and its harmful effects upon pupils and teachers, curricula and pedagogy, led to the ending of the Revised Code. Nevertheless, the twentieth-century extension of assessment and qualifications to all pupils was widely welcomed, as a means of providing formative and summative judgements and of countering bias based upon gender, social class and ethnic stereotypes, both in education and employment. Another significant change in stereotypes, attitudes and concepts, as Ian Copeland shows, was reflected in the transmutation of the designation ESN (educationally subnormal) into SEN (special educational needs).

Finally, at the start of a new century and a new millennium, what are the major continuing areas of educational concern? All of the ten topics covered in this book will be subject to further contest and change in the twenty-first century, but the most important issues for the first decade may well be found in the areas of secondary and further education and in a new resolution of the relationships between them. As Gary McCulloch argues in his chapter, it is at the secondary level that the harmful effects of the inequalities between independent and maintained schools, and between different maintained schools, are most clearly visible. These problems, and continuing debates over the purposes, character and role of secondary education, he attributes to the elite origins and continuities of secondary education and to the failure of both tripartite and comprehensive systems to win general acceptance. Further education has been another major area of concern, although in this instance, as Bill Bailey demonstrates in his chapter, more on grounds of its low profile and neglect. Indeed, it was wryly observed that the 1997 election cry of 'Education, education, education' referred to primary, secondary and higher, with further education overlooked once more. The Learning and Skills Act of 2000, with its unification of responsibility for all post-16 education outside of the universities, is but the most recent attempt at the resolution of such longstanding problems. It remains to be seen whether, in conjunction with the merging of academic and vocational qualifications and the IT revolution, a new foundation will be provided for the next century of education.

Notes

1 'El mayor negocio de un país es su educación', F. Aguilera (ed.) *César Manrique in his own words*, Teguise, Lanzarote, Fundación César Manrique, 1999, p. 62. For an assessment of the life and work of Manrique, 1919–1992, whose life was lived in Madrid, New York and his native Lanzarote, see F. Gordillo, *César Manrique*, Teguise, Lanzarote, Fundación César Manrique, 1999.

2 For example, between 1976 and 1997 the funding per university student fell by some 50 per cent, A.H. Halsey with J. Webb (eds) *Twentieth-Century British Social Trends*, London, Macmillan, 2000, p. 249.

3 H.C. Dent, *1870–1970. Century of Growth in English Education*, London, Longman, 1970.

4 Ibid., p. ix.

5 G. Smith, 'Schools', in Halsey with Webb, op. cit., p. 219.

6 For a discussion of education as initiation see R. Peters, *Authority, Responsibility and Education*, London, George Allen and Unwin, 1959, chapter 8.

7 See, for example, the mid-nineteenth-century controversies over the relative worth of scientific and religious knowledge generated by the publications of Charles Darwin and Herbert Spencer.

8 The terms 'traditionalist' and 'progressive' are used here in a general as well as a specifically educational sense.

9 J.A. Mangan (ed.) *'Benefits Bestowed'? Education and British Imperialism*, Manchester, Manchester University Press, 1988, p. 3.

10 For a further consideration of these issues see R. Aldrich, *Education for the Nation*, London, Cassell, pp. 23–39.

Index

Lightning Source UK Ltd.
Milton Keynes UK
09 September 2010

159675UK00003B/1/A